WITHDRAWN

Russian Animal Tales

THE COMPLETE RUSSIAN FOLKTALE

❁   ❁   ❁

This splendid multivolume work will acquaint readers with a rich folktale tradition that has not been easily accessible or well known in the West.

In the first volume of the series, *An Introduction to the Russian Folktale*, Jack V. Haney discusses the origin, structure, and language of folktales; the "discovery" and collection of folktales; Russian tale-tellers and their audiences; the relationship of folktales to ritual life; and the major folktale types.

Compared to other European traditions, the East Slavs have an extremely large number of tale types. Using the Russian version of the Aarne-Thompson index to folktale types, and drawing on both archival and written sources dating back to the early sixteenth century, Haney has collected examples of the full range of Russian animal tales, wondertales, legends, and tales about everyday life. These tales are translated in the subsequent volumes of *The Complete Russian Folktale*, beginning with the present collection, *Russian Animal Tales*.

Russian Animal Tales

Edited and Translated
with an
Introduction by

Jack V. Haney

M.E.Sharpe
Armonk, New York
London, England

Library of Congress Cataloging-in-Publication Data

The complete Russian folktale / Jack V. Haney.
p.   cm.
Includes bibliographical references and index.
Contents: v. 1. An introduction to the Russian folktale / by Jack V. Haney
v. 2. Russian animal tales / edited by Jack V. Haney —
ISBN 1-56324-489-6 (v. 1 : alk. paper). — ISBN 1-56324-490-X (v. 2 : alk. paper)
1. Tales—Russia. 2. Russia (Federation)
I. Haney, Jack V.,   1940–
GR202.C645   1998
398.2′0947   dc21
98-30059

CIP

Printed in the United States of America

The paper used in this publication meets the minimum requirements of
American National Standard for Information Sciences
Permanence of Paper for Printed Library Materials,
ANSI Z 39.48-1984.

♾

BM (c)   10   9   8   7   6   5   4   3   2   1

FOR GILLIAN AND ANDREW

CONTENTS

PREFACE

Russian Animal Tales is the second volume of *The Complete Russian Folktale*. The first volume, *An Introduction to the Russian Folktale*, has already appeared; subsequent volumes will feature Russian wondertales and legends, anecdotes and tales of everyday life.

The overall aim is to present to the reader of English at least one example of every type of folktale known to have existed in the Russian tradition. The sources are many and widely dispersed. I am indebted to the Interlibrary Borrowing Division of the Henry Suzzallo Library, University of Washington, for efforts to obtain copies of published materials. Aleksandr Bobrov of the Russian Academy of Sciences and Aleksandr Finchenko and his associates at TASK in St. Petersburg obtained archival materials for me that certainly made this collection more complete. Most of all, I am indebted to my wife, Barbara, without whose editorial skills, knowledge of English, and persistence this volume would never have appeared. I am happy to dedicate it to her, although the effort she devoted to the project can never be repaid.

TECHNICAL NOTE

In this and subsequent volumes of *The Complete Russian Folktale*, I will cite an Aarne–Thompson (A–T) type number when making reference to a type of tale in general and not some specific rendition of it. This number is given in its Russian (SUS) version. Sometimes the tale type number may be followed by a subscript, a Latin letter, and/or asterisks, indicating a particular variant or subclassification. Reference to a specific rendition of a tale is to the printed collection (e.g., Onchukov 110). The tales collected by Afanas'ev have been published in a number of editions, but the tale number is always the same regardless of edition. Thus, Afanas'ev 363 invariably refers to "The Vampire." When a tale appears without an identifying number in a collection, reference is made to the pages in the edition (e.g., Korol'kova, p. 152, "Fenist the Bright Falcon," or Sokolov 1932:147–150, "How the Landlord Gave Birth to a Calf").

When referring to a book or article in the text, I give the title in English; in the bibliography I cite the language of the original. The transliteration system used here is the Library of Congress system, with some simplifications to enhance readability.

GLOSSARY

Baba Yaga:	the Russian witch
Bathhouse:	the center of much ritual activity in old Russia
Boyars:	landed nobles of old Russia
Derevnia:	the Russian village
Diminutives:	a feature of speech that conveys affection or approbation by adding an ending to a noun, less often an adjective
Dvor:	a courtyard or yard
Gubernia:	a large administrative unit in tsarist Russia
Kolkhoz:	the collective farm of the Soviet era
Lubok/lubki:	booklet made of bast, woodcuts on bast often telling animal and other folktales; bast is the cambium layer of the bark of the lime or linden tree
Muzhik:	a Russian peasant

Sleigh: the means of conveyance of the bride in the peasant wedding or of a corpse

Sleigh wagon tongue: the shaft of the sleigh or wagon attached to the horse

Stove: the heart of the peasant's hut; the oven was at the bottom, and this then heated several layers up to the rafters, on which the family slept

Tsar, tsarina, tsarevna, tsarevich: the Russian royal family, equivalent to king, queen, princess, and prince

Zavalinka: a low earthwork surrounding the peasant hut

INTRODUCTION

Few children in the English-speaking world grow up without hearing "Goldilocks and the Three Bears," "The Race Between the Tortoise and the Hare," or "The Three Little Pigs and the Big, Bad Wolf." These well-known children's stories, or others like them, entertained children on the long overland wagon treks to the American West. Versions of them, ancestors if you will, were earlier told around fires in simple peasant huts throughout Europe, throughout Asia, throughout the world. Such tales represent the common heritage of mankind, and we know of no society that has not told similar tales and carefully retold them.

Most parents quickly find out that a vast store of stories and an ability to tell them to squirming children are helpful adjuncts to parenthood. On the odd occasion a story will actually send the young ones off to their own story-dreamland. I remember a long summer night's drive with my wife and children from my sister's ranch in the Wallowas back to Seattle. At the best of times it took a good ten hours; the nearest interstate highway was nearly three hundred miles away. The idea was to get Gillian and Andrew to drift off to sleep. They were tired and rather cranky from days of play with their cousins. The magic of a story was clearly called for.

But what sort of story? Parents soon become aware that certain stories just do not satisfy, others can be told but rarely, and some become favorites. Some are better for small children, some for those a little older. Certain stories are well told by some people, while others trying a hand at the same story will invariably lose the attention of their audience.

The first folktales children usually hear are animal tales. Then come the fairy tales, or wondertales, as they will be termed here. These may also be some of the earliest texts a child will read.

Animal tales are stories in which human beings are not the main actors. Animals, less commonly birds and fish, are the chief "movers and shakers." Occasionally, a story is about inanimate objects: a straw and a bubble, or a pancake, or the wind, or the months of the year. Folklorists, somewhat arbitrarily, refer to all these stories as animal tales.

The Russian tradition has a far greater number of animal-tale types than any other tradition except Ukrainian. Unfortunately, only very few of these Russian tales have been made available to the English-speaking public.

The Russian animal tales were first brought to the attention of the English reader by W.R.S. Ralston, an acquaintance of the most important Russian folklorist, A.N. Afanas'ev, in his *Russian Folk-Tales,* published in London in 1873. This outstanding collection of tales and commentaries from the published tales of Afanas'ev, Khudiakov, Erlenvein, and Chudinskii contained few animal tales, however. Ralston's scattered remarks about animal tales suggest that he was not interested in them as a subgroup of folktales. He tended to regard all tales as manifestations of Slavic, specifically Russian, mythology, a position he shared at least partially with Afanas'ev himself.

The earliest American writing about Russian animal tales dates to 1891, when the Modern Language Association of America published Adolph Gerber's *Great Russian Animal Tales.* Gerber included fifty Russian animal tales, which he translated and edited from a manuscript collection of the German Slavist August Leskien, and he accompanied these retellings with notes indicating analogues in the literary and oral traditions.

Both Ralston's and Gerber's works are long out of print. For the past half-century, the English-reading public has had to rely on the translation of tales from Afanas'ev published in 1945 by Norbert Guterman. Guterman's translation of one hundred seventy-eight tales and anecdotes contains only twenty-eight animal tales, all derived from the one source (Afanas'ev). The commentary by Roman Jakobson is not without interest but has little to do with the animal tales *per se.*[1] Most recent English editions of Russian folktales have relied on the Guterman translation, or they are translations of tales written or adapted by Russian writers.

This volume of tales seeks to present a much broader selection. There are tales from the eighteenth century as well as from the nineteenth and twentieth centuries. There are tales from the far northern regions, from the Baltic area, from the central region, and from Ukraine. There are tales from western and eastern Siberia, from the Caucasus, and from the Volga and Don River regions.

In this volume I have included animal tales representing at least one of each type of tale known in the Russian tradition. It thus provides the reader with the most extensive and comprehensive collection of Russian animal tales available in English, or for that matter in Russian.

Classification

Folklorists have given animal tales classifying numbers from one through two hundred ninety-nine. This numbering system represents tales arranged according to what folklorists call the "International Tale-Type Index," devised at the beginning of this century by the Finnish scholar Antti Aarne, edited and expanded by the American Stith Thompson, and then used to classify the thousands of East Slavic folktales by Lev Barag and his colleagues in the *Comparative Index of Tale Types. East Slavic Tale* (Barag et al. 1979). Barag's volume is often cited by the abbreviation SUS, taken from the Russian title. According to the Aarne–Thompson (A–T) system, each type of folktale recorded anywhere in the world can be given a number such that analogues to the tale will have the same number wherever encountered. Not that any two renditions of a tale in the oral tradition are exactly the same. But all tales given the A–T number "2" will deal with one animal's being instructed in fishing through the ice, although the animals may differ, as may the consequences of the ensuing and inevitable trickery. The tales share nothing more than a basic structure. For example, the Grimms' tale, no. 74, "The Fox and His Cousin," is classified as A–T 4 (Aarne–Thompson 4), a type termed by Thompson "Carrying the Sham-Trickster." According to the German story, a fox is invited to a wolf cub's christening and there suggests that the young wolf will grow up especially strong if he has a lot of nourishing food. The fox invites the mother wolf to go hunting for that good food and leads the wolf to a sheepfold. The wolf is about to take a sheep when a dog discovers her. The farmers are aroused and catch the wolf. They pour lye on her, but she escapes and drags herself away with her badly burned coat. The fox pretends to be injured even more severely and tricks the wolf into carrying her back into the forest, where the fox runs off with a parting, insulting remark.

In a well-known Russian version dating from 1795, the incident about the wolf's carrying the sly fox is part of a larger tale that begins with the fox's teaching the wolf to fish by lowering his tail into the water through a hole in the ice:

And when the tail had already frozen solidly in the ice hole, the fox said that it was "time to pull the basket [fish trap] out of the water and perchance many fish would be in it." However hard the wolf endeavored to pull his tail out of the water, he couldn't at all. His efforts were in vain, and he began to roar and shout. Peasants, hearing such an unusual roar, ran with stakes to the river, and seeing that the wolf had frozen his tail, they began to beat him. He suddenly gave such a strong jerk that he tore off a great part of that tail, and, without thinking what he was doing, he rushed into the forest. The fox, Lisa Ivanovna, seeing that the wolf had suffered such a misfortune and fearing that he would rip her to shreds, ran into the village and into a hut in which a kind old woman had a batter mixed in a pitcher. Lisa Ivanovna several times satisfied her hunger, and then, having thrust her head into the pitcher, she proceeded to smear herself with the batter. Then she ran out to meet the disfigured wolf, who at first was furious with her but then, seeing that she was beaten to a pulp, asked, "How did such a thing happen to you, cousin?"

"Well, cousin, I imbibed too much at the wrong feast. You went on to catch fish, and they beat my brains out."

"Oh, I'm so sorry for you, cousin," said the wolf. "But I don't know how to be of assistance."

"Never mind, cousin," answered the fox. "I'll remember your hospitality." Then she proposed to the wolf, "Let's cast lots, cousin, to decide which of us shall carry the other one, for we are both crippled." The luck of the draw fell to the wolf to carry the fox on his back. So sitting on top of the wolf, the fox said, "Beaten carries unbeaten," and she repeated this about three times.

The wolf listened to the fox's mumbling, but he didn't grasp her words and asked "What are you saying, cousin?"

"I am saying," said the fox, "that beaten is carrying beaten."

"You are right, cousin," answered the simple-hearted wolf.

The tale might well go on, and in this version it does, but the point here is to show the similar features of the episode and not to examine the tales in detail. Both of these episodes are classified A–T 4, according to the Aarne–Thompson system, because both involve a weaker animal's tricking a stronger but more stupid animal into carrying him or her.

One of the problems with the A–T classification system is that relatively few of the tales in this volume can be classified by a single A–T number. Many of these tales have always, or almost always, been told as links in a larger chain. Others, however, seem complete as they are encountered and are never, or almost never, "contaminated," as the Russians refer to the linking process. Thus, in all three East Slavic traditions (Russian, Belarusian, Ukrainian), A–T 1 and A–T 2 are frequently combined, as are these two with A–T 3, and then the three of these with A–T 4. Only in Russian, however, does one find A–T 15 combined with A–T 43 (SUS 395). The first tale in the present collection, "Sister Fox and the Wolf," consists of no fewer than eight tale types strung together: A–T 1 + 2 + 3 + 4 + 43 + 30 + 170 + 61. This chain of tales is uncommon, indeed unknown, outside the Russian tradition.

The tale types that are linked together to form a single folktale need not always occur in the same order. It is quite true that A–T 1, the story in which the fox teaches the wolf (or bear) to fish through a hole in the ice, is most commonly encountered in the Russian tradition as the first episode in a chain, but it may also occur last in the chain, as in the tale "The Hare and the Fox" (no. 19).

It is important to bear in mind that not all the types are equally well or completely represented in each tale, and some of the types occur merely as transitional elements in the larger tale.

Within the broad category of "Animal Tales," subdivisions are used to identify tales more precisely: one-third of the tale numbers (1–99) are reserved for tales featuring wild animals, while another group consists of tales that involve the interaction between wild and domestic animals. A third category comprises tales depicting the interaction of man and wild animals, but there is no category for man and domestic animals, although such tales do exist: they are so infrequent that they can be subsumed in another group. Separate categories are needed for birds and fish, and finally there is a catch-all subdivision for other animals and objects, including body parts, grains, and the seasons and months of the year. Both the latest version of the A–T index published in English (FF Communications No. 184, Helsinki 1987, second revision, fourth printing) and SUS describe each tale briefly, pointing to the salient feature that distinguishes one type from another.

So many types of animal tale have been collected in the Russian tradition that the index no longer contains sufficient numbers, and thus Russian and Ukrainian scholars make use of an array of subcategories, marked with asterisks (*) and capital letters (A, B, C, and so forth). These are preserved in this edition as an aid to locating the tale's analogues in other collections.

The Tales in This Collection

There are one hundred fifty tales in this volume, with at least one example of each of the one hundred nineteen tale types listed under "animal tales" in the SUS. I have also included a few tales that represent types that escaped the notice of the editors of that remarkable book. The overwhelming majority of the Russian animal tales were recorded in the nineteenth century, and that is reflected in this collection. There are fewer representatives from the eighteenth and twentieth centuries.

For the collector of tales, whether amateur or professional folklorist, the charm is in the details, the interest in the differences among tales of the same type. When ten people paint a picture of a poplar tree, two or three of those trees are going to be "better," by some criteria, than the others. So, too, with tales. There are some storytellers who are masters, whose every word, gesture, and intonation add up to the performance. Others either conceal their art or do not in fact possess it, which explains why there are some tales that are obviously better told than others in this collection. In one or two cases, the text as it has survived is unfinished. In such instances I was guided by an effort to complete the coverage, and the truncated tale is included if it is the only one of that specific type surviving. The tale from Smirnov's collection, "The Fox and the Crane" (no. 36 in this collection), is a well-told story and the sole Russian example of A–T 68A known to me (it is not in SUS), but the ending is missing. The integrity of the tale is not threatened, however, as the missing portion is A–T 1, and the reader will know that the wolf is about to be tricked by the fox into going ice fishing.

My translations reflect the art of the storyteller as much as possible. These tales are, however, for the most part tales told by peasants, and the language leaves a lot to be desired if one is accustomed only to the polished prose of a Turgenev or Tolstoi. It is often elliptic; predicates are frequently omitted when the narrator apparently regarded them as unnecessary. On the other hand, narrators add much that is parenthetical, a characteristic of oral narration in general. It is not always easy to catch the meaning of this linguistic local color, nor can the humor that was no doubt so often a part of the story in its original form be successfully translated across the years and over the language barriers. Where the language of the original tale seems too polished, one may often find an editor zealous to "preserve the purity of the (literary) language." These translations seek to be faithful to the original, and the reader will not always find literary English in the text. It would be most artificial, however, if the Russian were rendered into some form of English not known to the translator! The course chosen for the translations presented here is to reflect the original tale as closely as possible while presenting a text to the reader that is pleasing to read. Those who require the flavor of the original in its pristine form will have to seek out the Russian text.

A further point to be made is that narrators of folktales invariably use a larger or smaller number of oral formulae in their narration. While such expressions as "Once upon a time," "In the deep, dark, and dreamy forest," or "Over the wide blue sea" will rightly be considered clichés in the literary language, these and many similar formulae are the building blocks of oral art, in which linguistic innovation was considered less important than the continuation of tradition. The Russian formulae are not, however, the same as those encountered in English. Many of them will not jar the reader, but others may seem rude. Thus, "A peasant lived with his old woman" is not only acceptable, it is expected and even endearing. He certainly will address her as "Old Woman," and she will respond, "Old Man." Foxes become "dear little sister" or "cousin" to a wolf, and for the bear there is a whole range of names, from such diminutive forms of Mikhail as Misha or Mishenka to Heathen, which is obviously a pejorative. All these nuances are difficult if not impossible to translate, but generally I have tried to tackle the problem in the text unless to do so results in something that is absurd or silly.

Occasionally a tale bears signs of a narrator's failing memory, or distraction. The narrator of "The Fox as Carpenter" (no. 75; A–T 130**), from Kuibyshev, frequently breaks into his tale, distracted by the student who is taking down his every word. "The Billy Goat and the Ram" (no. 69) seems to be little more than a sketch for a story. Tales recorded in the eighteenth century were nearly always severely edited before publication to reflect the taste of the times. They may in fact never have been told at all, at least in the form in which we have them: such is the state of the documentation. On the other hand, some tales from the twentieth century were taken down by skilled students of folklore, who went to great lengths to preserve as many of the speech peculiarities of the narrator as possible. Some are in fact a part of a linguistic study of a particular dialect and were not originally intended for study by folklorists. Translation cannot possibly do justice to these subtleties.

Very occasionally I have given more than one version of a particular tale. I had two reasons for doing so: first, tales classified with the same

A–T number may differ enormously, and more than one example is needed to demonstrate the type fully; second, the alternate selection of tales given permits the reader to compare versions of a single tale told by different storytellers in different times and places. An excellent example is provided by two versions of A–T 210*, in which animals and objects go on a journey. In the Russian version an old man is very much part of the traveling party. In the South Russian variant, "Verlioka" (no. 104), the old man seeks to find and destroy the one-eyed giant Verlioka, who has killed the old man's wife and granddaughters. Along the way he is joined by a bob-tailed drake who speaks in proverbs, a rope, a maul, and an acorn. A North Russian variant features an old man and his three sons who seek to cut bast in a wood belonging to a powerful enemy. This enemy beats the sons, one at a time. They respond by making a calf, which they daub with pitch. On the way to the enemy's hut they are joined by an awl, a cowpat, a crayfish, and a mortar and pestle. In both tales the outcome is the same and expected. The differences, however, are more obvious than the similarities.

A few of the tales in this collection are quite vulgar. I have not made any extraordinary efforts to "clean up" such tales; the coarseness is part of them. Neither have I tried to include here any great number of such tales.

The complete source citation for each tale is given in the commentaries. In these commentaries, the reader will also find some information about the narrators, who are men and women, old and young, from all parts of Russia, and from lands with Russian populations that are now independent countries. The sole criterion is linguistic: if the language is demonstrably Russian (and that is not always easy to say), then the tale is eligible for inclusion. Occasionally I refer the reader to a similar tale in the West European tradition or to a fable attributed to Aesop. Some Russian tales are no doubt borrowings from other linguistic cultures, although fewer than has often been thought. The borrowings in an earlier period, before the eighteenth century, would almost always have been by word of mouth, although some tales may have entered the popular repertoire from the lives of the saints or stories of the monks, themselves influenced by oral traditions. Certainly the presence of a tale in two unrelated linguistic cultures cannot be regarded as foolproof evidence of borrowing. Both may have developed from a common third source, but there is also the possibility that storytellers have created similar tales from similar raw materials, as it were.

If a tale is known only in the Russian tradition and only in a single recording, I usually make that information available, too. It should be noted, however, that a single rendition of a tale may indicate nothing more than the failure of ethnographers and folklorists to record it more often. No doubt many types of tales told in Russia in the past have completely disappeared, leaving no trace whatsoever. It may also be the case that recordings of all the tales told in our time do not exist.

The Origins and History of the Animal Tales

Russian animal tales taken as a whole resemble the animal tales of related peoples, especially the Ukrainians and Belarusians. There are, however, a number of tale types that are unique to Russia; many others are limited to East Slavic and the East Baltic area. There are also quite a few animal tales that were told in Western Europe that seem never to have been told among the Slavs. Some Slavic animal tales find their analogues only among peoples of Indo-Iranian stock. A few types are found pretty much throughout the world.

One of the leading scholars of the folktale, Stith Thompson, argues that there were four main sources for European animal tales: (1) "the literary fable collections from India; (2) the Aesop fables as they were elaborated, especially in the early Middle Ages; (3) the medieval literary animal tales brought together in the cycle of Reynard the Fox; and (4) the purely oral tradition, a very important part of which was developed in Russia and the Baltic states" (Thompson 1977: 217). However, the history of a tale is extremely complex, and Thompson really did not know much about the Slavic tales.

One can agree that in the European world the fables of Aesop are among the oldest documented animal tales. The tales attributed to him were apparently told as long as 2,500 years ago; but perhaps there was no such person as Aesop, or perhaps he was a storyteller, or perhaps he was only a scribe. He may have collected the animal tales from the Attic countryside and edited them, supplying each with a moral that was missing in the original. It is not known. It is established, however, that collections of stories attributed to Aesop were not uncommon in Western Europe a thousand years ago, and they seem to have entered the repertoire of popular storytellers after that.

Aesop seems to have remained unknown in Russia until 1607, when one Fedor Gozvinskii, a translator in the Foreign Office (*Posol'skii Prikaz*), translated into Russian Church Slavonic a collection of one hundred forty-four fables attributed to Aesop. This is not to say, of course, that Aesop's tales had not arrived in Russia before the actual translation—as folktales! But there is no direct evidence for that.

Aesop's fables were not the first foreign folktales to appear in Russia. As early as the fifteenth century, translations originally derived from the Sanskrit *Panchatantra* had come to Muscovy in a Bulgaro-Russian translation from the Greek, which in turn was based on a Persian text. Even though the translation is far from perfect, and at times well-nigh incomprehensible in some of the extant manuscripts, this text, known as *Stefanit i Ikhnilat*, became in its Muscovite versions one of the most popular texts of the seventeenth century. I am familiar with only one Russian oral tale that could possibly be traced to the *Stefanit i Ikhnilat*, A–T 178A, "The Hound and the Grass Snake" (no. 100 in this collection), which bears a strong resemblance to the story of the couple who unexpectedly became the parents of a son. The infant was once left alone, and a serpent attacked it. A pet weasel killed the snake. When the father returned, he found the bloody weasel but could not find the child. Suspecting that the bloodthirsty weasel had killed his son, the man killed the weasel and only later discovered the living child and the dead serpent. The Sanskrit story features a mongoose and a boy but is recognizably the same. The version given in this volume is the only East Slavic one known, and that uniqueness again suggests the possibility of a borrowing.

It seems likely that in Russia neither the *Panchatantra* in its Greco-Bulgarian form nor the fables of Aesop, and certainly not the stories of Reynard the Fox of Western Europe, had any very great diffusion, and the majority of Russian animal tales are more or less "homegrown," derived from the oral tradition of which Stith Thompson made mention. Unfortunately, concrete evidence that the animal tales go back deep into antiquity is missing. Nevertheless, most folktale scholars agree that animal tales may in some cases reflect extremely ancient notions about the relationships between men and animals, or the animal world. One must therefore seek to understand the animal tale as oral narrative or, in the absence of texts, content oneself with the identification of motifs in a given tale that may antedate the narrative and, indeed, be found in completely unrelated contexts. In the latter case, the motifs may be very old indeed, three thousand years old or even more. As far as the Slavic tales are concerned, motifs found among the detritus of prehistoric cultures, such as carvings, etchings, embroideries, or funereal accoutrements, really cannot be used to establish the existence in prehistoric times of narratives known more recently. The Russian chronicles, lives of saints, and tens of other medieval narrative texts preserve much that is undoubtedly "folklore," by which I mean "popular belief and tradition," but certainly there are no animal tales to be found. The earliest Russian animal tale of which I am aware is classified A–T 1900A and therefore appears in the last volume of this set. Because of its obvious relationship to animal tales and because it can confidently be dated to the sixteenth century, even though it is known only from a Latin version, I offer it here:

> The Muscovite ambassador Dimitrii, distinguished by his cheerful and clever character, told, to the great mirth of all present, how not long ago a certain villager who lived not far from him, while searching for honey, had jumped from a considerable height into a very large hollow tree, and the deep mass of honey sucked him in up to his waist. For two days he feasted on the honey, alone, because the sound of his cry for help in these isolated forests could not reach the ears of passersby. Finally, when he despaired of being rescued, by a most extraordinary coincidence he was pulled out [of the honey] and climbed forth [from this hollow] by the kind act of an enormous she-bear, since this beast quite by chance, just like the man, had climbed down there to eat some honey. What actually happened was that the villager grabbed hold of the bear's rump from behind, and she took such fright from his pulling on her and his loud shouting that he caused her to jump out. (Novikov, 1971:40)

Strictly speaking, this is not an animal tale, although the untrained reader may be forgiven for missing the difference. Thompson's rubric for A–T 1900 places the tale among "lies," but that is certainly not a distinguishing feature among Russian folktales! The editors of SUS generally classify this tale as an anecdote of a type known as *nebylitsa*, a word occasionally translated as "cock-and-bull story." This tale is a legend, that is to say, a fictive account that tradition has ascribed to an historical figure but at some remove. It is known that Dimitrii Gerasimov was a Muscovite diplomat who served Grand Prince Vasilii III in a variety of positions. Note, however, that the narrator, in this case a distinguished papal official, states that the story was related by Gerasimov as a true incident that actually happened to a near neighbor of his in far-off Muscovy. The tale can thus be termed a "fabulate," to use the accepted term for second-hand narratives purporting to be true.[2] It is thus, strictly speaking, not a traditional story, not a folktale. This is despite the fact that there are a great many folktales that resemble this one more than superficially. A common Slavic tale, classified 1900B, relates that a man somehow got stuck in a bog. A duck came along and built a nest on his head. When she had laid her eggs, a wolf, or bear, came by and decided to enjoy some fresh eggs. As the beast prepared to help himself, the peasant grabbed hold of him, and the wolf, or bear, pulled the peasant out of the bog. Clearly a related tale, this example also shows some of the limits of the Aarne–Thompson classification system; what differentiates these tales is not their content but the degree of veracity claimed for the story by its narrator. It is possible that Gerasimov added the personal elements to a current folk story and thus, for the modern specialist, removed a very traditional tale to the category of a fabulate. Certainly there are many occasions in the Russian folktale corpus when just such intrusions occur. To my knowledge, no alternative to the A–T system has been proposed, and thus, despite its imperfections, one is forced to work within it.

Almost certainly, animal tales are among the oldest tales the Russians knew. Animal tales seem to antedate wondertales, which can be dated no earlier than the Muscovite period. Obviously they are much older than the modern (post–sixteenth-century) tales of social and class conflict. My conclusion is that the motifs encountered in them are old, sometimes truly ancient, spanning two or even three millennia, but the narrative structure is probably in most cases more recent. It would be useful to know more about the distribution of tale types across the entire Slavic world. This might enable one to suggest Slavic predispersal (ca. 600 A.D.) dates for tales that have survived in all Slavic languages. No such comprehensive Slavic index exists.

One may indeed ask what is the basis for the claims of antiquity for the subject matter of animal tales. Obviously, the existence of *Stefanit i Ikhnilat*, Aesop's fables, and the medieval European miscellanies of tales is one kind of evidence that animal tales have been told by neighbors and relatives of the East Slavs for a thousand years and more. Some of the animal tales, as has been pointed out above, may not as such be terribly old, but they may reflect ancient practices and beliefs. Thus, the Russian tale "The Bear," which is no. 90 in this volume, is often said to reflect the totemistic practices of pre-Christian Russians. Evidence from a number of sources suggests that there were still many Russians in the nineteenth and twentieth centuries whose beliefs about the bear went beyond the purely natural. As Russian scholars have shown, some of these involve verbal formulations, but there is much more to the matter than that.[3] The practice of nailing the bear's paws to the barn is probably not just an extension of the hunter's pride in the kill, for instance. It may well represent deep-seated beliefs in the animal's kinship with humans. Stories like "Masha and the Bear" (no. 101) reflect beliefs in the totem animal's marriage with humans, a notion expressed in a number of tales about a young hero who is the offspring of a bear and a human. Not infrequently this hero will be named something like "Ivan Bear's Son" or "Ivan Bear's Ear." A tale such as "The Case of the Beekeeper and the Bear" (no. 83) clearly reflects ancient beliefs connected to sacrificing the bear as noted below and in our *Introduction to the Russian Folktale* (the first volume of *The Complete Russian Folktale*).

Eighteenth-century collections of Russian tales contain few animal tales, and, indeed, it is not until the middle of the nineteenth century that they appear in appreciable numbers. The reason is likely that collectors found Russian animal tales to be too primitive for the sophisticated tastes they imagined their readers possessed. The few that were included in the eighteenth-century collections bear the marks of heavy editing and often an attempt to provide a moral the tales probably never had. It is of more than passing interest that the nineteenth-century fableist I.A. Krylov (1769–1844) remained largely indifferent to Russian animal tales. His nearly two hundred animal fables were modeled on those of Aesop and Phaedrus from the classical world or those of Jean de La Fontaine, which he read in the French. Many of these had been retold in Russian by Kheraskov, Sumarokov, Viazemskii, and others. Krylov's fables bear no resemblance to Russian animal tales. They are in verse form in fine literary Russian, and the animals that are featured are often exotic to Russia. Many of the fables are thought to have been satires against living persons, especially politicians and church officials. The fables also bear witness to their author's classical education. References to Latin and Greek mythological figures abound. Krylov's fables very frequently end, less frequently begin, with a statement of the moral of the tale. Often the fables prove to be based on a well-known proverb, but this is usually a French proverb. Even in cases where Krylov (kn. vi, xii) appears to be retelling a Russian folktale, as in "The Wolf and the Crane," he does not refrain from altering the ending and thus the impact of the tale. In the folktale "The Crane and the Wolf," the crane somewhat stupidly removes a bone lodged in the wolf's throat, and the wolf repays the crane by biting off his head. In Krylov's version, the wolf politely informs the crane that he is repaid sufficiently by being permitted to remove his head from the wolf's mouth. To the extent that his sources are Russian at all, Krylov's fables thus take their place with the adaptations of other Russian writers.

In the nineteenth century, the greatest number of animal tales appeared in the collections of Avdeeva and Afanas'ev. The majority of the tales in Avdeeva's collection (1860) were animal tales, but Afanas'ev's collection contained the larger number of them. By the end of the nineteenth century, few new animal tales were being recorded, and scholars began to note that those animal tales they did find often bore the marks of a written source. The decline in their popularity was linked to the spread of literacy among the peasantry. D.K. Zelenin was told in the northern villages before World War I that most animal tales were in fact derived from books published for children and others learning the rudiments of reading. If that is the case (and on the face of it there seems little reason to doubt it), then the process leading to the extinction of the animal tale must have begun long before, with the appearance of the popular *lubki* (bast books), cheap productions from the eighteenth century that often featured animal tales in one version or another.

By the time of the revolutions of 1917, the demise of animal tales in Russia was noticeable to all, and collections made after World War II, such as the tales of A.N. Korol'kova or D.M. Balashov's tales from the White Sea, contain very few animal tales. This is not to suggest that new tales are not occasionally to be heard: tale no. 45, "The Mouse, the Sparrow, and the Pancake," is an example of a Russian tale recorded for the first time in 1976! Furthermore, this is the very first recording of this tale type (A–T 85) among the East Slavs.

Structure of Animal Tales

From a structural point of view, animal tales present a rather untidy picture, especially if compared to wondertales (which are the subject of our next volume). Nearly seventy years ago, the Russian folklorist Vladimir Propp established that all Russian wondertales could be said to have a single structure.[4] Animal tales, on the other hand, have no discernible common structure. They do not begin with a common introductory formula ("Once upon a time . . ."), nor do they conclude with anything or anybody living "happily ever after." Animal tales are structured around a trick, verbal or physical, and they are rarely more complicated than that. In some of the simplest there is scarcely any discernible plot. Thus, Afanas'ev 88 makes little sense to the contemporary reader, and one can only wonder whether something has been lost in the transmission.

> Two old men were walking along a road, and they stepped into an empty hut to warm themselves by the stove. They were a bubble and a beard. The bubble sent the beard off: "Go and get some fire!" So the beard went off and blew on a little fire, which set him alight, and then the bubble laughed and laughed, fell off the stove, and burst. (Afanas´ev 88)

There are some other structural features of animal tales that stand out, although they are not necessarily unique to this kind of tale, nor do all animal tales exhibit them equally. The reader cannot but note the triple repetition of simple actions, verbal formulae, episodes, and so forth. This is a feature that animal tales share particularly with wondertales. There seems little reason to doubt that this triplification goes back to Indo-European antiquity, although what its original role or significance might have been is open to discussion. The fact that it is the more "archaic" texts, such as animal tales and wondertales, that exhibit this phenomenon and that it is common throughout all the European traditional cultures suggests antiquity. Its presence in texts intended for younger people may well argue for an educative function: "Repetition is the mother of learning," as the proverb has it.

But the triplification is not without its consequences, and in animal tales these often show up as a variation in the given theme that occurs in the third round, so to speak. By knocking with her tail against the floor, the fox twice manages to simulate the knock at the door that summons her to be a midwife (A–T 15, for instance). Each time, she uses the diversion to steal butter from the bear or hare, but the third time the situation is altered by the fox's having finished off the supply. Obviously, something different has to be introduced by the narrator. The last episode does not begin with a knock at the door. In one version the fox pretends to be ill for some reason and asks her "friend" for some butter. When the bear discovers that all the butter has been eaten, he is furious and suspects the fox, quite rightly. For the final episode in this tale of deceit, I refer the reader to tale no. 5, "The Bear and the Fox."

One major difference between the animal tale and the wondertale is that, in the latter, the crucial episode tends to occur precisely in the middle of the narrative, while in the animal tale it is the final episode that is decisive in determining the outcome. In this sense the animal tale is much more like modern narratives than is the highly ritualized wondertale.

The reasons for this grand finale in the animal tale are likely to be sought in the fact that these tales were never associated with ritual but rather with childrearing. Though they were intended for children, they had nothing to do with the transformation of boys and girls into young adults, which was accomplished by a series of tests, the results of which could only be known as time passed.

Magic is not a dominant feature of animal tales and plays little or no role in structuring them. However, this is not to say that the magical use of words is not important. The use of the imperative verb almost invariably brings about the desired result; and the use of rhymed refrains, choruses of songs, or recognized formulae also are seen to have a magical function, a function well documented outside the animal tale.

Russian animal tales differ from other types of folktale, and wondertales especially, in that animals (or at least nonhumans) play the leading roles. I.I. Kruk, who has produced the most thorough and interesting work in the academic study of animal tales in recent times, has argued that the types of animal tales are differentiated by the specific actions of the characters (and not the characters themselves).[5] These actions fall into four rather broadly defined categories: dissembling or shamming; imitation and copying; falsifying the voice; and failing to recognize the antagonist, a kind of disguising of the character. The animal tales in this volume provide many examples of all these actions. Trickery, dissembling, and shamming are most frequently associated with the fox, but other animals are not averse to this sort of trickery, as the case of the March hare in the tale "The Fox and the Hare" (no. 16) obviously proves. In a good number of animal tales, the variants of a tale type allow one to suggest that, although the vixen or fox may have been the original trickster, a little old woman can and does make a fitting substitute.

Examples of failure to imitate are also readily met. The wolf is the most frequent unsuccessful copyist, as the very first tale in the collection demonstrates. In other tales the dog tries to imitate the wolf's behavior in front of the cat and fails dismally. The wolf is more successful, at least initially, when the task is to disguise his voice. The goat kids are taken in, thinking the wolf is their mother, and get eaten. Finally, in what may be called a variation on the theme, the villain takes over a weaker animal's abode. He is driven out not by the strong and mighty, the wolf or bear, but by the cock, whose threats and disguised voice cause the villain, usually the fox, to misjudge his adversary and give up his squatter's residence.

The Animals of the Animal Tale and Their World

Many of the animals familiar to Western folklore will be encountered in the Russian tales, although sometimes their behavior may be quite different. By far the most popular figure is the fox. The female fox usually has a name, Lizaveta Patrikeevna or Ivanovna, although male foxes do not seem to have names in the Russian tradition, perhaps because the Russian word for fox, *lisa*, is a feminine noun, although it is applied to a fox of either gender. Very rarely the obsolete *lis* is used to indicate a male, while the common *lisitsa* refers specifically to a vixen. Most often in the Russian tales the female is meant, whereas in the Western tradition "Reynard" is usually a male. In these tales I use only fox, although pronouns and possessive adjectives may refer to a particular sex.

Oddly, the Russian Lizaveta is frequently said to be married to a tomcat, Kotonail Ivanovich, who may be a burgomaster or mayor from the Siberian forests. On the whole, the character of the foxes in Russian tales is well-rounded. Their behavior swings from the utterly unscrupulous and malicious to the wily and clever to the good-natured and even helpful. Their innate curiosity not infrequently results in their undoing, although misplaced trust is sometimes to blame for the fox's perishing, especially when she is involved with men.

Some idea of the composite image of the fox is revealed in the various forms taken by her name. In addition to Lizaveta Ivanovna and Lizaveta Patrikeevna, she is frequently called "Little Sister Fox," "Cousin Fox" or "Dearest Friend Fox," "Beautiful Fox," "Lovely Fox," "Little Mother," "Fox of the Buttery Lips," "Fox of Sweet Words," "Fox of Sugary Lips, Sweet Words, and Flattering Tongue," "Maiden Fox," and many others. These rather pleasant-sounding appellations notwithstanding, the fox has a well-deserved reputation as a trickster.[6] She tricks the old man out of his fish; she tricks the wolf into freezing his tail in the ice, then into carrying her back to the forest when the wolf has been beaten by the villagers; she tricks the bear into revealing where his store of butter or honey is and then devours it; she tricks the cock into descending from his safe perch in a tree to confess his sins and devours him. Occasionally a variant of one of the above episodes will feature the escape of the victim, and that will be possible usually because of the fox's greed.

The fox is certainly not always lucky. Several Russian animal tales relate how the greedy fox sticks her head into a pitcher containing food and gets it stuck there, resulting either in the peasants' beating the fox or in a futile and fatal attempt on the fox's part to get her head out of the jug by sinking it into a river. The witless creature fails to remove her head and drowns as the heavy jug descends to the bottom of the stream. In another, humorous story, a March hare dishonors a fox and then mocks her cruelly as she seeks revenge. Even birds have occasional success. In one story (A–T 225A), a crane undertakes to teach a fox to fly but ends up sending her to her death by shaking the fox off her back so that she lands on a peasant's pitchfork.

There is a wide range of victims in stories involving the fox. Some are the weak and defenseless animals of the forest such as birds and hares, but her most celebrated victim is of course the wolf. In the Russian tradition the wolf is generally regarded as greedy, stupid, clumsy, and male, but he is also cruel. In the well-known tale "The Wolf's Song" (A–T 163), the wolf hears of a prosperous peasant household and coerces the peasant into giving him all his livestock and then his children and finally his wife. Having devoured them all, the wolf goes away, leaving the old man to his miserable existence. In a very few Russian tales the wolf actually attempts to deceive his adversaries subtly, but he usually fails. In a story known not only to the East Slavs but throughout Scandinavia as well (A–T 123), the wolf attempts to dupe the seven goat kids by imitating their mother. At first he is successful, but in the end the nanny goat rips open his stomach and saves her kids (no. 67). Farm animals are not always so lucky. The fox is most successful against the wolf, but man is not far behind. Men unhesitatingly terrify, beat, and even kill the wolf in virtually every encounter, some of which are bloody indeed.

The bear features in many stories and seems to have been popular in a number of roles, judging from the tales that have survived. The bear is undoubtedly a very ancient figure in Slavic mythology and cult, far antedating any of the texts that have survived in the oral tradition. Russian scholars point to versions of A–T 161A, "The Bear with the Limewood Leg," as containing some of the most archaic features in any of the animal tales. In this story the old man is sent into the forest, encounters a bear, and chops off one of his legs with his hatchet. The old woman prepares a bear-paw stew, and she uses the fur and skin for a cushion or in her weaving. The bear comes to take revenge and devours the old couple, who are guilty of the sacrilege of harming the totem animal and failing to seek forgiveness. Ample evidence exists to show that similar beliefs obtained among the Russians of Siberia even well into the twentieth century. (This is discussed in volume 1, *An Introduction to the Russian Folktale*.)

There is one story, no. 83, in which the bear functions as a sacrificial animal (A–T 154**). This rare tale may be even older than the story of the bear with the limewood leg. The story, from Smolensk District, takes place at the end of September, we are told, in what is a unique mention of concrete time in these tales, and features a bear who has taken to robbing a peasant's honey. The peasant undertakes to kill the bear and tries strong drink to poison him, then binds him, and finally, with his sons' support and the aid of all the people of the steppe (despite the apparent fact that the bear is a resident of the forest), the bear is clubbed to death. The community marks the occasion by drinking wine and celebrating a requiem for the bear in the evening.

It can scarcely be an accident, one suspects, that strong drink laced with poison, strangulation or binding, and clubbing were the three means by which the ancient bloodless sacrifice was accomplished. The autumnal equinox, marking the day when bears began their hibernation, in the belief of the Russian peasant, was actually celebrated on 25 September, which is St. Sergius's Day. St. Sergius of Radonezh is regarded as the patron saint of bears in popular Russian culture.

In more modern stories the bear has quite a different character. He is slow, trusting, lazy, and dangerous in his stupidity and strength, but man (or, less often, the fox) is more than a match for him.

Only a few other denizens of the forest figure in animal tales. One is the wily hare, who more often than not ends up a victim of the strong predators. I have but three animal tales in which the much-loved hedgehog appears (A–T 83*, 125E*, 293G*), and in a very few tales the lion figures. Rare also is the boar. As far as I know, few if any tales feature deer, or any of the smaller carnivores so common to the Russian forests such as mink, fishers, or otters, and yet crayfish appear, as do owls, partridges, and even a polar bear.

With regard to domestic animals, the situation is quite different. Many of them serve as victims of the forest animals, or they become victims when their master discards them in old age. The horse that plays such a prominent role in wondertales, the Russian *kon´*, is in animal tales the very domestic *loshad´*, most often a peasant's draft animal.[7] Cows are practically nonexistent, and bulls and oxen are only somewhat more common. Goats and sheep appear in several tales, and rams can be effective adversaries of the wolf.

There are a number of birds that figure in this group of "animal" tales, including the crane and the heron, the eagle, the crow, the raven, and even the sparrow. Most common, however, is the cock, whose role is not limited to a victim in the Russian tales and whose reputation as a prodigious seducer of pullets is as widespread in the Slavic as in the Western tradition. It is worth noting that several of these same birds, and animals, too, for that matter, also appear quite often in wondertales. As will be seen, however, their role is very different. In animal tales they tend to act no differently than the other animals, but in wondertales they are most frequently associated with psychic, spiritual, or physical journeys that are made by the hero to the otherworld.

Fish appear in the animal tales, especially those that are indigenous to the northern Russian waters, such as the pike, the whiting, and the bream. These fish apparently made their first appearance in written satirical tales dating from the early seventeenth century, and from then on these tales were disseminated by the *lubki*, eventually passing into the oral tradition. The original written tales were aimed at the attempts of the Muscovite serving nobility to gain control over lands long held by the Russian peasantry of the central and northern regions. In time the focus of the legal procedures of one or more "small fish" against the bully of the lake was widened to take in the judicial system and its corrupt officials as a whole. By the twentieth century, tales collected in the north of Russia focus less on corruption than on the general conflict among the various fishes, and collective-farm workers make a surprise appearance in more than one such tale. In general, however, humans appear but rarely, and when they do, they are merely another actor, behaving in a manner similar to the animals.

It should be noted that the portrayal of an animal is far from constant from tale to tale within the tale type. It has already been pointed out that the fox is not always so clever, sly, and perspicacious as she and most readers are inclined to think. Even the wolf, typically portrayed as stupid and cruel, turns out to have a good heart when he helps the dog regain favor in his master's house (A–T 101).

The animals in animal tales are almost always solitary. In any one tale there is just one bear (Mishka), one fox or vixen (Lizaveta), one wolf, one hare. The exception might be a pig with several piglets, eaten one at a time by a villainous wolf, thus lengthening the tale. These animals do not live in their own separate special communities. They wander around the forest and seem to have no fixed abode. They may well build a house, only to have it destroyed. It would seem that the various individual animals in the tales might well represent their species collectively. In other words, each one figuratively represents a clan, and as such the animal makes alliances, intermarries, but also competes for food and shelter with the other clans. Trust in animal tales is to be found only among one's own kind, if at all.

Vladimir Propp has given a comprehensive summary of the behavior of the animals in his posthumously published book on the Russian folktale. He noted that even if the cock crows, the horse kicks, and the fox lives in a burrow, it is still difficult to accept the friendship of a dog and a wolf or the marriage of a tomcat to a fox or a hare's building of a hut of bast (Propp 1984:301–2). For him the tales were pure fantasy, without any hint of realism, a view with which it is difficult to disagree.

It is hardly surprising that the locus of animal tales is overwhelmingly rural Russia and its vast forests, and even the few beasts not indigenous to Russia seem quite at home there. The lion, for instance, becomes a resident in the few stories in which he is encountered. Polar bears admit to their lack of familiarity with the land beasts, particularly man, but are otherwise fully at ease. Occasionally a mention of the steppe may intrude. Even more rarely one encounters a city, usually St. Petersburg or Kazan, but it is always far, far away and unreachable. When an inhabited place is brought into the tale, it is usually the village, the *derevnia*, distinguished by its anonymity and never described in any detail. Only the fact that human beings live in these villages is worth noting. The people are usually a peasant or his wife or occasionally a landowner, who may well end up the butt of a joke. It is usual to find more village women than men appearing in the tales. The activities that are depicted tend to be those of Central Russian peasants: building houses, harvesting, cutting wood, stripping bast, hunting, and fishing. There are rather detailed descriptions of the peasant hut and the bath house but surprisingly none whatsoever of the church.

There is nothing in animal tales to indicate time other than "past," but time is really irrelevant to these tales, unless of course it is the point of them: building an icehouse is not done in summer, the hare is not likely to lust after the fox except in spring, and so forth.

Many of the motifs found in animal tales are of great antiquity, perhaps surviving from a period reflecting totemistic beliefs. But in their existing form the tales are generally far removed from such ancient beliefs. Despite the evidence, if such it can be called, that the stories were first told when men, birds, and animals all spoke the same language, this seems as unlikely as a tomcat's beheading the famous witch, Baba Yaga. Although some of these tales may indeed be ancient, it is much easier to understand them as reflecting Russian society in its dominant historical mode—patriarchal, inward-looking, and self-sufficient. Modern ethnographic research in Russia has established that many of the most archaic rites and rituals associated with the basic rites of passage still persist in the late twentieth century. All of the more common of these rites and rituals, such as those associated with birth, naming, puberty, weddings, and funerals, and many of the less frequently performed rites, survive in animal tales. The fox can serve as midwife; the beasts get married but not divorced because the church disapproves of it. Some are involved in ritual confessions of sins; others in the commission of the sins themselves. There are animals at funerals, and they may even be involved in the disposal of the corpse. Mainly, however, and this is true for perhaps ninety percent of animal tales, the actors in the tales are concerned about getting a meal, and in this activity the animals pay little attention to moral niceties or polite table manners. The pig on a pilgrimage to Piter (St. Petersburg) may well lead the wolf, bear, fox, hare, cock, and mouse into a pit. The animals will be hungry and have a contest to see who will eat whom, and the mouse, cock, hare, pig, and wolf will be the initial victims. When it comes to the final contest between the little fox and the enormous bear, it is no contest at all. The fox, having hidden the scraps left over from the previous victims under her tail, pretends to be pulling them out of her bowels. The bear is most curious about this new source of food and inquires of the fox, who says she is so hungry that she is eating her own innards. The bear tries pulling out his own intestines, and, not surprisingly, dies. The fox has a number of good meals lined up (A–T 21)!

Interpretation and Purpose of the Tales

Animal stories in general do not lend themselves to a clear and obvious interpretation, although nearly every one involves the search for food and shelter—in other words, the struggle for survival. Each tale is a self-contained episode featuring villains and victims, but the identity of the latter changes. In many tales brute force obtains the desired results, while in others it is deceit and connivance that achieve this end. There seems to be no limit to the bestiality that animals practice: murder, theft, adultery, and overindulgence are rampant in this violent, dog-eat-dog world, a world that clearly resembles the world of man.

What then was the purpose of animal tales? They do seem to have served a very serious purpose in Old Russia. Many of the tales served to illustrate proverbs and sayings, as has been demonstrated by Grigorii Permiakov (1970), and there is very likely an ancient connection among proverbs, riddles, and animal tales.

I have searched in vain for any kind of overriding and positive message that might be gleaned from the tales. The lessons they teach are the following: take advantage of every opportunity to enrich yourself, strike while the iron is hot, do what it takes to survive, trust only one's own kin, and mistrust those who are different in any way. These are in fact the conservative values, the inculcation of which, I believe, constituted the didactic purpose of animal tales in Old Russia. Judging from the scanty evidence available, it would seem that in earlier times the tales were used by the peasantry of Russia to illustrate these negative aspects of social behavior, notwithstanding the fact that the actual moral of any particular story is rarely spelled out so blatantly as in the fables of Aesop or the tales of Charles Perrault, although Röhrich argued otherwise.[8] Most commentators on the animal tale have completely ignored this original purpose of the tale, merely mentioning its function in later times. Gerber, for instance, noted that the Russian tales were unlike their Western counterparts from the Middle Ages and the Aesopian fables in that they were "neither allegorical or satirical, nor intended to impart a teaching or a moral. They are often humorous, to be sure, but they never aim to chastise or ridicule any class of people or any abuse of society: they may convey a moral incidentally, their purpose, however, is not to teach, but to entertain." Gerber is only correct when one considers the role of animal tales from the nineteenth century onward.

Before the beginning of the nineteenth century, the function of animal tales had certainly changed. By then they had come to be regarded as nursery tales and were relegated to the printed page. They occupied a conspicuous role in the spread of literacy among the peasantry of all ages, appearing in the *lubki* and in primers published by the Ministry of Education. They also provided models for writers such as Lev Tolstoi and Kornei Chukovskii, whose books are still read and enjoyed by Russians today. It is hoped that this volume will amuse and instruct, and not offend, just as animal tales amused and instructed the peasants of Russia in the past.

Notes

1. There are no contemporary academic studies of Russian animal tales in English. Stith Thompson only briefly mentions the tales in *The Folktale*. Neither do they receive more than a passing mention in the work of Lüthi or Röhrich.

2. The best study of fabulates and memorates in English is certainly that by Linda V. Ivanits, *Russian Folk Belief* (Armonk and London, 1989). The outstanding Russian study is E.V. Pomerantseva, *Mifologicheskie personazhi v russkom fol'klore* (Moscow, 1975).

3. The interested reader is directed to Jack V. Haney, *An Introduction to the Russian Folktale* (volume 1 of *The Complete Russian Folktale*), where there is extended discussion of the bear and his role in Russian folklore.

4. V.Ia. Propp, *The Morphology of the Folktale*. Propp has contributed more than any other Russian to the study of the Russian wondertale, but his remarks on animal tales are more limited.

5. Published in Russian in Minsk in 1989, Kruk's *Vostochnoslavianskie skazki o zhivotnykh* (East Slavic animal tales) is a summary of current Slavic thinking about animal tales. It embodies the points of view expressed in the twentieth century by Russian scholars, notably V. Bobrov (see Bobrov 1906–8).

6. Every folk culture identifies a trickster. For instance, among the Pacific Northwest Coast Indians it is the raven. The coyote is predominant in a large number of other North American Indian cultures. Among the Europeans the fox is the most common trickster.

7. The word *kon'* was an ancient borrowing from Celtic and in ancient times referred to a warhorse, a horse belonging to and ridden by a warrior. It is thus an entirely appropriate word for the horse of a hero in the wondertales and that is the word encountered. The word *loshad'* first appears in 1103 as a borrowing from a Turkic language, possibly Chuvash. This was always the beast of burden in Old Russia and does not figure as a warhorse. As a rule, Russian peasants, even in the nineteenth century, did not ride their horses but led them, and this is reflected in the folktales. They invariably referred to them as *loshad'*. Overall, the word *loshad'* gradually replaced *kon'* as the standard word for horse, and *kon'* was relegated to poetic usage.

8. Röhrich argued that the tales close with didactic or moralizing statements whenever possible (Röhrich, 1991; 164). This definitely is not the situation with regard to the entire Russian corpus. If a moral can be drawn, it is more subtle than the German scholar suggests.

Bibliography

Aarne, Antti and Stith Thompson. 1987. *The Types of the Folktale*, 2nd rev., Helsinki.

Afanas'ev, A.N. 1973. *Russian Fairy Tales*, transl. Norbert Guterman, 2nd ed., New York.

Azadovskii, Mark. 1974. *A Siberian Tale Teller*, transl. James R. Dow. Austin.

Barag, L.G.; I.P. Berezovskii; K.P. Kabashnikov; N.V. Novikov. 1979. *Sravnitel'nyi ukazatel' siuzhetov. Vostochnoslavianskaia skazka*, Leningrad.

Bobrov, V. 1906–1908. *Russkie narodnye skazki o zhivotnykh*, published in the *Russkii filologicheskii vestnik*, Warsaw, 1906 (vol. 56), 1907 (57, 58), and 1908 (vols. 59, 60).

Gerber, Adolph. 1891. *Great Russian Animal Tales. A Collection of Fifty Tales.* Baltimore: Modern Language Association of America. Baltimore.

Kruk, I.I. 1989. *Vostochnoslavianskie skazki o zhivotnykh*, Minsk.

Legman, G. 1998. *Russian Secret Tales*, 2nd ed., Baltimore.

Löwis of Menar, August von. 1912. *Der Held im deutschen und russischen Märchen*, Jena.

———. 1923. *Die Brünhildsage in Russland*, Leipzig.

Lüthi, Max. 1976. *Once Upon a Time. On the Nature of Fairy Tales*, trans. of *Es war einmal*; transl. Lee Chadeayne and Paul Gottwald. Bloomington and London.

Mokhin, V.N. 1975. *Russkaia narodnaia skazka v sovremennom bytovanii*, Gor'kii.

Novikov, N.V. 1971. *Russkie skazki v rannikh zapisiakh i publikatsiiakh XVI–XVIII vv.*, Leningrad.

Permiakov, G.L. 1970. *Ot pogovorki do skazki: Zametki po obshchei teorii klishe*, Moscow.

Pomerantseva, E.V. 1963. *Russkaia narodnaia skazka*, Moscow.

Propp, V.Ia. 1990. *The Morphology of the Folktale*, 2nd ed., Austin.

———. 1984. *Russkaia skazka*, Leningrad.

Ralston, W.R.S. 1873. *Russian Folk-tales*. London.

Röhrich, Lutz. 1991. *Folktales and Reality*, trans. of *Märchen und Wirklichkeit* by Peter Tokofsky, Bloomington and Indianapolis.

Thompson, Stith. 1977. *The Folktale*. Berkeley, Los Angeles, and London.

Russian Animal Tales

1. Sister Fox and the Wolf

There lived an old man and an old woman. The old man said to the old woman, "You, old woman, bake some pies, and I'll go catch some fish."

The old man caught the fish and was bringing home a whole cart full. On the way, he saw a fox curled up like a biscuit lying in the road. The old man got down from his cart and went up to the fox, but she didn't move; she just lay there as if dead. "Well, that'll be a present for the wife," said the old man, and he took the fox and put her in the cart. Then he rode on. Now the fox waited for just the right time and then began ever so gently to toss all the fish one after another from the cart. And when she had thrown them all off, she herself departed.

"Well, old woman," said the old man, "look what a collar I've brought you for your fur coat!"

"Where?"

"There, the fish and the collar are both in the cart."

The old woman went up to the cart: no collar, no fish, so she began to curse the old man. "You old horseradish, you so-and-so. Who did you think you could fool?" Just then the old man figured it out: the fox hadn't been dead. He grieved and was bitter, but there was nothing to be done.

Now the fox collected into a pile all the fish she had thrown off along the way, and then she sat down and began to eat. A wolf came up to her.

"Hello, dearie!"

"Hello, my dear!"

"Give me a bit of fishy!"

"Catch it yourself, then you'll eat."

"I don't know how."

"Oh, I've already caught my lot. You, dear, go out on the river and let your tail down into the ice hole. A fish will hook onto your tail by itself. Then you sit a bit longer, or you won't catch your lot."

The wolf went out onto the river and lowered his tail into the ice hole. It was winter, you see. And he sat and he sat, he sat a whole night through, and his tail was frozen solid. He tried to get up, but there was no way he could. There was just nothing to be done. "Oh, so many fish have clamped on, I can't even pull them out."

He looked up. Some women who were coming for water had caught sight of him and were shouting: "Wolf, wolf! Kill him!" They came and began to thrash the wolf, some with yokes, some with buckets or what-

3

ever was at hand. The wolf tried and tried to jump up; then he tore off his tail and ran away with nary a glance back.

"Very well then," he thought. "I'll pay you back, my dearie."

But sister fox, having eaten up the fish, decided to try getting something else. She climbed into a hut where the women were making pancakes and fell head first into a barrel of batter, got it smeared all over her, and fled. The wolf happened along and met her. "So this is what you taught me! I've just been thoroughly thrashed!"

"But my dear," said sister fox, "you've just lost a little blood, while I've had it far worse than you. My brains have been beaten out. I'm just staggering along."

"That is true," said the wolf. "Wherever you need to go, I'll carry you."

So the fox got on his back, and the wolf set off carrying her. So sister fox sat quietly and sang quietly, "The beaten one carries the unbeaten one, the beaten one carries the unbeaten one."

"What are you saying, dearie?"

"I'm saying, 'the beaten one carries the beaten one.'"

"Well, that's it, dearie, that's it."

"Say, let's build huts for ourselves, my dear."

"Let's, dearie."

"I'll build a bast* house, and you build one of ice."

They set to work and built the huts: for the fox a bast one, and for the wolf one of ice. And they lived in them. Spring came, and the wolf's hut melted. "Oh, dearie," said the wolf, "you've deceived me once again, and now I'll just have to eat you for this."

"Let's go, friend, let's have another try to see who can find something to eat."

So sister fox led him into the forest to a deep pit and said, "Jump! If you jump across the pit, then you eat me, but if you don't jump across, then I'll eat you!"

The wolf jumped and fell into the pit. "Well," said the fox, "just sit there." And she went away.

She walked along, carrying her rolling pin in her paws, and invited herself into a peasant's hut. "Let sister fox spend the night."

"It's already crowded without you."

---

*Bast is the inner bark of the linden or lime tree. A paper-like material could be made from thin strips of it and used to make simple woodcuts. These same strips served as the material for the common boots of the Russian peasant.

"I won't crowd you, I'll lie on the bench, my tail beneath the bench, the rolling pin next to the stove." They let her in. She lay down on the bench, her tail beneath the bench, her rolling pin next to the stove. Early the next morning the fox got up, burned up her rolling pin, and then asked, "Where's my rolling pin? I'll take nothing less than a goose for it!" There was nothing else the peasant could do, so he gave her a goose for the rolling pin. The fox took the goose and walked along singing:

> *Sister fox went walking along the road.*
> *She was carrying a rolling pin*
> *And for that rolling pin got a goose!*
> *Knock, knock, knock!*

She knocked at the door of another peasant's hut.
"Who's there?"
"It is I, sister fox, let me in to spend the night."
"It's already crowded without you."
"I won't crowd you. I'll lie on the bench, my tail beneath the bench, my goose next to the stove." They let her in. She lay herself down on the bench, her tail beneath the bench, and the goose next to the stove. The next morning she jumped up early, grabbed the goose, plucked her, ate her up, and said, "Where's my goose? I'll take nothing less than a turkey hen for her!" The peasant—there was nothing else he could do—gave her his turkey hen for the goose. The fox took the turkey hen and walked along singing:

> *Sister fox went walking along the road.*
> *She was carrying a rolling pin*
> *And for that rolling pin got a goose!*
> *And for that goose she got a turkey hen!*

Knock, knock, knock! She knocked at the door of a third peasant's hut.
"Who's there?"
"I am, sister fox. Let me in to spend the night."
"It's already crowded without you."
"I won't crowd you. I'll lie on the bench, my tail beneath the bench, my turkey hen next to the stove." They let her in. She lay down on the bench, her tail beneath the bench, the turkey hen next to the stove. Early in the morning the fox jumped up, grabbed the turkey hen, plucked it

and ate it up, and said, "Where's my turkey hen? For her I won't take less than your bride!" For the peasant there was nothing to do except give up his bride for the turkey hen. The fox put her in a bag and walked along singing:

> Sister fox went walking along the road.
> She was carrying a rolling pin
> And for that rolling pin got a goose!
> And for that goose she got a turkey hen!
> And for that turkey hen she got a bride!

Knock, knock, knock! She knocked at the hut of a fourth peasant.
"Who's there?"
"It is I, sister fox. Let me in to spend the night."
"It's already crowded without you."
"I won't crowd you. I myself shall lie on the bench, my tail beneath the bench, my bag next to the stove." They let her in. She lay down on the bench, her tail beneath the bench, the bag next to the stove. The peasant stealthily let the bride out of the bag and kicked a dog into it. Well, next morning sister fox prepared for the road, took her bag, walked along, and said, "Oh bride, sing some songs!" And that dog started yelping! The fox was so frightened that she flung away the bag with the dog and ran.

So the fox was running and saw that on the gate there sat a cock. She went up to him and said, "Cock, oh cock! Come down here, and I'll hear your confession: you have seventy wives and are always sinning!" The cock came down, and she grabbed him and ate him up.

A–T 1 + 2 + 3 + 4 + 43 + 30 + 170 + 61

2. Where Does the Wind Blow From?

Once a bear was strolling about the forest. He walked and walked, and suddenly this black grouse flew up off the ground. And it flew right into the bear's mouth: he had let his mouth hang wide open as he was walking along. The bear quickly caught it and trapped it with his jaws, and then he walked on. He was most satisfied because he would have something for dinner, a bite to eat.

Then up came cousin fox Liza Patrikeevna. She noted that the bear was holding this grouse in his mouth, and she wondered about a plan to deceive him so that the grouse might fly out of the bear's mouth. She got an idea and asked the bear, "Misha, tell me, there's something I just don't get: where does the wind blow from?"

Now that fat-footed fool ought to have answered, "From the east," because then he would have had to clamp his jaws down firmer, but he said, "From the south." He opened his mouth, and the grouse fell out. The fox grabbed it and was off. She grabbed it and ran away.

A–T 6

3. The Tale of the Gray Wolf

In a certain small town there lived and dwelt this merchant who conducted trade in fish and by this means provided sustenance for his entire family. Once it occurred to him to take some smelt to the next village, and so, as he was riding through a field, a fox was lying in the middle of the road, pretending to be dead. The merchant hit it once or twice with his whip, but not only did it not get up, it didn't even move. The merchant, considering it dead, got down from his sleigh and lifted up the fox, and laid it next to the smelt, for which the fox was glad indeed. As it was still quite far to the village, the fox gnawed a hole in the sleigh, threw down a few smelt onto the road, and then, having herself eaten to complete satisfaction, she jumped out of the sleigh and ran away into the forest. She noted that the simple-hearted merchant had driven far into the distance, so she ran out of the forest and began to collect the smelt scattered along the road. Having gathered them up, she ran back into the forest, sat down on a little stump, and continued eating. It happened that at that very moment the gray wolf walked past Lisa Ivanovna, the fox. He came up to her and said, "May God be with you, Cousin Lisa Ivanovna!"

"Thank you, cousin and little father," answered the fox.

"What are you doing, cousin?" asked the gray wolf.

"I'm eating smelt."

"Let me determine what their taste is. Never since my birth have I eaten any."

"Please, do help yourself, cousin," and she gave him several smelt.

"What a splendid food! Where pray, cousin, did you obtain them?"

"I caught them, my friend. I am not so lazy as you idlers."

"Do me a great favor, cousin, and teach me how to catch fish, for which I shall be eternally grateful to you."

"Very well," said the fox. "Go fetch a basket from somewhere, and we'll go together to the ice hole."

The wolf, after hearing all this, purposefully ran into the settlement and in one empty hut found an enormous basket, and grabbing it, he ran to the fox, who took him to the ice hole, attached the basket to his tail, and ordered him to lower it into the water and then sit there. The wolf sat for a long time, and the fox, pacing alongside him, said, "Clear, clear is the sky, freeze, freeze wolf's tail in the ice hole." She repeated these words up to five times.

The wolf, hearing the fox talking as she walked about him, asked, "What are you saying, cousin?"

"I'm telling the fish," said the fox, "to get into the basket quickly."

"God grant it, foxy!" said the wolf.

Then the fox ordered the wolf to get up, but, seeing that his tail had still not frozen in the ice hole, she ordered him to wait a little longer.

And when the tail had frozen solidly in the ice hole, she said that it was "time to pull the basket out of the water and perchance many fish would be in it." However hard the wolf endeavored to pull his tail out of the water, he couldn't do it. And his efforts were in vain, and he began to roar and shout. Peasants, hearing such an unusual uproar, ran with stakes to the river, and seeing that the wolf had frozen his tail, they began to beat him. He suddenly gave such a strong jerk that he tore off a great part of that tail and rushed mindlessly into the forest. The fox, seeing what a misfortune had befallen the wolf and fearing that he would rip her to shreds, ran into the village and into a hut in which a kind old woman had a dough mixed. Lisa Ivanovna several times slaked her hunger, and then, thrusting her head into the pitcher, she smeared herself with the dough. Then she ran out to meet the disfigured wolf, who at first was furious with her but then, seeing that she was beaten to a pulp, asked, "How did such a thing happen to you, cousin?"

"Well, cousin, I imbibed too much at the wrong feast. You went on to catch fish, and they beat my brains out."

"Oh, I'm so sorry for you, cousin," said the wolf. "But I don't know how to be of assistance."

"Never mind, cousin," answered the fox. "I'll remember your hospitality." Then she proposed to the wolf, "Let's cast lots, cousin, to decide which of us shall carry the other one, for we are both crippled." The luck of the draw fell to the wolf to carry the fox. So sitting on top of the wolf, the fox said, "Beaten carries unbeaten," and she repeated this about three times. The wolf listened to the fox's mumbling, but he didn't grasp her words and asked, "What are you saying, cousin?"

"I am saying," said the fox, "that beaten is carrying beaten."

"You are right, cousin," answered the simple-hearted wolf. But as their route lay through a meadow, a little bird flew by, and seeing it the wolf said, "Where is that little bird going? I'd like to turn into one."

"That's not so extraordinary," said the fox. "If you want, I'll do it right away, because I made that little bird out of a hare."

"Do me such a kindness, cousin," the wolf asked the fox. "Turn me into a bird."

"Very well," said the fox. "Now, go to the village and bring back a lighted splinter and come to this place," she said, indicating to him a stack of hay.

The wolf ran into the village for the fire and splinter, and the fox made a small hole in the middle of the haystack, just so that the wolf could crawl through into it, for she intended to burn him up in it. As soon as the wolf brought the lighted splinter, the fox ordered him to make his way into the middle of the haystack, and she lit fires all around it, and started to burn it up, and with all due haste ran into the forest, wishing to get away from the wolf.

Running along the road, she thought to herself, "Little ears, listen to me! Whom do you serve?"

"You, Lisa Ivanovna!"

"Little eyes of mine! My guides! Whom do you serve?"

"You, Lisa Ivanovna!"

"Little legs, quick walkers of mine, whom do you serve?"

"You, Lisa Ivanovna."

"And you, dogtail, whom do you serve?"

"I serve the wolf," answered the tail, "and hinder your running so that the gray wolf will catch you and eat you."

"Very well, you [son-of-a-] bitch, I'll deal with you." And she ran up to the forest, sat in a hollow tree, and hung her tail out so that the wolf would tear it off for its insubordination.

Meanwhile, the gray wolf, sitting in the middle of the haystack, began to feel an extraordinary heat. He jumped out and ran in search of Lisa Ivanovna, wishing to eat her. Running by the hollow tree, he caught sight of the fox's tail. He ran up to the hollow tree, grabbed the fox by the tail, and ate that fox! Then he went into the forest, where even now he prowls, not having the slightest acquaintance with foxes and other beasts.

A–T 1 + 2 + 3 + 4 + 8

4. The Peasant, the Bear, and the Fox

A peasant and a bear were great friends. Once they took it into their heads to sow turnips. They sowed them, and then they began to discuss who should take what. The peasant said, "I'll take the roots, and you, Misha, take the tops." So the turnips grew, and the peasant took the roots and Misha the tops.

Misha saw that he had made a mistake, and he said to the peasant, "You have tricked me, brother! When we sow something else, you won't fool me so easily."

A year passed. The peasant said to the bear: "Well, Misha, let's sow some wheat."

"Let's," said Misha.

So they sowed the wheat. And the wheat ripened, and the peasant said, "Now which will you take, Misha? The roots or the tops?"

"No, brother, you won't fool me now! Give me the roots, and you take the tops."

So they gathered in the wheat and divided it. The peasant ground some wheat and baked himself some fine wheat rolls. He went to Misha and said, "Well, Misha, and this is what the tops give."

"Well, peasant," said the bear, "now I am angry with you, and I'm going to eat you!"

The peasant went off and started crying.

Then a fox came along and said to the peasant, "Why are you crying?"

"Why should I not cry, why should I not be sad? The bear wants to eat me."

"Don't be afraid, uncle, he won't eat you." And the fox went off into the bushes, but she ordered the peasant to stay in the same spot. Then she came out and asked, "Peasant, aren't there any lobo wolves or bears around here?"

And so the bear came up to the peasant and said, "Well, peasant, don't say anything, I won't eat you."

The peasant said to the fox, "Nope."

The fox started laughing and said, "What's that lying in the cart there?"

The bear quietly said to the peasant, "It's a chopping block."

"If it were a chopping block," said the fox, "it would be tied to the cart." And she ran off into the bushes.

The bear said to the peasant, "Tie me up and put me in the cart." The peasant did just that.

So the fox came back again and asked the peasant, "Peasant, aren't there any lobo wolves or bears around?"

"Nope," said the peasant.

"Well, what's that lying in the cart?"

"It's a chopping block."

"If it were a chopping block, it would have an axe stuck in it."

So the bear quietly said to the peasant, "Well now, peasant, stick an axe in me." The peasant stuck an axe in his back, and the bear died.

Then the fox said to the peasant, "Well, now, peasant, what will you give me for my labors?"

"I'll give you a pair of white hens, and you carry them off, don't peek."

So she took the bag from the peasant and set off. She carried and carried it along and then thought, "Let me have a peek!" She looked in and there were two white dogs! The dogs jumped out of the bag after her. The fox ran and ran, then popped under a stump into her burrow, and she got away, and she sat there talking to herself, "What did you do, little ears?"

"We listened."

"And what did you do, little legs?"

"We just kept on running."

"And what did you do, little eyes?"

"We just kept on looking."

"And tail, what about you?"

"I kept you from running faster."

"So you bothered me, just you wait, I'll give you one." And she stuck her tail out at the dogs. The dogs grabbed hold of it, pulled out the fox, and tore her to bits.

A–T 9 + 154

5. The Bear and the Fox

A bear and a fox became friends and began to live in the same hut. Once the bear let slip, "Well, fox, I've a whole platter of butter, you know."

Now the fox was very fond of butter and began thinking about how to eat up the bear's butter. One evening when the bear was lying on the stove and the fox was sitting on a towel rail spinning, it occurred to her to eat some of the butter. She took the thread up on her spindle, stuck it in the spinning wheel, and shouted, "Who's there? I'll put this down and come." She ran into the hallway and came back, and the bear asked, "Who's there, foxy? Who's banging so?"

"Oh, they're calling me to be a godmother at a christening."

"Well go, foxy, go!"

Well, the fox quickly turned and left, ran up into the attic and started gnawing at the butter. But the butter was frozen so that she froze her lips and got chilled to the bone. She ran back and sat down on the towel rail. And the bear asked, "Well, and what did you name your little peasant, foxy?"

"Oh, lie still, fat belly, I'm completely frozen and you want to know everything."

"Well, tell me, foxy, tell me!"

"Begun."

"A good name is that! Very good."

Again she sat, she sat on the rail, warmed up, and thought of gnawing some butter. Once more she stuck her spindle in the spinning wheel and said, "Who's there?" She ran into the hallway, and the bear asked, "Who's there, foxy, who's banging so?"

"I'm called to be godmother at a christening again. Such a cold spell, everything is frozen."

"Well, off you go, poor foxy, off you go!" (He doesn't know his butter's being eaten!)

So the fox went out and went back into the attic and gnawed up more than half the platter of butter. She ran back and sat down on the stove, on the towel railing to warm herself. And the bear asked, "Well, what did they name your little peasant, foxy?"

"Oh, fat belly, I'm just frozen—nobody calls you out!"

"But tell me, foxy, tell me, what did they name the little peasant?"

"Lapped-up-to-the-middle"—because more than half the butter had been eaten.

"Oh, a good name! Very good."

The fox warmed up and again thought of going to gnaw some butter. Once again she stuck her spindle in the spinning wheel and said, "Who's there?" She ran out into the hallway, stood there for a bit, and came back into the hut. And the bear asked, "Who's that banging there, foxy?"

"Once more they're calling me to a christening."

"Well, off you go, poor foxy, off you go."

So the fox ran up into the attic and gobbled up all the butter. She came back, sat down on the railing, and said to herself, "Oh, to hell with it. I'm not going out to be godmother anymore! I'm frozen stiff."

On the stove the bear said, "Listen, poor foxy, what did they name the little peasant?"

"Licked-to-the-bottom."

"A fine name that. Very good." So they lived and lived on a while, and the bear remembered about the butter and said to the fox, "Foxy, make some pancakes. I've got a platter of butter, so let's eat some pancakes with butter."

Well now the fox heated up the stove, and the bear clambered up into the attic and looked: his platter was empty! He came back into the hut with a roar. "Oh, oh, foxy! Someone has eaten my platter of butter! Are you sure you went to those christenings?"

"Oh, fat belly, maybe you ate it yourself and are blaming me! Let's sit up against the stove and the one the butter runs out of is the one who ate it."

So the stove got really hot, and the fox moved two tables to the stove, laid down two frying pans on them, and they sat down in the frying pans. The bear went to sleep on account of the heat, but from the fox a full frying pan of butter poured out. She took her frying pan full of butter and moved it over to the bear. She took the empty one for herself and woke up the bear. The bear believed her and said, "Probably I'm the guilty one, poor foxy, I ate up all the butter." And so that's all there is to that.

A–T 15

6. The Beasts in the Pit

A pig was going to Piter* to pray to God. Along the way she chanced to meet a wolf. "Pig, oh pig, where are you going?"

"To Piter, to pray to God."

"Take me with you."

"Come along then, cousin."

They walked, and they walked, and they chanced to meet a fox. "Pig, oh pig, where are you going?"

"To Piter, to pray to God."

"Take me with you!"

"Come along then, cousin."

So they walked and walked, and they chanced to meet a hare. "Pig, oh pig, where are you going?"

"To Piter, to pray to God."

"Take me with you."

"Come along then, cross-eyes!"

Then a squirrel asked to go along, and so they all walked and walked.

But then right there, right in the road, was a deep and wide pit; and the pig jumped and fell into the pit, and behind her the wolf, the fox, the hare, and the squirrel.

They sat there for a long time and got really hungry—there was nothing to eat at all. So then the fox thought, "Let's drone out a note, and we'll eat up the one who can't hold it as long as the others." So the wolf started droning his note in his deep voice: "O-o-o-o-o-o-o." The pig was a little softer: "Oo-oo-oo-oo-oo." The fox was still softer: "E-e-e-e-e-e." But the hare and squirrel with their thin little voices managed only a little "Ee-ee-ee-ee." Immediately the beasts tore the hare and squirrel apart and devoured them and all their bones.

The next day the fox again said, "Whoever has the deepest voice we'll eat." So the wolf started singing deepest of all: "O-o-o. . . ." And so they ate him up.

The fox ate the meat but hid the innards underneath her. About three days later she sat there eating the guts. The pig asked, "What is that you're eating, cousin? Give me some."

"Oh, pig, I'm pulling out my insides. Slit open your belly, pull out

---

*St. Petersburg.

your guts, and start eating!" So that's what the pig did, she slit open her belly and the fox got the lot for dinner. The fox was left alone, all by herself in the pit. Whether she climbed out or is still sitting there, I don't know.

A–T 20A + 21

7. Miss Mousie—The Burrower

Here's Miss Mousie with a little Housie, sailing along, squeaking away, she's singing a song. A weasel came running and asked, "And whose little ship is running over the lake, and what is its master called?"

And she replied, "I'm the mouse's daughter, the daughter of the bell ringer;* I am the young Snafidia Davidovna. And who are you?"

"I am Weasel Silky-sides! Take me along!"

"Let's go!"

And they set off, they started singing in various keys, they rode along and sang, and they made quite a racket. And up ran a little white hare. "And whose little ship is this running over the lake, and what is its master called?"

"I am the mouse's daughter, the daughter of the bell ringer; I am the young Snafidia Davidovna."

"And I'm Weasel Silky-sides."

"Take me along!"

"And who are you?"

"I'm Little White Hare!"

And so the third one jumped on. They rode, they rode along, and in various keys they sang, they made quite a racket. And up ran a young hound. "And whose little ship is this running over the lake, and what is its master called?"

"I am the mouse's daughter, the daughter of the bell ringer; I am the young Snafidia Davidovna."

"And I am Weasel Silky-sides."

"And I am Little White Hare."

"Take me along!"

"And who are you?"

---

*She has a tinkling voice.

"I am Young Hound." And so the fourth one jumped aboard.

They rode, they rode along, and in various keys they sang, they made quite a racket. And up ran a fox. "And whose little ship is this running over the lake and what is its master called?"

"I am mouse's daughter, the daughter of the bellringer; I am the young Snafidia Davidovna."

"And I am Weasel Silky-sides."

"And I am Little White Hare."

"And I am Young Hound."

"Take me along!"

"And who are you?"

"I am Sister Fox." And so that one jumped on.

They continued on, they sang songs, they made quite a racket. Up ran a big wolf with a huge gray tail. "And whose little ship is this running over the lake, and what is its master called?"

"I am the mouse's daughter, the daughter of the bell ringer; I am the young Snafidia Davidovna."

"And I am Weasel Silky-sides."

"And I am Little White Hare."

"And I am Young Hound."

"And I am Sister Fox."

"Take me along!"

"And who are you?"

"Wolf Big Gray Tail."

And he jumped on. They went on, they sang songs in various keys, and they made quite a racket. Then up came running Bear Eating Warm Food: "And whose little ship is running over the lake, and what is its master called?"

"I am the mouse's daughter, the daughter of the bell ringer; I am the young Snafidia Davidovna."

"And I am Weasel Silky-Sides."

"And I am the Little White Hare."

"And I am Young Hound."

"And I am Sister Fox."

"And I am Wolf Big Gray Tail, and who are you?"

"I am Bear Eating Warm Food, take me along."

"Come along."

They turned toward the shore. The bear thrust one paw on board and wanted to get the other one on, but the boat turned upside down, like an upturned trough, and all started swimming. Miss Mousie of the Little

Housie, weasel, hare, hound, fox, and big wolf with the big gray tail. And they all swam to shore and sat down: the mouse's daughter; the daughter of the bell ringer; the weasel Silky-Sides; Little White Hare; Young Hound; Sister Fox; Big Wolf with the Big Gray Tail; and Bear Eating Warm Food. They all sat according to rank. And they began singing. They sang and sang. Then the fox spoke, "Let's sit a bit and sit a bit more, then whoever's smallest, we'll eat him up!" So they ate the little mouse—the fox tore her up, weasel got a haunch, hare a haunch, hound a shoulder, and fox a shoulder, then wolf got the torso, and the remainder went to the bear—just the head. And the bear could scarcely feel it on his tongue.

Again they sat and sang songs. The fox ran about, ran in a circle. She had bitten off a piece of her share and shoved it under her ass, under a stone. And she said, "We'll sit a bit, we'll sit a bit more, whoever's smallest, we'll eat him up."

They tore up the weasel. For hare a haunch, for hound a haunch, for wolf a shoulder, for fox herself a shoulder, and for bear the torso and the rest. And the fox ate a little bit and put the rest beneath a stone. And again she ran, not sitting down anywhere, and said, "We'll sit a bit, we'll sit a bit, and whoever's smallest, we'll eat him up!"

It was the hare's turn. They ate up the hare. The fox gave the hound a haunch and took a haunch for herself. The wolf had two shoulders, and the bear all that remained. They sat and told tales and sang songs. The fox said again, "Let's sit a bit, let's sit a bit, and whoever is smallest, we'll eat him up." So they ate the hound. They divided the hound too. She took some for herself, gave some to the wolf, and gave a little to the bear too. They sat and sang songs. And the wolf looked around. The wolf said, "I," he said, "am going for a short run." And he ran into the forest.

The fox sat on a knoll. She took some meat out from under her ass and ate it. "And what are you eating, fox?"

"I stick my paw up my ass and get some meat. You can get some too, I gave you more." Again they sat for a while, the fox still getting some meat and eating it. The bear asked her, "What are you eating, fox?"

"I stick my paw up my ass and get some. Stick yours in and you'll get some." He stuck in his paw. What? Nothing?! But the fox said, "Stick it further, stick it in further still!" He could hardly breathe. She took him by the throat and strangled him. And she ate him. Though not all at once. And just the fox remained. And that's the whole tale.

A–T 20A + 21

8. The Pig Set Off for the Games

An old man lived with an old woman. The old woman said, "Let's butcher the pig. Brother-in-law is coming, and there'll be nowhere to get any pork."

The pig heard and decided to run away. She was walking along when she met a dog. "Where are you off to, pig?"

"To the games."

"Take me along."

"Let's go, the more the merrier." They continued on. They met a hare. "Where are you going, pig?"

"To the games."

"Take me."

"Let's go! The more the merrier."

So the pig, the dog, and the hare set off again. They met a fox. "Where are you going?" asked the fox.

"To the games."

"Take me."

"Let's go. We'll go together. The more the merrier." So the pig, the hare, the dog, and the fox set off. They met a wolf. "Where, oh pig, are you going?"

"To the games."

"Take me with you."

"Let's go. The more the merrier."

So the pig, the dog, the hare, the fox, and the wolf set off again. They met a bear. "Where are you going, pig?"

"To the games."

"Take me with you."

"And why not? Let's go. The more the merrier."

The pig, wolf, bear, fox, hare, and dog set off again. They walked and walked. They came to a pit. How could they cross it? A thin pole was laid down. The pig set out first, behind the rest came the bear. When they came to the middle, the pole broke and they all fell in. They sat and sat. They wanted to eat. The fox said, "Let's all see who can drone a note the longest." They all stretched out their voices, but the hare didn't stretch his in the slightest, so they tore him up.

The fox put the guts under herself. But the bear didn't stretch his voice out either: he was master of them all. They sat there one day, a second day they sat. And again they started to drone out a note. The pig didn't quite stretch the note far enough, so they ate her, and then the dog and wolf were torn to bits. Each time the fox put the intestines under herself.

Finally the fox was left sitting with the bear. They sat and sat. The fox put her paw beneath her and sat there, eating the intestines. The bear asked her, "What are you eating, foxy?"

"I'm pulling out my intestines and eating them." The bear stuck his paw into himself, took out all the innards, and died. The fox ate him.

The fox sat in the pit, but she did not know how to get out. She looked and saw a woodpecker flying over the pit. "Woodpecker, dear little father! Let me out!"

"And how am I to let you out?"

"Peck out some steps for me!" So he pecked out the steps and out she crawled.

"Woodpecker, little father, bring me some beer."

"And how shall I?"

"Over there a peasant is carting some beer. Sit first on the horse, then on the barrel, then the horse, then the barrel."

The woodpecker flew off. The peasant began to use his whip chasing the bird, and he whipped the barrel apart, and the beer spilled out, and the fox drank it up.

Then the fox asked, "Woodpecker, dear little father! Feed me with pancakes."

"And how shall I feed you?"

"When the old woman has mixed the batter, drag away the pancakes." He fed her.

Again the fox asked, "Woodpecker, dear little father? Make me laugh!"

"And how shall I make you laugh?"

"Over there four peasants are threshing grain. Fly over there, alight on them, first one, then another, and they will whip each other with their flails."

The woodpecker flew off. Then the peasants did whip each other, crosswise. And the fox giggled behind the threshing floor. They heard it, and the dogs leapt after the fox. The fox ran and ran, got herself into a hollow tree, and asked, "Eyes, little eyes, what have you been doing?"

"We saw everything and helped you run, fox!"

"Feet, little feet, what have you been doing?"

"We kept on running, fox, and saved you from the dogs."

"And you, tail, what did you do?"

"I just twitched between your legs."

"So you twitched, intending to hand me over to the dogs to perish." She stuck her tail out of the hollow tree. The dogs tore off the tail. And so the fox started running about without a tail. The other foxes laughed, but she said, "You just tear yours off, and you'll find out how easy it is to run!" And that's all.

A–T 20A

9. The Hen and the Cock

A cock was living with a hen. The cock got blind drunk and shit his pants. The hen went to the river to wash them. She washed and washed, and a lump flew out of the trousers into her forehead. She ran home, where the cock was lying on the stove. "Cock, do you know what?"

"What should I know?" he said.

"Oh," she said, "the Germans have invaded Rus*!"

"Who told you that?"

"I saw it myself, I heard it myself, and a bullet flew into my forehead."

"Let's run," they said, "into the forest." And off they ran.

They ran, and a weasel came running by. "Where are you running?"

They said, "We're running into the forest." The cock said, "The Germans have invaded Rus!"

"And who told you that?" he said.

"The hen told me."

"And who told you, hen?"

"I saw it myself, I heard it myself, and a bullet flew into my forehead."

"Let's run farther," they said.

They ran on, and a hound suddenly came running by. "Where are you running?" he said.

---

*Rus: Russia

"We're running into the forest, the Germans have invaded Rus," the hare said.

"And who told you, hare?"

"The weasel told me."

"And you, weasel, who told you?"

"The cock told me," he said.

"And you, cock?"

"The hen told me."

"And you, hen?"

"I saw it myself, I heard it myself, and a bullet flew into my forehead."

"Well," they said, "let's run into the forest."

A fox came running. "Where are you running?"

"We're running into the forest," the hound said. "The Germans have invaded Rus."

"And who told you, hound?"

"The hare," he said.

"And you, hare, who told you?"

"The weasel told me."

"And you, weasel?"

"The cock told me."

"And cock, who told you?"

"The hen told me."

"And who told you, hen?"

"I saw it myself, I heard it myself, and a bullet hit me in the forehead." And they all ran away into the forest.

Suddenly a wolf came running. "Where are you all running?"

The fox said, "We're running into the forest, the Germans have invaded Rus."

"And you, fox, who told you?"

He said, "The hound."

"And you, hound?"

"The hare."

"And you, hare, who told you?"

"The weasel."

"And you, weasel?"

"The cock."

"And you, cock?"

"The hen."

"And you, hen?"

"I saw it myself, I heard it myself, and a bullet flew into my forehead."

"Let's run into the forest!" they all said.

And then the bear appeared. "Where are you running?"

Now the wolf spoke, "We are running into the forest, the Germans have invaded Rus."

"And you, wolf, who told you?"

"The fox."

"And you, fox?"

"The hound."

"And you, hound, who told you?"

"The hare."

"And you, hare?"

"The weasel."

"And you, weasel?"

"The cock."

"And you, cock?"

"The hen."

"And you, hen?"

"I saw it myself, I heard it myself, and a bullet flew into my forehead."

"Let's all run," they said. "Farther."

They ran and ran, and suddenly they came to a deep pit—deep, ever so deep. They all jumped into the pit. They sat and sat and wanted to eat. They said, "What will happen to us?" (There's no way out of the pit. It's a very deep pit.) And they decided, "Whoever is smallest, we'll eat him up!"

Now the hen was smallest, so they ate up the hen. Yet a hen for such a family is but little, so they went and ate up the cock. They ate up the weasel, they ate up the hare, the hound they ate up, and there remained only three—the fox, the wolf, and the bear.

"Now," they said, "Who shall we eat? The fox is smallest."

"No," said the fox to the wolf, "I am older than you in years."

They went and ate up the wolf. And there remained but the fox and the bear. Now the fox, as she had been eating, put all the bones and scraps beneath her ass; she'd not quite finish a morsel and then stick it up her rear. Now she began to pull out all the bones and polish them off. And the bear asked, "Where are you getting those bones from, cousin?"

"I am getting them from up my ass. I stick a paw in there and pull one out."

"How can you?" he said.

"Just so, I stick a paw in and get one. You can also stick a paw up your ass and you'll get a bone." The bear stuck his paw up his ass and pulled his paw out, and he had grabbed his guts with his claws and did he begin to howl! No way could he pull them out. He howled and howled and died. And the fox quietly ate up the bear and then quietly hopped out of the pit and ran away.

A–T 20C + 20A + 21

10. How the White Bull Ruined the Gentleman

There lived and dwelt an important, influential gentleman. And he had a large herd of horses, cattle, and swine. That's the kind of gentleman he was! And a herder looked after the herd! Once after dinner he fell asleep. And in that herd there was a white bullock. And he began to shit. Then he looked and saw that the stuff was smoking and burning. The bull shouted, "The end of the world! Run!" And he started running. And the whole herd ran after him. He ran and he ran. He met a herd of horses. A stallion was herding them. The bull shouted, "The end of the world! Run!" And the horses galloped after him.

They ran and they ran, far and wide, and they met some ducks with a drake. The bullock shouted, "The end of the world! Run!" The ducks also started running. They ran and they ran, and they met some pigs with a boar. "Run," shouted the bull, and the swine also ran after him.

They ran and saw a lake: deep, oh so deep, and big, so very big. They all stopped and looked at the bull, and he said, "The earth is burning. Let's cross the lake and we'll be saved."

They went into the water, and they all drowned. Only the ducks remained; they flapped their wings and flew away. And that is how all the gentleman's wealth was destroyed.

A–T 20C

11. The Beasts in a Turnip Pit

A fox set off to pray to God, and she met a bear. He asked her, "Where are you going?" And she answered that she was going to pray to God, and she invited him [to go] with her. Then a wolf happened to come along, and he asked, "Where are you going?" And she answered that she was going to pray to God. And he went with her.

A hare happened to come along and asked, "Where are you going?" And after her answer, he set off with her. Then she came to a pit. She didn't know how to cross over the pit. She placed a pole across it and started praising the bear so that he would set off across. "Since you have such thin little legs and wide paws, you will go right across, you won't fall!" Truly, that bear set off, but he had just stepped off onto the pole when he pitched into the pit. Then she said to the wolf, "You go, cousin wolf; you have fine little paws, sharp little claws, you have an understanding of things." So the wolf set out and pitched into the pit.

Then she began to ask the hare to go. "So you, hare, you plaything! You have the thinnest little legs, you're so slight yourself! Quickly run along the pole!" The hare set off and pitched into the pit. And then the fox crept into the pit and ate them all. And from then on she lived well, prospered, and became wealthy.

A–T 20D*

12. There's Nothing to Be Gained from the Company of a Rogue

A peasant was riding to market with all sorts of things—with mushrooms, with smelt, with Kaluga† pastries, and so on. . . . A fox caught sight of him and slyly thought, the clever one did, about getting the edibles for nothing. She ran on ahead, lay down in the middle of the road, and pretended to be dead. The peasant rode along and saw this fox lying in the middle of the road. "Let me take her," he said. "I'll bring her to market and sell her there, and that way there'll be a little clear profit for me. . . ." The peasant was thinking in vain how to make use of this trove, for it all turned

---

†Kaluga: a provincial town one hundred twenty miles southwest of Moscow.

out quite differently—the clever fox tricked him. No sooner had he laid her on the cart and covered her with a bast mat than she gnawed through the bag of smelt and started flinging those smelt out along the road. And then, when the peasant was sitting there with his mouth gaping wide open, she climbed down and was gone. She gathered up the smelt, ran off into the forest, and began to enjoy them there in wide open spaces.

So she was walking along and eating when out of nowhere a gray wolf, her cousin, came running right toward her: "Welcome, welcome, cousin!"

The fox was not happy with this guest, she'd wanted to eat it all by herself, but there was nothing else to be done. She said, "Eat something, cousin, you are most welcome."

Now the wolf is a beast with very little conscience. He sat down with cousin fox and tucked into those smelt. He ate and sang their praises. The fox was vexed. Just look, she thought, just look how he's putting them away, as if he'd obtained them himself.

Well, there were only a few smelt. It was obvious that the wolf had come late to the feast at his cousin's. They had soon eaten everything, and the wolf asked, "Now then, cousin, where did you get such a trove? You don't have any more?"

"No," answered the fox, "that's it, cousin, there just aren't any more."

"But could one get some more?"

"Probably, why not? Nothing's impossible in this world." And she thought to herself, "Wait a minute, my darling, I'll pay you back for taking someone else's goods; I'll teach you a trade that I've been skilled at since my birth."

"And where can one get them?" the gray wolf asked again. "Over there, on the river, in the ice hole. You can catch as many as your little heart desires."

"Well, and how are they caught?"

"It's the simplest thing. You just have to get a jug and tie it to your tail and then lower the jug through the ice hole and sit and wait. The fish will come running on their own."

"That's all?" said the wolf. "Oh, that's a simple business. I'll go off and bring a jug, then you can teach me to catch the fish."

The wolf ran off, got a jug, came to his cousin fox, and bowed low: "Don't just do half the thing, teach me all of it: tie the jug to my tail, and lead me to the ice hole."

That's just what that fox wanted. In a flash she had found some string and tied it to that gray wolf's tail, and then she brought him to the ice hole and taught him how to sit there. "Stay with me, cousin," the gray wolf implored the fox. "It's more fun together."

"No, cousin, if we're both too close, we'll frighten off the fish. So I'll go off a little ways and watch you, and you sit here and don't move."

The wolf obeyed his cousin and sat submissively at the edge of the ice hole, his tail lowered in the water and his head hanging down. He didn't move, he just waited—for soon a fish would come swimming up.

But cousin fox strolled along the shore, looked at the sky, and chanted, "Shine, little stars, shine! Freeze the tail of that gray wolf!"

"What are you saying, cousin?" the wolf shouted from the ice hole.

"Sweet nothings, cousin! I was just counting the stars; I was casting a spell so that the fish would be caught better!"

The wolf sat there an hour, he sat another—he didn't move. And the fox kept on walking along the shore, looking at the stars, and chanting, "Shine, little stars, shine! Freeze the tail of that gray wolf!"

And it happened just as was said, just as was written: that wolf's tail froze—why you could take an axe to it! And the wolf asked the fox, "Isn't that enough, cousin? Couldn't I pull it out now?"

"Oh, no, what are you thinking, wait a minute! I'll count at least forty stars, and then you can pull it out, but I've only counted to twelve so far."

The wolf sat, he was silent. But impatience ruled: "Hey, cousin! Truly, it's time to pull it out. I'm shivering all over." But the fox kept on persuading him, and she got him to sit there until morning. And then, look! The peasant women were coming to the stream for some water, and the wolf was just sitting there on the edge of the ice hole.

The fox saw the people and took to her heels. The wolf was about to go after her, but his tail wouldn't let him; it was frozen fast. The women came up closer and saw the wolf. They started shouting at the wolf; they yelled. They saw that he didn't run from their shouting, so they came up closer and started poking him in the sides with their yokes. . . . The wolf became terrified. . . . He howled, poor thing, and strained with all his might, trying to loosen his tail from the ice hole. . . . He strained and strained, and somehow he broke off half his tail and ran away.

From some distance the sly fox saw the wolf run off into the forest with his torn-off tail, and she took fright: "Well," she thought, "I'll be getting it from my cousin! If he guesses that I sat him down at the ice hole intending . . . What should I do?"

But it came to her, and she decided to outwit, to deceive him. She rushed into the village and out behind the yards. She glanced into one hut and saw an old woman's dough rising: she was going to bake bread. The moment the old woman left the hut for a minute, the fox ran up to the bread trough, smeared her whole head with dough, and tore off again into the forest.

The gray wolf came up to meet her, and the fox ran straight up to him. "Cousin, kin of mine, save me! Some old robber-women have attacked me; they've beaten me instead of you! They said I was trying to catch all their fish with you!"

"How's that?" asked the wolf. "So that's what they beat you for? I got a heck of a beating too. Just look, half my tail's been torn off."

"But don't even speak of me: they grabbed me by the head and then knocked all my smarts out."

The wolf looked at the fox's head a little closer. "Oh, cousin, just look! Why, your brains are pouring out."

"Yes, dear cousin, and my head is just swimming from it all. Oh, what a misfortune! What slanders I've endured for you! Oh, my poor head! . . ." And the sly fox lay down as if she could no longer stand up.

"What shall we do, cousin? Why you'll never manage to drag yourself home. Perhaps I should carry you."

"Oh, cousin! Please do me the favor."

There was nothing else to be done; the gray wolf took the sly fox on his back and carried her into the forest. The wolf dragged himself along with quiet steps—he had a considerable burden on his back—and out of boredom that fox quietly sang a little song, sitting on the wolf's back. "Beaten is carrying unbeaten! Beaten is carrying unbeaten!"

"What are you saying, cousin?" asked the gray wolf.

"Oh, I'm saying a spell, cousin, so that it will be lighter for you to carry me and my head will get better."

The wolf carried the sly fox; he carried her for a long time, and sitting on his back she kept chanting, "Beaten carries unbeaten!"

They noted that on the road, just to one side, a stake was sticking out and to that stake a duck had been fastened. And that duck was quacking with all her might. The wolf stopped and said to the fox, "Well, now, cousin, that's a splendid find! Just look over there, a duck is calling on that side, next to that stake. . . . Oughtn't one somehow drag it off? Go on, try it; you are certainly most adroit at that sort of thing!"

"No, cousin, I've a got a really bad head, I've got no desire to eat anything at all, only perhaps a chunk of meat, perhaps, to ease the pain. . . . Better you go get it, and I'll keep watch; I'll look all around so that no one will hinder you."

And then that stupid wolf heeded her. He set the fox down and set off to get that duck. But she was a difficult prey. Where the stake was sticking out was a deep hunter's pit, and the duck was serving as bait. As soon as the wolf rushed onto it, he fell into the deep pit. . . . And the wolf turned coward, seeing that the whole business had turned out so painfully badly, and he was getting ready to shout, to call on his cousin for help, when the clever fox, finding the wolf in such an unfortunate situation, began to cry out with all her might, "Cousin, help me! . . . Kinsman, don't abandon me! Oh, how badly it's all going; they're going to catch me! . . ."

Anyway, that sly fox shouted out something like that at the top of her lungs, and the wolf, upon hearing her, became even more cowardly. He couldn't utter even a word, and he didn't call her to help him. He just hid in that pit, all scrunched up as if he weren't even there.

The sly fox shouted and shouted and then turned heel. And the gray, stupid wolf paid for it with his skin.

And nothing would have happened to him, if he hadn't been greedy, if he hadn't been stupid. You won't be deceived if you don't go around with a deceitful companion.

A–T 1 + 2 + 3 + 4 + 30

13. The Bear and the Fox

There lived in the taiga* this sow-bear and a fox. They were great friends. They often visited each other. The bear treated the fox to honey, and the fox treated her with chicken. They would have remained great friends if once at an evening party the bear had not been dancing with the fox and crushed her foot. From that time on the friendship was at an end. The bear embarrassed the fox before the other beasts. The beasts laughed at her and teased her for being lame.

So the fox thought about how to take revenge on the bear. Once the

---

*Taiga: the huge coniferous forest belt that extends across Russia and western Siberia.

fox watched while the bear hid her honey. When the bear had gone off for a walk, the fox took the barrel of honey—and home she went! The bear returned from her walk and desired a bit of honey. But there was no honey there! The bear started growling in vexation, and she set off to the fox's to ask her whether she hadn't seen who had taken the honey.

The bear came to the fox's as she was just licking the bottom of the honey barrel, slurping it up with her tongue. "Oh fox, what a misfortune!" the bear wailed. "Someone has stolen my barrel of honey. You didn't see the thief, did you?"

"No, bear, I didn't see him. I was visiting a collective-farm friend. When we parted, he even gave me a little barrel of honey. It's a pity you didn't come a little earlier; I would have shared with you. It was such tasty honey, why I'm afraid my lips are stuck together!"

As a result of the fox's words, saliva began to trickle down the bear's chin. She looked at the barrel and said, "That barrel wouldn't be mine, would it?"

"What do you mean, bear? I told you, that collective farmer gave it to me. If you don't believe me, let's go and ask him."

The bear declined to go to the collective farmer, became angry, and went home. She grumbled all along the way and thought, "Just you wait, fox, I'll show you a collective farmer or two. I'll teach you to cast your eyes on other folks' larders."

The bear wandered about the woods for three days looking for some honey. And then in a certain tree she saw some combs with wasp honey. She wanted to eat it, but she thought deeply about it. "Wait a minute! I'll go and invite fox and treat her to some wasp honey. The wasps will show her how you savor other people's honey." So spoke the bear, and she waddled off to the fox's.

She came to the fox's place and said, "I'm inviting you to visit, fox, to taste a little honey. Let's make peace and afterward, 'Whoever brings up the past, let her eyes be gone!'" The fox agreed, because she really liked honey. The bear took her by the hand, and off they went.

So here was the honey tree. "Climb up after me into the tree, fox!" said the bear. "Do you see where the honey is?"

"I see it, but I won't be able to climb up to it," answered the fox.

"Alright, I'll pull you up," the bear said, and she helped the fox into the tree. "Eat and enjoy, fox, for your health!"

The fox stuck her nose into the honeycombs, and the wasps fastened onto her nose, and her eyes, and her tongue, and did they ever sting and sting her! The fox got frightened and started shouting, "Chase them away, bear, they'll eat me up!"

The bear started chasing away the wasps. But they turned on her and started stinging her in the nose and eyes. The bear got mad and let the wasps' nest have it. Out of sheer carelessness one swat landed on the fox and knocked her out of the tree.

The fox groaned, "Oh, oh, bear, you've broken my ribs, you've ripped my fur coat, take me home." The bear apologized to the fox and took her home. When they were parting, the bear bowed and said, "I beg you not to take my hospitality amiss; I treated you to what I could," and then went away.

"Just you wait, pigeon toes," the fox thought. "I'll treat you so that you won't pay with just your skin." The animals all saw the fox's torn coat and started mocking and teasing her. "Rag bag," they called her. "Rag bag."

The fox soon recovered, and her coat grew out again. She set off for the village. There she sought out the collective-farm poultry yard. In the yard stood a big rough-hewn chicken coop. The fox dug a hole through the roof and crawled into the chicken coop, and she grabbed a hen from the roost. Then she ran away into the forest and ate the hen, but she carried the head and feet to the bear.

"Here, bear, eat this—I got it to try from the collective farmer. If you like the chicken meat, we'll go take as many chickens from him as we need. He has so many hens, you can't count them! That's the same collective farmer who stole your honey and gave it to me. If you want some chicken, let's go to him."

The bear ate up the head and chicken feet—and she wanted more. They chose a night darker than usual and ran into the village. The fox led the bear to the collective-farm poultry yard. "You stand watch here, bear, and I'll go throw the hens out," said the fox and climbed up onto the roof. She tore open her old gap and plopped onto the roost, but it broke—and crash! onto the floor she went. She wanted to jump out, but that wasn't possible—she could see the stars shining through the hole, but she couldn't climb out.

"Bear," she shouted, "climb up here! I can't lift all the hens up. Help me, please!" So the bear clambered up onto the roof, made the hole a bit bigger, and climbed onto a roost. The roost broke, and the bear and all the hens went flying onto the floor. She raised herself up on her hind legs in the darkness in order to look around, and the fox got onto her shoulders and then went out onto the roof. "Well, bear, a debt paid off is beautiful," she shouted. That's for my crushed foot, for the wasp honey, and for my torn sides. Eat chickens to your heart's content, but I'm leaving."

And the fox hopped down from the roof and ran up to the watchman's window. "Hey, watchman, there's a bear in your henhouse eating hens— and you are always blaming me! Run and have a look!"

So the watchman ran out into the yard. The hens were clucking away in the henhouse, and the bear was roaring because she couldn't get out. So the watchman ran to summon all the collective farmers. They soon gathered together, some with pitchforks, some with rifles, some with ropes, and they surrounded the henhouse. They opened the door, and, when the bear showed herself, they tied her up with ropes.

"Let me out, I'm not the guilty one! The fox has accused me falsely! She's the thief who steals your hens, and I'm in no way involved!" the bear roared.

When the fox heard that the bear had slandered her with the word "thief," she wanted to clear her name before the collective farmers. She ran into the yard and kept shouting and shouting, "She's lying, she's lying! Don't believe her. One hen was enough for me, but she wanted to kill them all."

The farmers grabbed the fox and tied her up. The watchman looked at the fox and then at the bear, and he said sternly, "A quarrel never brings any good! But your skins are both first-class; tomorrow we'll release you from them! A good fur always brings a price." And so it was.

A–T 31

14. The Wolf, the Fox, and the Crane

Well, now, a wolftrap had been constructed. A crane was flying by and decided to land and feed a bit, and it got caught in this trap (which was a pit covered over with brush so that it couldn't be seen). So the crane sat there. It would rise up to fly out of there, this crane, but when it got up to the brush, there was no way it could get through it, and so back down it went.

Then a wolf fell into the wolftrap, and then a fox. So they sat there— they'd all of them fallen in there together. And then the fox said, "Well, I'll still be alive."

"How will you stay alive?" they asked.

"That's my affair," she said.

So the wolf answered the fox, "Dear cousin, all three of us are going to perish. We shouldn't have gotten in here!"

But the fox said nothing; she was just thinking her own thoughts, about how to save herself. The fox heard someone coming. She fell to the ground, stretched out her long tail, spread out her legs, bared her teeth, and lay there as if dead, sort of.

So the master came up, the one who'd made the wolftrap. "Look! A crane has gotten into the pit, and there's a wolf there! And there's a fox lying over there too." And he went on: "The wolf didn't get along with the fox. See, he's chewed up the fox; the fox has already died."

The hunter loaded his rifle and killed the wolf. Then he put a smaller cartridge in and killed the crane. "Well, now I'll crawl into the pit; I'll have to drag them out of it."

Then he said, "Oh, poor fox! I didn't have to waste a shell on you! The wolf took a bite out of you!" He took the fox and flung it away, and the fox pulled herself together and started running, and she said, "I said that I'd be alive, and alive I still am!"

Then the peasant said, "Oh, you crafty fox! How you fooled me! I never dreamed you were alive. . . . I had some luck, but I let it go." Then he skinned the wolf and carried the crane home. He cooked it and ate it, and so the hunt ended. And that's that.

A–T 33

15. Let the One Who Fasts Look to Heaven (The Fox and the Wolf)

Once a fox was running through the forest. She saw a goose lying in the road. She rejoiced at this find and came up closer: things weren't so fine—a snare was set out in front of the goose. She understood the trick and began thinking about how to make use of this goose without falling into the snare. She thought and thought and finally ran up to a wolf and said, "Cousin, I've caught a goose, and I can't eat it because today is Friday. You wouldn't like to eat it, would you?" The wolf, fool that he was, believed the fox and set off with her to the loot. He saw the goose and immediately rushed at it. The snare caught him by the neck and raised him up. The wolf was hanging there, unable to touch the ground with his hind legs. That was just what the fox needed. She ran up to the goose and ate.

"But you said that today was Friday, that you were fasting. And now you are eating?" the wolf asked her.

"It's Friday, cousin, for those who can't reach the ground with their soles," the fox answered. She ate the goose up and ran away.

A–T 35B*

16. The Fox and the Hare

Spring came, and the hare's blood began to heat up. (Though he's poor in strength, he's frisky at running and full of youthful pranks.) So he set off into the forest, and he thought of dropping in on the fox. He came up to the fox's hut, and at that very time the fox was sitting near the stove, and her children were near the window. She caught sight of the hare and instructed her kits, "Now children, if that cross-eyed one comes up here and starts asking, you tell him that I'm not at home. Oh, he brings the very devil. I've been angry with him for a long time, the villain. Now somehow I'll catch him." And she hid herself.

The hare came up and started knocking.

"Who's there?" asked the kits.

"It's me," said the hare. "Greetings, dear little foxies! Is your mother not at home?"

"No, she's not at home."

"What a pity! I was in the mood for a hump, but she's not at home." So spoke the cross-eyed one, and he ran off into a thicket.

The fox heard him and said, "Oh, you son-of-a-bitch, you cross-eyed devil! You mischief-making miscreant! Just you wait, I'll give you a charge!"

She got down from the stove and started standing watch behind the door, just in case the hare should come again. She glanced up, and the hare was coming back along the same path, and he asked the kits, "Greetings, little foxies! Is your mother at home?"

"She's not at home."

"What a pity!" said the hare. "I was going to give it to her in my own special way!"

Suddenly the fox jumped out: "Hello, my darling!"

All of a sudden the hare wasn't up to it, and he tore out of there as fast as his legs could carry him, gasping for air in his nostrils and dribbling nuts from his ass. And the fox tore after him: "No, you cross-eyed devil, you won't get away!"

And so the chase was on! The hare leaped and jumped through two birches that had grown firmly together. And the fox tried to jump through the same way, but she got caught. She couldn't go one way or the other. She struggled and struggled but she couldn't crawl out. The cross-eyed one looked around and saw a good thing. He ran up from behind, and did he hump that fox, all the while intoning, "This is how it's done our style, this is how it's done our style."

He worked her over and ran out onto the road, and there, not far away, was a charcoal pit where a peasant burned charcoal. The hare raced into the pit, rolled around in the dust and soot, and came out a real monk!

He went back to the road, let his ears droop, and sat there. Meanwhile the fox somehow got free and ran off looking for the hare. She caught sight of him and took him for a monk. "Greetings," she said, "Holy Father! You haven't seen a cross-eyed hare somewhere?"

"Which one? The one that just worked you over?"

The fox leaped into the air in shame and ran home. "Oh, that villain! And he'll already have spread my ill fame throughout the monasteries!"

However clever that fox was, the hare still put one over on her!

A–T 36

17. The Fox as Keener

There lived an old man with an old woman, and they had a daughter. Once she was eating beans and dropped one onto the ground. The bean grew and grew and grew right up to heaven. The old man climbed up to heaven. He climbed up and walked and walked about, admiring everything, and he said to himself, "Let me bring the old woman here; she would be overjoyed!" So he climbed down to the ground, placed the old woman in a sack, held the sack with his teeth, and climbed up again. He climbed and climbed, grew tired, and dropped the sack. He descended most quickly, opened the sack, and saw the old woman lying there, gnashing her teeth. Her eyes had popped out. And he said, "What are you laughing at, old woman? Why are you baring your teeth?" Then he noted that she was dead, and so he burst into tears.

They had lived alone, quite alone in the middle of a wilderness. There was no one to mourn the old woman. So the old man took a sack with three pairs of white hens and set out to look for a keener. And he saw a bear coming. So he said to the bear, "Weep, o bear, for my old woman! I'll give you two white hens!"

The bear roared out, "O you, my own grandmother! How I pity you!"

"No," said the old man, "you don't know how to keen." And he continued on. He walked and walked and met a wolf. He got him to keen, but the wolf didn't know how either.

So he continued on and met a fox, and he got her to keen for a pair of white hens. And she sang out, "Tra la, Grannie, tra la, your old man has killed you."

The peasant liked the song, and he got the fox to sing it a second, third, and fourth time, but then he was short a fourth pair of white hens. The old man said, "Fox, fox, I forgot the fourth pair at home. Come to my place." So the fox followed on his trail.

And they came home. The old man took the sack, put a pair of dogs in it, and on top put the fox's six hens and handed it over to her. The fox took it and ran. A little later she stopped beside a stump and said, "I'll sit on this little stump, and eat a white hen." She ate it and ran on. Then she again sat on a stump and ate another hen. Then a third, a fourth, a fifth, and a sixth. And then she opened the sack for the seventh time, and the dogs leaped out at her.

That fox did run! She ran and ran and hid beneath a log, she hid and asked, "Ears, ears, what did you do?"

"We listened and listened so that the dogs didn't cat the fox."

"Eyes, little eyes, what did you do?"

"We watched and watched so that the dogs wouldn't eat the fox."

"Legs, little legs, what did you do?"

"We ran and ran so that the dogs wouldn't catch the fox."

"And you, tail, what have you done?"

"Through stumps and bushes, through the logs, I got hung up so that the dogs would catch the fox and rip her apart!"

"So that's what you are! Well, take this, dogs! Eat my tail!" And she stuck out her tail, and the dogs grabbed her by the tail, dragged out the fox herself, and tore her apart.

A–T 218B* + 1889K + 37 + 154

18. The Wolf, the Bear, and the Fox

There lived and dwelt—indeed, there had long lived and greatly prospered—a wolf and a bear. So then the bear said to the wolf, "Let's go
break some branches and put together a lean-to for the winter." But the
wolf answered, "We can get by without the branches; better let's dig a
pit in the earth." So the bear agreed, and they started digging a pit.

So they dug and they dug and they dug out a deep, really deep pit.
The wolf said, "Now let's make the paths to it." So they started making
the paths, and they went their separate ways. Suddenly the bear saw
something: something was shining up above. He looked, and it was gold
glistening. He went up, took hold of it, and unfortunately dropped it
onto the ground. And it was heavy. As it hit the ground, hares suddenly
appeared out of the gold.

So the bear started in eating them. He ate and he ate, and he finally ate
them all up, but he was so fat that he couldn't get out of the den. He stood
there, he stood and he really felt like going to sleep. So he lay down. And
he listened, and in his belly the hares were talking: "Let's gnaw through
his stomach and crawl out!" The bear took fright and said, "Don't gnaw
me, my dear friends, otherwise I'll die, you see. I'd better belch you up!"
The hares answered, "Very well." So he belched them up.

Suddenly the wolf came along. By this time the bear had become thin
again and was thinking, "I need to have a little something to eat." So he
took and ate the wolf.

"Well," he said, "now I won't let you get away!" And he lay down to
sleep. He fell asleep, and the wolf somehow went and crawled out, out
of the bear's mouth, and was free, and he said to himself, "Well, I'll just
have to pay him back!" So he dug a hole upward and climbed out of the
pit; he was overjoyed and went off to visit sister fox.

He came and told her everything, and she said to him, "Let's go, you
see, he's still sleeping there, and along the way I'll think something up
to do to him."

They climbed back down through the opening to the bear. The fox
took some scissors and slit open his belly, stuffed it full of pine cones,
and sewed it up; then she and the wolf went off home and began to live
and prosper together.

But the bear woke up, got up, and went off to the river for a drink. He slipped and went straight into the water. But the pine cones were light, and they carried him along the river. They carried him away, no one knows where!

A–T 41

19. The Hare and the Fox

There lived and dwelt a hare and fox. The hare had a bast hut, but the fox's was ice. So then came spring, and the fox's hut melted. And so she came to the hare's to ask to stay over, and she said, "Cousin, dear cousin, let me in onto the threshold." The hare said, "Crawl in, cousin, my dear."

So they sat for a while; they sat for a while on the threshold, and the fox said, "Cousin, cousin, let me onto the stoop."

"Crawl on in, cousin, my dear."

The fox sat awhile, she sat awhile, and then she said again, "Cousin, dear cousin, let me into your cellar well."

"Crawl on in, cousin, my dear."

So then the fox sat a while; she sat a while and said, "Cousin, cousin, let me into your loft."

"Climb on up," said the hare, "dear cousin, climb on up."

So the fox climbed up into the loft, lay down to sleep, and said, "Cousin, wake me up in the morning, I'm going to be called out to be a midwife."

"Very well, dear cousin."

So then in the night the fox knocked with her tail. The hare said, "Listen, dear cousin, get up: they're calling you to be a midwife." The fox jumped up and ran up into the attic to eat some butter; that hare had some butter up in the attic. So she started on that butter, and then she came back into the hut; the hare asked her, "Well, what did God give?"

"A Starter."

The next night the fox again gave instructions to the hare: "Dear cousin, wake me up, they'll be calling me to be a midwife."

"Very well."

So night came. The fox knocked with her tail in the loft. . . . "Hey, listen!" said the hare. "Get up, dear cousin: they're calling you to be a midwife." The fox jumped up and ran up into the attic again to eat some butter. So she ate, and then she went into the hut. "What did God give?"

"The Half of't."

On the third night the fox again instructed the hare: "Cousin, wake me in the morning. They'll be calling me to be a midwife."

"Very well, dear cousin."

And so in the night the fox again knocked with her tail against the rafters. "Listen! Get up, dear cousin, they're calling you to be a midwife."

The fox jumped up and ran away into the attic to eat butter. So she ate it and came into the hut. "What did God give?" asked the hare.

"Scrapings."

So then the next morning the hare thought of making some griddle cakes, and she said to the fox, "Dear Cousin, go and fetch it; there was some butter in the attic, bring it here."

The fox ran up to the attic and back and said, "No, cousin, there's nothing up there in the attic."

"How's that, cousin dearie, nothing? There was some! I'll go myself." So the hare made the trip and said, "It's clear, cousin dear, you ate it!"

"No, cousin, you ate it yourself and forgot."

The hare said, "Let's lie down on the grating. The one the butter melts out of is the one who ate it."

"Very well, cousin."

So they lay down on the grating. The hare soon warmed up, and he went off to sleep. But the butter just oozed out of the fox. So she smeared the hare with it and woke him: "Cousin, cousin! Just look! Why, you ate the butter!"

"Well now what are we going to eat, dear cousin?"

"Well, cousin, we shall have to obtain something." So the fox ran out onto the highway. She saw a cart coming along with some fish. So she lay down as if dead. A certain peasant saw her and shouted, "Lads, there's a fox lying there!" The peasants took the fox and threw her into the cart with the fish.

They rode along, not suspecting anything. But she ever so quietly ate a hole through the sleigh and dropped the fish onto the road, one after the other. And when she had emptied the whole cart, she hopped down and ran away to the hut, to the hare. "Cousin, cousin, let's go collect some fish."

And so the fox and the hare, they collected the fish. And from then on they lived and prospered and ate fish.

A–T 43 + 15 + 1

20. About a Wolf and a Fox

A wolf and a fox lived in the same place. The wolf had a root house, but the fox's was made of ice. So along came beautiful spring and the fox's house melted, as if it had never been there. What should she do? Well, foxes are clever, and she went up under the window at the wolf's house and said, "Dear, precious little wolf! Let this poor and miserable one in onto your porch." And he replied in a deep voice, "Okay, fox!"

"Dear, precious little wolf! Let me into your courtyard."

"Okay, fox!"

"Dear, precious little wolf! Just let me into your hut!"

"Okay fox, come in!"

"Dear, precious little wolf! Let me onto your step."

"Okay fox, come on!"

"Dear, precious little wolf! Let me onto your stove."

"Okay fox, come on!"

So the fox was lying on the stove, wagging her tail. But then, you see, well, for three whole days she hadn't eaten a thing. "How can I find out whether the wolf has any bread?" she thought. Well, she started looking for some bread. She looked and looked and in the wolf's shed found a punnet of oatmeal and a pitcher of butter. And then she was back on the stove. "Knock, knock, knock," the fox said beneath her coat. And the wolf asked, "Fox, who is that knocking?" The fox answered, "Dear, precious little wolf, they're calling you out to be a godfather and me a godmother."

"Go on, fox, but I'm not up to it." Now the fox was pleased with this. She hopped down from the stove, hopped into the shed and there she licked the butter, she licked some oatmeal, she licked and licked and stuffed it all in. Then she hopped from the shed, and hopped onto the stove, and she lay there as if nothing had happened at all. The wolf slept and slept and then he wanted to eat something so he wandered off into his shed. "Oh, my goodness! How awful!" the wolf howled. "How awful, who has eaten the butter? Who's lapped up the oatmeal?" And the fox said, "Dear, precious little wolf, don't think I did it!"

"Oh, stop it, cousin! Who would think it of you?" And so that's how the matter was settled, but they didn't staunch their hunger.

"Well, let's go to Rus," the wolf said to the fox, "and whatever we find there, we'll bring back so that we won't starve to death." The fox offered not a single word in reply and—pop!—they were off to Rus.

The fox ran out onto the road and saw a peasant riding along with some herring. She threw herself down and lay flat out across the road, as if dead. The peasant rode up to the fox. "Oh, a fox! And what fine hair! What sort of tail is that?" And he threw the fox into the cart.

This was most pleasing to the fox, who dug into the herring. She dug right to the bottom and then gnawed the matting. And then she gnawed the sleigh runners. She let the herrings down through the hole and then hopped off herself. All the while the peasant slept and knew nothing. So the fox collected up all the herring and carried them to the wolf in their hut. "Well," she said, "dear, precious little wolf, eat, be merry, there's no reason for sadness!"

The wolf could not but be amazed at his cousin's booty. "But how, my dear cousin, did you get hold of the herring?" the wolf asked the fox.

"Oh, my dear cousin! I let down my tail into an ice hole. I got a couple of herring, then a couple more." The wolf just had to try this unheard of thing. So he packed himself some bread and set out herring fishing, just like his cousin had done, just like she had taught him. So he came to the river, dropped his tail into the water, and held it there. And all the while the fox intoned, "Shine brighter, still brighter in heaven! Freeze the wolf's tail, freeze it!" And then the frosts crackled, and that wolf's tail was frozen fast!

The priest's daughters came and battered that wolf with their pokers, and from the skin they made themselves fur coats. And the fox remained there, living alone, and she still lives there and will outlive us all!

A–T 43*

21. The Sheep, the Fox, and the Wolf

A sheep ran out of a certain peasant's fold. She chanced to meet a fox, who asked her, "Where is God taking you, cousin?"

"Oh, oh, cousin, I was in a peasant's sheepfold, but my life was very hard; whenever the ram misbehaved, I, the ewe, was accused of being guilty. So I made up my mind to go away wherever my nose might take me."

"It's the same with me," answered the fox. "Whenever my husband catches a chicken, I, the fox, am always held responsible. Let us run off together."

After some time they met a lone wolf, a lobo. "Good day, friends," he said.

"Good day," said the fox.

"Are you going far?" he asked.

"Wherever my eyes take me," the fox said, and told him her woes.

The wolf said, "It is the same with me: whenever the she-wolf kills a lamb, I, the wolf, I am accused. Let's go together." So off they went.

On the way the wolf said to the sheep, "Well now, sheep, isn't that my coat you're wearing?"

The fox heard him and said, "Is it really yours, cousin?"

"It certainly is."

"Will you swear to it?"

"I will."

"Will you take a solemn oath?"

"I will."

"Then go and kiss the cross to affirm your oath."

At this point the fox saw that some peasants had set a trap near the road. She brought the wolf to the edge of the trap and said, "Now, go in there to take your solemn oath."

The wolf stupidly went into the trap, which snapped and caught his snout. The fox and the sheep speedily ran away from him for ever and ever.

A—T 44*

22. A Tale About a Fox and a Wolf

There lived and dwelt this sister fox, a terrible thief, and she especially loved geese, ducks, and hens. Once she stole a goose and ate it but kept the guts for herself. Now a little bit later a wolf came walking by, just famished, so hungry he could die. "Cousin," asked the wolf, "you might give me just a bit of the guts, I so much need to eat something!"

"Well, now, cousin, if I sate your hunger, if I feed you with the guts, then what happens? Over there's the priest's mare grazing, take her into the woods and eat her!"

"But she's tied up!"

"Well, so what? Untie her!"

"But she'll run away!"

"Why will she run away? Wrap the rope around yourself, then she'll come with you by herself."

So the wolf untied the rope and wrapped it around his belly, only the wolf didn't lead the mare—the mare led the wolf! The mare took fright and ran off, dragging the wolf behind her! "Cousin, cousin," yelped the wolf. "Cousin, grab hold of her legs with your jaws!"

"No, cousin, whether I grab hold or not, I'm off to the priest's yard!"

And so the mare ran on, but the wolf gave up his soul to God. Later this witch came along to the fox and said, "Sister fox, you are not acting according to the law. Why did you deceive that wolf?"

But the fox said to that, "Well, this is why—you have to teach fools!"

A–T 47A

23. How a Fox Taught a Wolf Intelligence

In a depression among some hills far off in the taiga a fox was finishing off a pheasant when an emaciated wolf happened by and caught sight of the fox. He was overjoyed and asked her, "Oh, cousin, I so want to eat something, give me just one wing."

The fox smiled thinly and with malice answered him, "Oh, cousin, for you—with pleasure, but what is a pheasant's wing to you, such a powerful, beautiful creature? Over there behind that hill in the valley there is a horse tied to a tree. Go and take it, and you'll have as much to eat as you really ought to have."

"But I'm exhausted. How am I supposed to deal with a horse?"

"Oh, you are such a stupid thing! I've just told you: you are powerful and beautiful, and the horse is on a rope; all you have to do is tie yourself to the other end, and then the horse won't be able to get away from you, and then, there and then . . ."

Now wolves are greedy, and then there was this hunger, and so the wolf quickly headed for the valley. When he had seen the horse, he stealthily stole up to it, untied the rope from a stump, tied it around himself, and then straightaway, happy and with a broad wolfish smile, he opened his toothsome mouth wide and set off for the horse, already salivating from his appetite. But as soon as the horse saw the wolf, she raised her proud head, stretched out her beautiful neck, and then reared up and snorted, and out of her nostrils there came a great heat, and she galloped off with all her strength toward the village.

Well, the wolf didn't have the strength to hold back the horse, and he soon toppled over and was dragged along after the horse by the rope through the stumps and stones, and in our Far Eastern Maritime provinces there are plenty of those, and not just for one wolf either. And then along the shores, and through the roots of trees toppled by a typhoon, the horse dragged him, and finally, from the long-haired wolf's skin, from that beautiful bearing, there remained just enough for some rags and some scraps for a ball, and that was all.

When he saw this, Mikhail Toptygin, the bear, came out of the forest, sauntered up to the fox, and said, "Well, miss foxy, you see everything, you know how to deal with suitors in your youth all right, and what's done is done, but why did you do that to brother wolf?"

With an utterly thin smile the fox, all the while playing saucily with her eyes, straightened out her bushy tail, and then, opening her mouth ever so slightly, she stated through her teeth, while moving just her lips, "That fool needed to be taught some intelligence, and so I taught him."

A–T 47C*

24. How the Fox Was Deceived

Once cousin fox came into the village and stole a pig from one of the peasants. She went into the forest, roasted the pig, flung it onto her back, and went on.

She walked along, and a wolf chanced to meet her. So the wolf said, "Cousin fox, let me join you!"

"Come along!" the fox answered.

So the two of them went along. And then a bear chanced to meet them. "Cousin fox, let me join you!"

"Well, come along!" the fox answered again.

So the three of them walked along. They walked and they walked and then they sat down to rest. Cousin fox said to them, "How shall we divide the pig?" And she sang out:

> *You were not yet in the world,*
> *And I, my children, was already old!*

And in answer the wolf went:

> *When first there was the light of day,*
> *I was already quite, quite gray!*

And then the bear growled out:

> *On me there is not one hair of white,*
> *And so for you there's not one bite!*

So he took the pig and set off. He really fooled the sly fox!

A–T 51A*

25. The Peasant and the Fox

A certain muzhik† lived in the forest, and he had this wife, and they had these seven children. The wife of this peasant died, and he remained

---

†Muzhik: a Russian peasant.

alone with the children. Once a fox came and said, "Grandpa Lupionushka! Give me a child, and if you won't, I'll chop down the oak and eat you up." And so she dragged off the children, one after another. As the peasant remained quite alone now, he sat down next to the window and began to weep.

A crow came flying by and said, "Why are you crying?"

"Why should I not cry, the fox has dragged off all my children but one."

The crow asked, "And what did she say?"

The old man said, "Grandpa Lupionushka! Give me a child, and if you won't, I'll chop down the oak and eat you up."

And the crow said, "You should have said to her, 'You have a very bushy tail, and you can't cut down a tree.'"

Afterward the fox came after the last one. "Grandpa Lupionushka! Give me a child, and if you won't, I'll chop down the oak and eat you up."

But the peasant said to her, "You have a very bushy tail, and you can't cut down a tree."

So the fox said, "Who told you that? Crow? I'll go eat her up." And off she went.

Now it was wintertime, and she sat down on a hill with her feet up, her tongue hanging out, and she just lay there. The crow flew up and cawed, and she flew deep into the fox's mouth and began to crow. The fox slammed her mouth shut and swallowed her. The crow begged the fox to let her out. "Let me out, and I'll bring you some flax fluff, then we'll go sledding." So she went and brought some fluff. The fox sat down first, then the crow behind, and they went off down the hill and straight into a pit.

The fox and the sleigh stayed in the pit, but the crow fluffed out her feathers and flew away.

A–T 56A

26. The Blackbird

There was this blackbird. She hatched some eggs. She sat and sang little songs with the children. And then a fox came running up. "Blackbird, blackbird, stop singing, you've sung long enough! By now the horses have fled throughout the open field, and seeds have been scattered over the crossroads. I'll cut down that tree with my tail! Give me a baby!"

She was very sad to give up a baby, but anyway, hand over a baby is what she did! On the next day the fox came running up again: "I'll cut, I'll cut down that tree with my tail. Give me a baby."

So now she wept and sat and wept, and a magpie came flying by. "Why are you crying, blackbird?"

And the blackbird said, "The fox came and said 'I'll chop down the tree with my tail,' she said, 'give me a baby!'"

"Oh, you," said the magpie. "Why did you give up a baby? For what reason did you give up a baby? Say to that fox, 'You have a tail, not an axe, not a knife, not a sharp sword.'"

The next day the fox came running up again, and the little bird said, "Why are you deceiving me? Your tail is no axe, no knife, nor a sharp sword."

"Who taught you that?"

"The good wife magpie."

"Oh, I'll catch her." So off ran the fox. She went along, then flopped down on the ground and put a piece of meat on her body. The magpie flew up, grabbed the meat, and the fox went and caught her. And she began to torment her. She tortured and tortured her, and the magpie said, "Your grandfather never tortured my mother like that! He went up a hill, took a bottomless bucket, and set it rolling."

The fox listened and wanted to get the bucket, so she let the magpie go, who flew away. She said to the fox, "You are clever, but I am more clever than you." Now that's all of that tale!

A–T 56A*

27. About a Thrush

A thrush wove a nest right opposite a fox's window. The fox sang to him:

> *Thrush, you whore's son,*
> *Thrush, you slut's son,*
> *You wove your nest opposite a fox's window,*
> *You booze and carouse, won't let my children sleep.*
> *I'll chop and I'll chop your bush down,*
> *I'll eat up your little ones.*

Well, poor thing, he threw the fox a little one. But he still had a few of them left. Well, the next morning the fox came again and sang the little song:

Thrush, you whore's son,
Thrush, you slut's son,
You wove your nest opposite a fox's window,
You booze and carouse, won't let my children sleep.
I'll chop and I'll chop your bush down,
I'll eat up your little ones.

Now the hare heard this. He came up and started scolding the thrush:

Silly thrush,
Stupid thrush,
How will she chop it down?
She has no axe.
There's never been a knife.
She can't chop with her tail
Nor cut it down with her tongue.

On the third day the fox came again, and again she sang her song:

Thrush, you whore's son,
Thrush, you slut's son,
You wove your nest opposite a fox's window,
You booze and carouse, won't let my children sleep.
I'll chop and I'll chop your bush down,
I'll eat up your little ones.

The thrush sat and sat there, unperturbed, and gave her nothing. Somehow the fox figured out what the hare had said to him. "Oh, perhaps that cross-eyed hare has coached you. I'll go and chase that hare away right now!"

The hare heard the fox. He walked along. Some women were burning brush. He got into the soot and rolled around in it. Then he whacked the fox in the ass. Then he quickly made a raft and got away. Well, he was punting about among the stones with a pole.

The fox came to the shore to wash. Well, she saw him and changed her mind, she wouldn't wash, and she said, "Well, Brother Monk, where are you coming from?"

And the hare said, "From Moscow, my lady, from Moscow."

"And what good news have you of Moscow?"

"Well, all's well in Moscow, and the good news heard there is how the hare whacked the fox in the ass!"

"Oh, alas! alack! My oh my! That didn't take place so long ago, and they already know about it in Moscow. I'll run, I'll go away, and I'll never show myself again. (Everyone finds out everything by radio!)

A–T 56A

28. The Fox and the Woodpecker

There lived and dwelt a woodpecker in an oak tree, and she wove herself a nest, brought forth three eggs, and hatched out three little ones. A fox took up the habit of visiting her. Knock, knock went her big tail on the dry old oak! "Woodpecker, woodpecker! Come right down from that oak. I need that oak to bend into things for my work."

"Oh, fox, you haven't let me hatch out even one little one."

"Oh, woodpecker, just throw it down to me; I'll teach it to be a smith!" So the woodpecker threw it to her, and the fox was off from one bush to another, one wood to another, and then she ate it up.

She came back to the woodpecker again and knock, knock went her big tail against the dry old oak. "Woodpecker, woodpecker! Come right down from that oak! I need that oak to bend into things for my work."

"Oh, fox, you haven't let me hatch out even one little one."

"Oh, woodpecker, throw it down to me, and I'll teach it to be a cobbler." So the woodpecker threw it down, and the fox was off from one bush to another, one wood to another, and then she ate it up.

She came back to the woodpecker again and knock, knock went her big tail against the dry old oak. "Woodpecker, woodpecker! Come right down from that oak! I need that oak to bend into things for my work."

"Oh, fox, you haven't let me hatch out even one little one."

"Oh, woodpecker, throw it down to me, and I'll teach it to be a tailor." The woodpecker threw it to her, and the fox was off from one bush to another, one wood to another, and then she ate it up.

A–T 56B

29. The Fox and the Crow

The little crow caught sight
At a peasant woman's house
Of a piece of cheese on the sill;
The little crow grabbed up
That piece of cheese from the sill,
And dragged it away to a fir,
And there she pecked away at it;
The fox she did catch sight
Of some very rare marvels,
And she felt like having a bite,
Of enjoying a morsel or two.
"Oh, you strange little bird,
Oh, what a beak you have!
Let me hear your little voice!"
"Caw-w-w," the crow called out,
And thus she didn't note,
That the cheese was hers no more.

A–T 57

30. The Fox and the Crane

A fox and a crane became good friends; they even swore everlasting friendship at somebody's house when a baby was born. So once the fox took it into her head to entertain the crane, and she went and invited the crane. "Come visit, cousin, come visit me, my dear one! Oh, how I will entertain you!" So the crane went to the banquet, and the fox boiled up some fine wheat groats and buttered a plate for each of them. She set it out and suavely bid the crane, "Eat some, my dearest cousin! I cooked it myself!" So the crane pecked away with her nose: tap, tap, but couldn't get anything! All the while the fox was lapping and lapping the groats, and soon she had eaten them all.

The groats were eaten, and the fox said, "Don't fret about it, kind cousin, but there's nothing else to come."

"Thanks, cousin, for even that! Come visit me!"

The next day the fox came, and the crane had been preparing a fine ale soup. She put it in a pitcher with a little neck, put it on the table, and said, "Do eat, cousin. Forsooth, that's all there is." So the fox began circling around the pitcher, and she tried one way and another, she licked it and sniffed it, but she couldn't get anything! Her head wouldn't fit into the pitcher. And meanwhile the crane kept pecking away, and she pecked until it was all gone. "Don't fret about it, kind cousin, but there's nothing else to come." Vexation overcame the fox. She had thought she'd eat enough for a whole week, and she went off home as if she'd tasted something nasty. She had gotten just what she deserved. But since that time the friendship between the fox and the crane has tapered off.

A–T 60

31. The Fox as Confessor

A fox was walking toward a peasant's farmyard. She wanted to carry off a chicken from the henhouse or a calf from the shed. A cock heard her and stamped his feet, and he started shrieking.

The peasants heard it, grabbed their weapons, and ran off to shoot the fox. Out of fright the fox started running, and she lay three days beneath a certain bush. Bright weather came. The cock flew to the wood to fly around. He flew from tree to tree, he flew from one branch to another.

The fox heard the cock in the wood. She went up close to the cock and bowed low. "Greetings, oh, child cock! For thirty years I've not eaten any meat, and now I want to see you and hear your confession! You have had," she said, "about twenty wives, about thirty wives even; you are supposed to have one legal wife, a second as bed partner, but you can't get along without a third."

The cock recognized these grievous, great sins of his and wanted to alight on the grass, but he landed on the fox's head. The fox grabbed the cock in her claws, sank her nails into him, and brushed the wings to one side.

The cock cried out in an unusual voice, "Oh, mother of mine! Oh, fox! So this is penitence!"

"Oh, thieving cock! You have laughed at me! When I was going toward the peasant's farmyard, desiring to drag off a chicken from the henhouse, or a calf from the shed, were you seized by a fever so that you started shaking all over?"

"Oh, mother of mine, fox! One slave does not serve two other slaves! I serve the master!" he said. "Listen, mother of mine, fox! I'll set you up in a cozy spot."

"Which one, you thieving cock!"

"I used to live at the metropolitan of Kritskii's, I served in the right-hand choir, sang the first lines.* The communion loaves were soft, and the holiday brews were sweet."

The fox listened intently and weakened her grip on the cock in her claws. The cock flapped its wings and flew up onto a branch. "We congratulate you, mother of mine, fox, on your new rank! Eat the white snow as if it were ham!"

A–T 61A

32. The Fox as Confessor

It was most extraordinary: a fox was coming from a far-off wilderness. And having caught sight of a cock in a high tree, she spoke sweet words to him: "Oh, my dear child, oh, fine cock! You are sitting there in that tall tree, and you are thinking dirty thoughts, accursed thoughts. You cocks keep too many wives. Some keep ten, others twenty, still others even thirty, and from time to time the number goes up to forty! And whenever you get together, you quarrel over your wives as if they were concubines. Come down onto the earth, my dear child, and confess! I am coming from a far-off wilderness, I haven't drunk anything or eaten,

---

*In a traditional Orthodox church, the male choir sang from the second level. The church did not discourage the congregation from joining in the singing, although it was not customary.

and I have endured many hardships, and all because I wanted to hear your confession, my dear child."

"Oh, mother of mine and fox! I have not fasted nor have I prayed; come at some other time."

"Oh, my dear child, oh, fine cock! You have not fasted and you have not prayed, so come down onto the earth and confess so that you do not die in your sins."

"Oh, mother of mine and fox, honeyed are your lips and sweet your words, but deceitful is your tongue. Judge not one another, and you will not be judged; whoever sows something will also reap. You wish to bring me to confession by force, not to save me but to devour my body."

"Oh, my dear child, oh, fine cock! Why do you say such things? Would I do that to you? Have you not considered the parable about the publican and the pharisee, where the publican was saved but the pharisee perished on account of his pride? Now you, my dear child, will perish on that high tree without confession. Come down lower, onto the ground, and you will be closer to confession: forgiven and absolved and allowed into the heavenly kingdom."

The cock recognized the heavy sin on his soul, and he was deeply moved and weeping, and he began to descend from branch to branch, from bough to bough, from stump to stump, and the cock descended onto the ground and perched in front of the fox. The fox leaped up, like a sly bird, and grabbed the cock in her sharp claws; she looked at him with her fierce eyes and ground her sharp teeth; she intended to devour him alive, just like some renegade.

And the cock said to the fox, "Oh, mother of mine, fox, honeyed are your lips and sweet your words, but deceitful is your tongue! Are you going to spare me, or will you devour my body?"

"Neither your body nor your bright clothing is dear to me; what's dear is to repay you some friendship. Or don't you remember? I was going to visit a peasant; I just wanted to eat a little hen, and you, fool, idler, were sitting up on a high perch, and you started shouting and wailing with your loud mouth, you stamped your feet, you flapped your wings, and then all the hens started chattering, and then the geese started honking, and the dogs started barking, and the stallions started neighing, and the cows started mooing. And all the peasants and their wives heard it. The women came with brooms and the men with axes, and they wanted to cause my death on account of that hen; yet that owl lives from generation to generation there, always eating chicken! But you, fool, idler, shall live no longer!"

Then did the cock speak to the fox: "Oh, mother of mine, fox, honeyed are your lips and sweet your words, but deceitful is your tongue! You see, just yesterday I was called upon by the metropolitan of Trinchinsk to serve as a deacon; I was singled out of the choir for special praise, and the congregation said, 'He's a handsome lad, well-clad, reads a great many books, and has a fine voice.' Now could I not, oh, mother of mine and fox, use my influence to get you into the group of ladies who bake the communion loaves? There would be great profit for us in that. They would be giving us sweet buns, fine white loaves, and a bit of butter and eggs and cheese!"

The fox recognized the cock's plan and held the cock a little less firmly with her claws. The cock tore away and flew into a tall tree and started shouting and wailing with his loud mouth, "Dear madam bread baker, greetings! Is your profit large? Are your buns sweet? Have you worn away your hump carrying all the baked goods? Or wouldn't you like some nuts, you villain? But maybe you don't have any teeth?"

So the fox went off into the forest with a long face and began weeping bitterly: "As long as I have lived on this earth, I have never in my life seen such a disgrace. Since when do cocks become deacons or foxes bakers!" Glory to him and power, now and forever, and that's an end to the tale.

A–T 61A

33. A Wolf—Gray and Daring

In a certain tsardom in a certain country, in the one in which we are living, beneath the number seven where we are sitting, snow burned, and they put it out with straw; many people were destroyed, as a result of which nothing was decided.

Twelve wolves ran, and old men with pikes ran after the twelve wolves. One wolf—gray and daring—said, "Old men, turn back, take pity, my father ate a hundred of your sheep, but I will never touch your flock!" So they turned back, took pity, and went off home.

Then came that wolf—gray and daring. And a pig with her piglets went strolling by. So he took the pig. "Let me go, wolf—so gray and daring—and take my bob-tailed, chicken-assed piglet!"

So he took the bob-tailed, chicken-assed piglet by the back, stripped the skin off it, and sat down to eat. Up popped a fox out of nowhere: "Good health to you, cousin, dearest friend! I came to visit you to swallow up the piggy's bones."

"What kind of creature are you, to tell me such rubbish? In Riga I learned to read the Lenten books. What happened to the bob-tailed, chicken-assed piglet will happen to you, creature!"

That fox stretched out her legs running along the road. That fox set off for the Briansk woods, and in the Briansk woods a cock sat in an oak. "Good health, little cock, dearest friend! I have been in the city of Jerusalem, where they praised you: you see, they say, the cock has a silken beard, speckled wings, and bright red boots. I am your mother confessor and go around to all chicken coops to hear the confession of you cocks. You are a sinner; you are a lawbreaker; you have seventy-seven wives. Climb down here to me, confess to me. In the otherworld there is spring wheat and winter wheat, and I'll let you go there; I'll regale you with fine food."

That cock was seduced by the fox's patter, from branch to branch he descended, said farewell to the tree, and sat down on the fox's head. The fox took the rooster into her lips, carried him into some thick bushes, and proceeded to wring the cock's neck. She ate up the cock, just the guts were hanging out, and she went to the river to slake her thirst.

Up popped that wolf—gray and daring—grabbed the fox by the back, stripped the skin off her, ate her all up, and sweet it seemed to the wolf! And with that this fable is at an end.

A–T 61A

34. The House Spirit

There lived and dwelt a tomcat, a sparrow, a house spirit,* and then a cock. And they all set off into the woods for firewood, but they left the cock at home. "You boil the porridge, and we'll cut the wood." The cock boiled the porridge, began to daydream, and started counting. "This is sparrow's spoon, this is tomcat's spoon, this is house spirit's spoon, and this is my spoon. Cock-a-doodle do, don't touch my spoon." A fox heard this, crept up, and said:

---

*Zhikharka.

Cock, oh, cock with golden comb,
Shiny head and silken beard,
Look out the window!
The boyars* have been riding,
They've strewn peas,
And there's no one to gather them up!

The boyars had brought the peas. The cock looked out the window; the fox grabbed it and dragged it away. The cock started shouting, "Tomcat, sparrow, and you, house spirit, a fox has dragged me beyond the deep forests, beyond the high mountains, beyond the squishy swamps!"

They heard him and ran to catch up. The tom ran and the earth shook; the sparrow flew and the woods murmured. But the house spirit galloped along, his eyes bulging, leaping over everything, knocking down everything—just like a bear. So they caught up and took the cock away from the fox. They came home, then set off again for firewood, but on going they said, "We'll go for firewood, and you boil the porridge, but mind you, don't open the window, or the fox will drag you off."

So again the cock boiled the porridge and sat there; he became bored, dozed off, and again began to count spoons. "This is sparrow's spoon, this is tomcat's spoon, this the house spirit's, and this my spoon. Cock-a-doodle-doo, don't touch my spoon." The fox heard him, went up to the hut, and said:

Cock, oh, cock with golden comb,
Shiny head and silken beard,
Look out the window!
The boyars have been riding,
They've strewn peas,
And there's no one to gather them up!

The cock looked out, and the fox grabbed him and dragged him away. The cock began to shout, "Tomcat, sparrow, and you, house spirit, a fox has dragged me beyond the deep forests, beyond the high mountains, beyond the squishy swamps!"

They heard him and ran to catch up. The tom ran and the earth shook;

---

*Boyar: one of the ancient aristocracy.

the sparrow flew and the woods murmured. But the house spirit galloped along, his eyes bulging; he leaped over everything and knocked
everything down. They ran and ran but couldn't catch up. The fox dragged
the cock far away. They went home. "How shall we rescue the cock?"
they all thought. They made little *gusli*, little guitars, and rode off to
rescue the cock. They arrived with their *gusli*, that is, they began to
approach the fox's house, and they started playing:

> *Play, play little* gusli, *little golden strings.*
> *Does Lizaveta still live at home?*
> *Does Ivanovna still live at home?*
> *With her little children,*
> *With her own little ones?*
> *The first is Suchenok, little biscuit,*
> *The second is Plachenok, little cape,*
> *And the third is Break-the-Pot,*
> *And the fourth is Give-up-the-Boat.*

All the fox's daughters heard this and said, "Mama, they're playing
gusli there, let's go out and dance."

"Well, you go dance." So they went out one at a time. The first went
to dance—and they cut off her head and threw it into the bushes. Again
they started playing. "Play, play, little *gusli*, little golden strings."

All the little maids came by and they cut off all their heads. The fox
waited for them, but no daughters appeared. "Well," she thought, "let
me dance myself. They play incredibly well." As soon as she went through
the gates, they chopped off her head and then entered the hut. The cock
sat there on a bench with his wings tied, head lowered. They rejoiced,
untied him, and went home. There they lived and prospered and became
wealthy.

A–T 61B

35. The Fox and the Black Grouse

A fox was running through the woods. She saw a black grouse in a tree
and said to him, "Terentii, Terentii, I've been to town!"

"Bu-bu-bu, bu-bu-bu, if you've been, you've been!"

"Terentii, Terentii, I've procured a new law!"

"Bu-bu-bu, bu-bu-bu, if you've procured it, you've procured it!"

"A law forbidding all you black grouse to perch on trees, and ordering you always to walk in the green meadows!"

"Bu-bu-bu, bu-bu-bu, if it's walk, then I'll walk!"

"Terentii, who is coming over there?" asked the fox, hearing the trampling of horses' feet and the barking of dogs.

"A peasant."

"Who is running after him?"

"A colt."

"And how does he hold his tail?"

"In a hook."

"Then farewell, Terentii, I have urgent business at home!"

A–T 62

36. The Fox and the Crane

A fox invited a crane to be his guest and made some fried eggs for her in a skillet, but it was difficult for the crane to peck them: the eggs kept flying away from her nose. So the fox lapped it all up herself. So then the crane invited the fox: "Now, fox, you come to my place, I'll entertain you," and she made some fried eggs in a pitcher. The fox poked and poked his head in, but it just wouldn't go, so the crane pecked just as he wished and pecked nearly all of them. The fox pushed and pushed his head and finally stuck it in and licked up the fried eggs. Then he started to pull his head out. The pitcher tipped up but it wouldn't come off. So he dragged it around and around, but nothing happened, and he said, "Pitcher, let me go or I'll go smash you against a corner or I'll sink you in a well." But the pitcher still wouldn't let go.

So he set off and lay down on the road. A peasant was coming from town, his feet dangling from the box he was sitting on, and in the box were some fish he had bought. He got down and hit the fox with his whip, but the fox didn't get up, she was pretending to be dead. So the peasant took the whip and hit the pitcher around the neck and put the fox in the box. She ate a hole through it, threw out the fish, gnawed a little bit more, and climbed out. She took the fish and carried it off to a haystack. She was sitting there eating when a wolf ran by. "Oh, cousin, what are you eating?"

"Fish."

"Give me some." So the fox tore off the head and threw it to him. "Oh, cousin, that's fine, how about a little more?" She gave him the tail. "Oh, cousin, that was still better, how about a little more?" She gave him the innards. "Oh, cousin, that was even better, how about a little more?"

"Go on." (The ending is lost.)

A–T 60 + 68A + 1

37. The Fox and the Jug

A certain peasant went into the field to work and took with him a clay jug. And in this jug there was some sour cream. A fox saw the peasant, and, the conniving good-for-nothing, she began thinking about how to get away with that sour cream.

She waited a while until the peasant turned his back, then zap! and she had the sour cream. The good-for-nothing ran away to a quiet spot, desirous of investigating that sour cream! So, you see, she stuck her head into the jug and lapped up some sour cream, and then she thought of pulling her head out of that jug. She wanted to pull her head out, she wanted to, but she couldn't. The head wouldn't budge; the jug's throat was narrow. She bashed her head against a stump, but the jug wouldn't break. And oh! how her head did hurt! The fox ran to the river. "I'll sink this wretched jug in the river." She sank her head in the water and started sinking together with the jug. And she drowned. And that's how an end came to that conniving fox.

A–T 68B

38. Cousin Fox and the Wolf

There was this cousin fox. Well, she ran off into the forest. Later there were two wolves. This cousin fox caught some fish. Well, then this cousin fox went up to them. "Hey, you, gray wolves, where have you been?"

"In the forest."

"Well, I'm going to deceive you."

"And how will you deceive us?"

"I'm going to catch some fish in front of you." And she caught some fish, climbed up onto a hayrick, and ate the fish.

Then they turned to her: "Cousin fox, give us a fish."

And she answered them, "Oh, you smoothy, you beauty, go and catch some yourself." And then she said to them again, "Here then, beauty and smoothy," and she threw them a fish.

They ate it up, and then they said to her, "Cousin fox, how did you catch them?"

"Here's how I caught them. Come on then and I'll teach you."

And so they set off. She tied a satchel to each one of them. And so they again set off and ran and then went with her, and she showed them the way to the lake. She had tied a satchel to their tails, and they went to fish. She walked around on the shore, but they waited. Well, after a time she said to them, "Frost, frost, be clear, be clear, freeze the tail of wolf and bear."*

Then they said to her, "Cousin fox, what's that you're saying?" And she said to them, "Oh, I'm just praying 'Get yourselves caught, you big fish and little fish!'" And this went on three times. Then she repeated again, "Frost, frost, be clear (be stronger still), freeze the tail of wolf and bear." Well, the tails of both wolf and bear froze. She ran to the village, did cousin fox, and shouted, "Women, come running, come running, look what a fine tale I've got to tell." And the women came out. She said, "Go, go there and look, what a fine little thing there is on your lake." The women set off running. "Do your running with axes and flails and hammers, because two wolves have gotten frozen in the ice there; they were catching fish, and cousin fox has deceived them!" Then they all ran off, only cousin fox stayed in the village.

Well, then, they all went away, but it was a feast day, the women were making pancakes, and cousin fox was there, and there was milk standing there on the table. She was as quick as a fox, she was! Soon they were coming back from the lake, talking away. But cousin fox had daubed the batter all over her head. She said to them, "Women, what a damnable village this is! I've been completely beaten up. They've broken open my head right to the brains!" Then that cousin fox ran off into the forest, she

---

*The narrator has forgotten that he began with two wolves. Now he continues with a wolf and a bear before returning to two wolves.

tore off the batter tub and then she said to herself, "I think I'll go to another village."

So she went there. "Women, let me in to spend the night!"

Well, they said to her, "We'd let you in to spend the night, dearie, but this is only a dough rising room and the kids' storehouse."

So she ran off, did cousin fox, to another household. Then, later, she went to yet another, where she asked to spend the night. And then again she begged. "Well, here's something. Here's my batter tub for you. But if that batter tub disappears, you'll have to give me a strap." So she spent the night, and then she said, "Women, give me my batter tub." The women searched and searched, but they couldn't find that batter tub. She had hidden the batter tub. "Well, give it to me, and if that batter tub has disappeared, then give me a strap." They gave her the strap.

Then she ran to the next village for the third night. She came running into the third village and knocked at the window: "Let me in to spend the night!" So they let her in, and she spent the night with these people. She gave them the strap. "You have to keep this strap secure for me. If the strap disappears, then you will give me a chicken for the strap." Later on she took this strap back too. So like it or not, they got up in the morning, and she said to them, "Women, give me my strap!" Well, the women searched and searched, but they couldn't find the strap, so they gave her a chicken for the strap.

So then later, she ran on into the next village with this chicken and again begged to spend the night, and she handed over the chicken. "Now, women, you have to look after this chicken, and if this chicken disappears, then you must give me a goose." And so in the night she got up, and she ate that chicken, and she put the feathers beneath the manure pile. So then, they all got up in the morning and they looked for the chicken. "Give me my chicken, women!" The women looked, but they did not find it, and so they gave her the goose for the chicken.

Well, then she ran off into the forest again, with the goose. And then cousin fox thought, "How could I get more? If I were to eat it, the goose, then I'd have nothing left."

So then she thought up a little plan with these little twists: as she was walking among the villages, she'd stop in a village again. "Well, women, let me in to spend the night." Some women refused, so off to the next household. "Women, let me in to spend the night." The women let her in. "Watch over my goose. If this goose of mine disappears, you'll have to give me a bullock." So then she spent the night there. And in the night she ate up her fine goose. Well then, in the morning she got up and spoke: "Women, give me my goose." The women went here, then they went there, but no goose. They quarreled and argued and fought, and then they gave up the bullock to the fox for the goose.

So then she took the bullock and led it into the forest. She harnessed it to a sleigh and then set off. Out of nowhere there appeared a couple of wolves. "Cousin fox, give us a ride."

And she said, "Oh, you beauty, and you smoothy, go and make your own way. I've walked so far, I've worked so hard."

But the fox settled them down on the runners anyway. And then cousin fox's sleigh shaft broke. So she sent one of the wolves out after another shaft. He cut a shaft and brought a big thick shaft back! Just great! "Smoothie, or beauty, what is this, why did you bring in such a thing? Take it back. It's much too thick."

Then a hare came running by. He asked cousin fox if he could sit in the sleigh. "Please, cousin fox, let me sit down."

She said, "Oh, you cross-eyed hare, go and make your own way. I've made my own way." But then she took pity on him, that cross-eyed hare, and seated him. And so they all continued on.

So they rode and rode along, and then the shaft broke. Well, she said to them, "Go, you cross-eyed hare, go and cut one." So he set off. He came back carrying a tiny little twig. And she said to him, "Well now, you cross-eyed hare, where do you think you're carrying that twig? It's much too thin; it's no use to anyone."

So she said, "Wait here, just remain here, and I'll go myself. Stay with the bullock." So then she set off into the forest. While she was gone, cutting away, the wolves ate that bullock, and they skinned that bullock and stuffed him full of straw. The fox came back, carrying the shaft, and they were waiting. They started to hitch up the skinned bullock, but he wouldn't go, so she hitched him up, did cousin fox, but he still wouldn't go. So then she said, "Haw! Giyup!" But he wouldn't go, this bullock.

Then the bullock swayed and fell. Cousin fox and all the wolves that were there with cousin fox, all ran away. Just the little hare was there, then he ran away.

Cousin fox was all alone, and she thought, "What is there for me to do? I'm left alone. Better that I take up some sort of handicraft trade again."

So cousin fox went to where the women were reaping in the fields. A large pitcher stood near them. Then she, cousin fox, knocked over that pitcher of milk. Cousin fox started scooping it up first with her paw. But that didn't go very well. "I'd better lick it up quickly; I'll stick my head in the pitcher." She put her head into the pitcher, but pull it out she couldn't! She worked and worked at it, but no way could she pull it out. Then cousin fox ran to the river. "I'd better sink it there." So she crawled into the lake with the pitcher. She thought she'd be able to sink the pitcher, but the pitcher sank her.

A–T 2 + 3 + 158 + 68B

39. The Fox and the Thrush

A thrush lived in a high oak with his two children. And then he saw a fox come running. "Thrush, thrush, feed me or else I'll cut down that tree and destroy your children."

"Oh, mother fox, don't cut down the tree, don't hurt my babies. Come, I'll feed you."

A country woman was walking along with her granddaughter. She was carrying a basket containing little pies to the bazaar. And the thrush flitted in front of her, lighting here, then flying off. The granddaughter said, "Grandmother, let's catch the thrush!" They started trying to catch the thrush, and the fox was there on the spot. She grabbed the basket of pies and was off! The grandmother and granddaughter returned, but there was no basket.

In the morning the fox was at the thrush's again. "Thrush, you fed me—now get me something to drink. Otherwise, I'll chop down the tree and destroy your babies."

"Oh, mother fox! Don't chop down the tree, don't hurt my babies!" The thrush led the fox off. A peasant was coming along, carting a barrel of beer. The thrush perched on the barrel. The peasant chased him off again and again, but he couldn't get him to leave. The peasant took his axe, aimed it at the thrush, but sank it in the barrel. The beer flowed out. The fox drank her fill—she could scarcely move. She went off, drunk.

In the morning she got up and came again to the thrush. "Thrush, you fed me and gave me drink, now amuse me, or else I'll chop down the tree and destroy your babies."

"Oh, mother fox, don't chop down the tree, don't hurt my babies. Let's go, I'll amuse you."

The thrush led the fox into the forest. A woman was milking a cow while her old man was braiding some bast boots. The thrush landed on the cow and pulled out some of her hair. The old man tried to hit the thrush but bashed the woman with the bast boot, and the old woman upset the milk. The fox was right there.

"Thrush, you've fed me, you've given me drink, you've amused me, now frighten me." The thrush bound her eyes and led the fox to the sheepfold (where they keep the ewes). He untied her eyes and the sheep-dogs rushed at her. The fox had just about reached her burrow, when the dogs seized her and tore her up.

A–T 68C

40. (Who Is More Cowardly Than the Hare?)

A hare became bored with his life, and he said, "Everyone is always insulting me; I'm afraid of everyone; I can't get a minute's peace; what sort of life is this? I'll go and drown myself from my grief." So he hopped, hopped to the river. And near the bank there was this frog. The frog was frightened by the hare, and so he hopped into the water away from it. The hare stopped and said, "Oh," he said, "now that's some-thing! There are folks who are afraid of me. I don't want to drown!" And so he didn't drown himself.

A–T 70

41. The Boaster Hare

There lived and dwelt this hare in the forest, and he played out his life. It was fine for him in the summertime, but in winter it was bad. He had occasion to frequent the peasants at their threshing shed to pilfer their sheaves.

He came to this one peasant's, and there was already a passel of hares there. So he began to boast to them, "I've no lip-strainer but a fine mous-tache, no paw but a real fist, no teeth but real fangs—I'm afraid of no one."

And once again he set off into the forest. But the others told auntie crow. Auntie crow heard about that boaster. She set off to search out the boaster and found him under a hollow log. The hare took fright and said, "I won't boast ever again!"

"But how were you boasting?"

"Well, I said 'I've no lip-strainer but a fine moustache, no paw but a real fist, no teeth but real fangs.'"

So she roughed him up a little and said, "Don't boast any more."

Now once the crow was sitting on the fence, and some dogs grabbed her and began to rough her up, and the hare saw this and said, "How could I help the crow?"

Then the dogs caught sight of the hare and were after him, and they started running, and the crow was on the fence again. The hare slipped away, and the dogs could scarcely drag their legs away, they were so tired. So the crow sat there, and the hare came running up.

"Well," she said, "good lad. You're no boaster, but a hero. You'll do for my supper." So she ate him.

A–T 70**

42. The Crane and the Wolf

So, a wolf went out after some booty. There was this dead sheep lying there. He took a run at it out of greed, grabbed hold of the carcass, tore a chunk off and swallowed it, with the bones, choked, and lay there gasping.

This crane was walking around the swamp. He asked the crane for help. The crane approached but was frightened. "Oh, crane, don't be frightened, nothing will happen to you."

The crane stuck her head down into his gullet and pulled the bone out. Then the wolf shook himself, stood up, thought the matter over, and didn't offer a word of thanks; he just intended to eat the crane. "But how can you, friend, I did you such a favor?"

The wolf stood there and said, "Old hospitality is soon forgotten." Crunch, and he ate that crane, head first. And that's all.

A–T 76

43. About a Grouse

A grouse wanted to build a house. He thought and thought. There was no axe, no blacksmith, no one to make the axe, no one to build a little house for the grouse. "Why," he thought, " do I need to put up a house? Just one night won't make a difference." And he plopped into the snow; He spent the night in the snow, in the morning he got up, flew around the whole world quite freely, cried out quickly and loudly, and sought out his comrades. He came down to the ground and visited with his comrades. They played about, cleaning the snot from their noses. They wandered through the brush, sought out good places to weave nests, laid their eggs, and brought forth babies. With the children they walked in the open steppe, fed the children on midges, took them out into the free world, flew about in the free world, and again in the winter they slept in the snow. "And one night with the children never made a difference, however it went. Why should we raise up a house? It's better to sit in the birch trees, stare into the steppe, greet beautiful spring, and go 'whirr-whirr-whirr.'"

A–T 81

44. The Squirrel and the Hedgehog

A squirrel lived in the forest. She had her nest high in the tree, and every autumn she would carry nuts there for the winter. Once she set off into the forest for nuts, and she encountered a hedgehog.

The hedgehog said, "Greetings, little squirrel!"

The squirrel said, "Greetings, hedgehog!"

"Well, little squirrel, how have you been getting along? Who is living in your house? Or do you live alone?"

"I live alone. And it's very difficult because I have to carry enough nuts there for the whole winter."

"Well, let me help you!"

So they ran off together to collect nuts. They came home, dropped them off, and then the little squirrel once more ran into the forest for nuts, but the hedgehog went home. In the forest the little squirrel encountered a wolf. And the wolf asked her, "Are you running far, little squirrel?"

"Well, you see, I have to carry home enough nuts for the whole winter."

"And do you live alone, or does someone live with you?"

"Of course not, I live all alone."

"Well, let me help you." So they gathered up a lot of nuts, dropped them off, and the little squirrel ran into the forest a third time. This time she encountered a fox. "Well now, little squirrel, where are you going in such a hurry?"

"Why, into the forest to collect nuts."

"And don't you have anyone to help you?"

"No, no one at all."

"Well then, I'll just have to help." So the fox helped the little squirrel. The next day the hedgehog came to the little squirrel and asked, "Little squirrel, how many companions did you find yesterday?"

"Three—hedgehog, wolf, and fox."

"Would it not be better for us if we all lived together?"

"Whether better or not, my hut is too small. The fox, you see, wouldn't even fit in my hut."

"But we could somehow live together." So the squirrel invited the hedgehog to live with her. And the wolf and fox lived lower down near the forest. Then the hedgehog decided to marry the squirrel. They called all the forest dwellers together and put on a wedding. When they had all been seated at the table, the hedgehog and the squirrel sat down with them, and the hedgehog accidently pricked her with his needles. The squirrel shouted out. The hedgehog took fright and ran off. The squirrel also jumped up from the table and started running. They collided in the doorway, and the hedgehog pricked her again. She screamed out again, and they ran off in different directions. And that was the end of the wedding. And the squirrel and the hedgehog started living as before.

Live and dwell and prosper!

A–T 83*

45. The Mouse, the Sparrow, and the Pancake

In a forest clearing, in a little forest hut, there lived and dwelt a sparrow, a little mouse, and a buttery pancake. They lived peaceably; they never offended each other. They had distributed amongst themselves all the household tasks. For whole days at a time the sparrow would fly about the forest and gather food, and the little mouse would drag in firewood and chew it with her sharp little teeth, and all day long the buttery pancake would be at home in charge of the household: it kept the stove going, swept the hut, made cabbage soup and porridge, and waited for its friends. In the evening they would all gather together, in a hut that was neat and clean, with the stove stoked, and they would eat this rich cabbage soup and sing its praises: "My, what a cabbage soup! The soup is excellent!"

And the buttery pancake would smile and say, "I dipped in and out of that cabbage soup, and that's why it's so rich."

For a long time, or a short time, they lived like that, but the sparrow got bored of flying about the forest for whole days at a time. One morning he got up out of sorts and said, "I'm not flying out today for any food; for whole days at a time I go flying around in every sort of weather; I feed you all."

So they debated, they squabbled, and they decided this: the pancake would go out to get the food, the mouse would stay in the hut, in the little house, and cook the cabbage soup, and the sparrow would chop the firewood. It chopped and it chopped, and it bent its bill to one side even, but there was still no firewood. The little mouse stoked the stove, swept the hut, and started cooking the cabbage soup. No matter what she put into it, no matter what she added to it, the cabbage soup was still not rich, the cabbage soup still wasn't tasty. The little mouse remembered that the pancake had dipped itself in it, so she went and dived in herself. She climbed out of the hot water all dripping and bedraggled and annoyed, hardly alive, and she sat down on the earthworks* and sat there crying. And all day long the pancake rolled around the forest, all day long it gathered food, but then it got into a wolf's teeth! The wolf grabbed it by one side and so bit off half a side. Toward evening the pancake crawled home, barely alive. They all sat down to eat supper that evening, but no one ate a thing, and they all got more upset than before. Then suddenly the sparrow understood that he'd done the wrong thing, and he started asking his friends for forgiveness. They forgave him, and the next day they each went about their own business: the pancake

---

*Zavalinka: a low earthen wall around the exterior of the peasant's hut that served to protect it from the elements. It was a favorite place for resting in summertime.

once more started making cabbage soup and porridge, the little mouse dragged in the firewood, and the sparrow flew off to get food.

So that's how it is, children, when someone puts the blame on somebody else.

A–T 85

46. The Bear and the Wild Boar

A certain hunter was walking through the forest when he saw a bear sitting in a tree. So he stopped: "How ought I to go about killing that bear?"

The bear climbed down from the tree and set off. And the hunter did not see that the bear and a wild boar were sparring about with each other. And up there in that tree was a great growth, a great toadstool. Suddenly the bear came tearing as fast as he could go, and behind the bear was the wild boar. The bear climbed up into the tree again, and he sat down on that toadstool. Then the boar came running up, and he walked around that tree, but he couldn't get at him, and so he went off again. The bear saw that the boar had gone. Once more he climbed down and set out after the boar. The boar once again chased after the bear. Then the bear again came charging up here looking for a place to hide himself, and he ran around with the wild boar running after him. The bear again got on top of the toadstool. The boar went away, and the bear again came down from that tree, from that toadstool (whenever he leaps up into that tree, he holds on to the toadstool), and again he set out after the boar. For the third time the boar came chasing after him. The hunter was enjoying all this and thought, "Whom shall I kill first: the boar or the bear?"

The boar went away, the bear also came down and set out after the boar. The hunter thought, "I'll go and just cut through that toadstool, then it'll tear loose, and the boar will tear open the bear's belly, and then I'll just have to kill the boar."

So that's what the hunter did. He cut through the toadstool stalk, then he himself climbed a bit higher into a snag and waited. Suddenly the boar was chasing the bear once more. The bear climbed up into that same tree, to sit again on that toadstool, and he grabbed onto the toadstool. Then the toadstool broke loose and the bear fell. The boar tore open his belly. The bear's guts came out, and the boar started eating them immediately. The bear died. The hunter shot at the boar, but hit it poorly. The boar rushed at the hunter's gunsmoke. (Both the bear and the boar go for the gunsmoke, the place from which it's fired. Nowadays there are few boar, but we used to have them. Also, the pig can become wild.)

Then the boar ran up to that old snag and walked around, but he couldn't get up into the snag. The hunter had already loaded his rifle, and he put a good bullet in him, right square in his forehead. And so the boar fell. The hunter readied the second shot and said, "This isn't going to waste." And he fired again.

So he killed the boar; he set off, took his horse, and brought in two trophies: the bear and the boar. And he told folks all about how he had had to kill them.

A–T 87A*

47. The Bear and the Beam

A bear wanted to satisfy his craving for honey. So off he went and hung around an apiary, but he was afraid. The owner took note of this, and hung a beam over the hive because the bear had already tricked him more than once on his hunts for honey.

And so it was that one fine day the bear got up the courage to satisfy his craving and went after the honey. And there's that beam hanging there. The bear took it in his paws and gave it an almighty shove away from him. The beam swung back and flew right at the bear and knocked him down. He got up and pushed it off again. And so it went on, time after time. The beam would swing away and then come flying back, and time after time it knocked the bear down. He got angry and gave it an even greater push, and he pushed it so hard that the beam came and hit him and knocked him off his feet. His legs could hardly carry him away. He lost all desire to go after honey and so never ventured there again.

A–T 88*

48. (The Dog and the Wolf)

A peasant lived with his wife. They lived neither richly nor poorly, just moderately. They had this dog, only they fed her badly. They went off into the field to harvest, and they took along a little baby in a cradle and set it up near the row where they were cutting. And the dog came running over there after them. And then up ran a wolf, caught the dog, and dragged her off, only then the dog said to the wolf, "Why are you dragging me away? You will just destroy my soul; the master doesn't feed me, and I'm all skin and bones."

"I'll leave you," answered the wolf, "and arrange it so that the master will feed you. Then will you come to me when you're fat?" The dog promised to come. "Then off you go, and lie down. And I'll carry the baby off from the cradle, and you run after me. I'll give up the baby to you."

The wolf ran up to the cradle, grabbed the baby out of it, and ran off with it. The mother and father took fright and ran after the wolf, and the dog did too. The wolf got farther and farther away. He ran out of sight of the peasant, but the dog just kept on running. The wolf gave the baby over to the dog. The dog, taking the baby by the swaddling, brought it to the father and mother at the row where they were cutting. When the father and mother saw that the dog had brought the baby, they rejoiced, and right then they gave the dog some porridge, and they started feeding the dog better than themselves.

After quite a little time the wolf came to the dog thinking that "she'll already be quite fat and I'll eat her up." He came and said to her, "Well, dog, are you fat now?" The dog answered, "I'm fat."

Just at that time the peasant was having a wedding. He had a shelter there. The dog said, "Let's go, wolf, I'll feed you," and she led him into the shelter.

The guests were having a good time, and the dog grabbed a chunk of meat and ran to the wolf. Then the guests started yelling, "The dog has run away with the meat."

The master said, "Don't touch her, whatever my dog wants, she gets."

So the dog ran in again and grabbed a pie, and that, too, went to the wolf, and then once more she grabbed a flask of wine, and that also went to the wolf. So then the wolf and dog set about drinking and eating. The wolf said to the dog, "Dog, I'll warble a little tune for you."

The dog said, "Don't you warble—they'll kill you."

The wolf said to her, "What nonsense you talk: kill me! Why, the guests are warbling away, and nobody's beating them!"

The dog said, "Oh, you wolf! Don't warble, or they'll kill you!"

The wolf said, "I can't hear you, I'm warbling." And so the wolf started warbling, and the dog accompanied him. Then the guests caught the sound of it and came running and killed the wolf. But the dog's life got still better. She had saved the child and caught the wolf.

A–T 100

49. The Wolf Was at a Wedding over the Hill

A wolf was hungry, and he went about begging the Lord God for something to eat. He stretched himself out and moaned, "Oh Lord, I want to eat. My legs are weak, my teeth are dull, I want to eat!"

So the Lord spoke to him: "Go then. There's a herd of sheep over there. Don't touch the ewes," He said, "but there's a ram there with big horns. Eat him."

So he came up to the ram and said to him, "Ram, I want to eat you."

And the ram said to him, "Go to the foot of that hill, and I'll go up on top of the hill. Then open your mouth, and I'll run right in for you."

So the wolf opened his mouth, and the ram came running and smashed his horns into the wolf's mug, such that he did a somersault and landed with his legs straight up.

After he had lain there for a while, he went up on the hill and asked the Lord God for something to eat. "Oh Lord, I so want to eat. My legs are weak, my teeth are dull, I can't live much longer," he said.

"Go then," He said, "there's a herd of cows over there. And there's a black cow with a star. But don't touch the others. Eat the black one."

Now a woman heard the Lord speak, and she went and smeared something over that star so that there was nothing on the cow's forehead. The wolf came and walked right up to the herd, but there was no cow with a star. Again he came to the Lord God. Once more he was up on top of the hill. "Oh Lord, I want to eat, my legs are weak, my teeth are dull, I so much want to eat!"

"Go then," He said, "there's a horse with a colt over there. Eat the mare, but don't touch the colt."

So he came up to the mare and said, "Mare, oh mare, do you know what?"

"No, what?"

"I intend to eat you."

She said, "Don't eat me, I haven't time! I'm just off to town with the letters."

"And where are these letters?"

"They're in a case, right next to my tail," she said.

Then he said, "Where are they? Show me."

And she said, "Go look behind me; I'll lift up my tail."

He went to have a look, and she kicked him in the snout so that he went rolling. Then he lay there for a while and once more went up the hill and said, "Oh Lord, I want to eat. My legs are weak, my teeth are dull, I want to eat."

"Then go," he said, "up by the threshing barn is a dog with some pups. Eat the dog, but don't touch the pups."

So the wolf came to the dog and said, "Dog, oh dog, do you know what?"

"No, what?"

"I intend to eat you."

The dog said, "Don't eat me. Let's go to Kuz'ma's to a wedding."

They arrived, and the dog said, "Let's go up onto the stove." So they got up onto the stove. There were lots of fish cakes there and vodka, too. So they drank vodka and ate the fish cakes, and they both started singing songs, and it was all very jolly. The dog sang in a fine little voice, but the wolf's was coarser. As they droned out the notes, you could hear the wolf clearly, and then the people all came rushing. The dog ran off, and the wolf ran onto a ledge, and that's where they killed him. Thus was Kuz'ma's fur coat sewn, and he is still going about in a wolf fur to this very day.

A–T 122A + 100

50. The Dog and the Wolf

There lived and dwelt this grandfather and his old woman. They had this dog. It got old and was no longer needed. So the mistress no longer gave it anything to eat. A son appeared for the mistress. At the same time it came time to start work in the fields. The woman took the baby and went with it into the fields. She put it next to a stack and went to cut the rye.

The dog was lying at home, unfed, and flies had eaten its ears. It lay there without moving. A wolf came up to the dog and said, "Where is your mistress?"

"In the field," answered the dog.

"I'll bring you back into favor," said the wolf to the dog. "I'll take the baby and drag it off, and you raise a rumpus and run after me; I'll give you the baby, and the mistress will again esteem you."

So that's what they did. The wolf came into the field, grabbed the child, and dragged it off. The woman raised a cry. The dog ran after the wolf, began barking, and the wolf gave the child back to the dog. The woman saw that the dog was carrying the child, and she said to it, "Until the last days of your life I shall feed you, and you shall be much honored by me."

Meanwhile the wolf found the dog and said to it, "Well, what will you pay me back with?"

"Now then, when they have the christening, I'll get you drunk."

So the christening came, and they threw some meat to the dog under the table; they also soaked a bun in vodka and gave it to him. But the dog gave it all to the wolf. And when the wolf got drunk, he raised a rumpus, and that's the tale.

A–T 101

51. The Wolf, the Woodpecker, and the Fox

A wolf was walking through the forest. He saw a woodpecker chiseling at a tree, and he said to him, "So, you, woodpecker, you chisel and chisel away, you work and work, but in your lifetime you can never build a hut."

And the woodpecker said to the wolf, "Wolf, you go on slaughtering and slaughtering, but in your lifetime you'll never sew a sheepskin coat."

The wolf thought that the woodpecker was speaking truthfully. The wolf came to a fox and said to her, "Lisa, miss fox, sew me a fur coat. And I'll bring you some sheep." The fox agreed.

So the wolf brought the sheep—one, two, three, but still there was no fur coat. The fox would eat the meat and sell the fleece at the bazaar. So finally the wolf asked, "When, oh fox, will my coat be ready?"

And the fox said, "Today, toward evening, the fur coat will be ready, only you need some fur for the trim. Go to the man's garden. There's a horse standing there. You slaughter it and bring the tail and mane for the trim."

The wolf set out and saw the horse. He crept up toward her from the

side, and he was about to sink his teeth into her when she struck the wolf
with her hooves and kicked him to death. And now in the field the wolf's
bones glisten.

A–T 102

52. The Fox's Wedding

There lived an old man and an old woman. They had no children. A fox
took to visiting the old man and old woman. She came one day, then the
next; she came a third day, and so she started coming to them every day.
She came and chatted away with the old folks.

Some time passed, and the old man and old woman died. The fox
buried the old folks and occupied their hut. The fox lived in the hut
alone without any trouble.

Once the fox went out after booty, and at that very time, out of nowhere at all, there appeared a tomcat. He climbed into the hut, locked
himself in, and just sat there.

The fox came running home. She pulled and pulled on the door, but
the door was latched. She ran around the house, then ran up to the door
in a sweat and asked in a sweet, endearing voice, "Who's sitting in my
little hut?"

And from the hut the tom answered:

> *I'm the tom of the bronze skull,*
> *With my feet I go tap-tap-tap,*
> *With my eyes clop-clop-clop.*
> *I sit on the stove*
> *And hold a sharp sword.*
> *Whoever enters this hut*
> *Will never leave it alive.*
> *Get out of here, fox,*
> *Don't plague me!*

The fox took fright and ran away. She sat down on the road and just
sat there. A wolf ran along and asked, "Why are you sitting on the road,
fox?"

"And why should I not sit? I had my own hut, but not any more. An unseen beast is sitting in it. He won't let me into the hut and won't come out of it himself."

"Don't cry! I'll go chase him out," said the lobo. He went up near the hut and asked angrily, "Who's sitting in foxy's house? Come out or I'll rip off the doors and tear you to bits!"

From the hut the tomcat spoke:

> *I'm the tom of the bronze skull,*
> *With my feet I go tap-tap-tap*
> *With my eyes clop-clop-clop*
> *I sit on the stove*
> *And hold a sharp sword.*
> *Whoever enters this hut after me*
> *Will never leave it alive.*
> *Get out of here, lobo!*
> *You won't escape my hands*
> *With my sword I'll cut off your head,*
> *And I'll put it in a basket!*

The lobo heard the threats of the tomcat and fled. "Where have you been, wolfie?" asked the fox. "I've no more time, cousin!" answered the lobo and ran away without looking back.

So the fox sat on the road and wept. A jackal came running by and asked, "Why, fox, are you sitting there crying?"

"Why should I not sit here? I had my own hut, but not any more. An unseen beast is sitting in it. He won't let me into the hut and won't come out of it himself."

"Don't cry, I'll go chase him out!" spoke the jackal. "The wolf tried but he didn't chase him out, so how could you ever chase out such a beast?" answered the fox. "I'll chase him out!" spoke the jackal.

The jackal went up close to the hut and asked, "Who's sitting in foxy's hut? Crawl out! Otherwise, I'll come in myself and remove your skin."

The tomcat heard, he listened to those words, and then he shouted out:

> *I'm the tom of the bronze skull,*
> *With my feet I go tap-tap-tap*
> *With my eyes clop-clop-clop*
> *I sit on the stove*
> *And hold a sharp sword.*

Whoever enters this hut after me
Will never leave it alive.
Get out of here, jackal,
Before I beat you up,
With my sabre I'll cut off your head,
And I'll put it in a basket!

The jackal listened to these threatening words and so didn't speak to the fox any more; he rushed off into the woods. He ran, looking back over his shoulder.

The fox sat on the road and wept. Night came and there was nowhere to go. So she sat there, she sat and thought to herself: "I shall go to the hut and speak sweetly with Tom." She went up near the hut and asked, "Who's that sitting in my hut? Come out, tomcat, show me your splendid face!"

The tomcat heard these words and answered:

I'm the tom of the bronze skull,
With my feet I go tap-tap-tap
With my eyes clop-clop-clop
I sit on the stove
And hold a sharp sword.
Whoever enters this hut after me
Will never leave it alive.
But will you marry me?
Then I'll open the door to you,
And let you into the hut, mistress foxy.

The fox listened but was silent. The tomcat waited and waited, and then he asked again, "Will you marry me, foxy? If you'll marry me, I'll open the door to you."

The fox answered, "I'll marry you." The tomcat opened the door. The fox crawled into the hut, and they made their peace.

The next day the fox went out into the yard, sat down near the hut, and just sat there. The wolf ran up, and she spoke to him: "Lobo, I'm getting married!"

"To whom, foxy?"

"To the tomcat. Come to my wedding!"

"I'll come, foxy!"

The wolf ran on, but foxy just sat there. Soon the jackal ran up, and foxy said to him, "Jackal, jackal!"

"What, foxy?"

"I'm getting married."

"To whom, foxy?"

"To the tomcat. Come to my wedding. It's going to be great fun!"

"I'll come, foxy."

The jackal ran on, but the fox kept sitting there. Up ran Tushkan, the hare. And she said to him, "Tushkan!"

"What is it, foxy?"

"I'm getting married!"

"To whom?"

"To the tomcat. Come to my wedding. It's going to be great fun."

"I'll come," said Tushkan and ran on.

The fox sat there, and the bear came along the road. The fox said, "Misha, I'm getting married."

"To whom, foxy?"

"To the tomcat. Come to our wedding."

"I'll come," said the bear, and off he ran.

Foxy began the wedding rituals. She glanced in the hut of a lonely cossack. The cossack was a fisherman; his wife had gone away to the city. The fox led all the invited guests to the cossack's hut. She obtained some wine and treated them all. The guests got drunk, and foxy said, "Dear guests! Eat! Each according to his custom!"

So the bear skinned the cossack's cow, the lobo butchered a sheep, the jackal chased the hens around the yard, and Tushkan ran through the garden, swallowing up cabbages. So the guests had fun, and they praised foxy: "What a good hostess she is!" And foxy went around saying, "Eat, my guests, eat, dear friends! Perhaps there is something not to your liking? Eat and be healthy!"

They were all making merry when just then the cossack came home and dispersed the wedding. The bear, the lobo, and foxy he shot, but the tomcat, Tushkan the hare, and the jackal ran away. The cossack skinned the bear, the lobo, and the fox and waited for his wife. When his wife came, he had a present for her.

A–T 103

53. The Fox as Tomcat's Wife

There lived this peasant and his wife. They had a tomcat. They fed him well and gave him plenty to drink. Then he started behaving really badly, breaking the crockery. So they started hitting him, and then he thought, "I'll run away from these masters into the woods."

So then later he ran away into the woods. In the woods he found himself some quarters and lived there by himself and made his way. And it just so happened that he started liking life in the woods. He would go outside to go walking. And once he encountered a fox. Well, she caught sight of him, too. "What sort of beast are you?" the fox asked him.

He said, "I am sent here from abroad; I am to be the commander over all the other beasts here."

The fox thought, "What a pity that I am to have a commander over me. That is not my desire, to carry out orders."

It occurred to the tomcat that he should get married. He started asking the fox. And she thought about it. "I'll be better off marrying him than living under his command; I'll be better off as his wife."

So then she married him, and she ran off to get some dinner for her husband. Along the way she chanced to meet a wolf. "Cousin, mistress fox, wherever are you going?"

She said, "I've no time to stand and talk to you. I've gotten married; I've entered into lawful wedlock."

"And whom did you marry?" he asked.

"Well, there's this beast sent from abroad who's to be commander over all the beasts."

"And what's he called?"

"Kotonailo Kotofeevich."

"How about our having a look at him?"

"It's possible, but gifts are requested."

So once more she ran off ahead. And she encountered a bear. "Greetings, mistress fox and cousin! Have you been far?"

She said, "I've no time to stand and talk with you. I've gotten married; I've entered into lawful wedlock."

"And whom did you marry?" he asked.

"There's this beast sent from abroad; he's to be commander over all the beasts."

"But how could one get a look at him?"

"Well, you can come and take a look, but don't come without gifts; you should bring something."

So later they all met up, she and the bear and the wolf. "Well, and how should we approach, how are we to get a look? We've got to take some gifts."

She also said to them, "When you come, don't let him see you, look from the side."

The bear brought him a bull and the wolf a ram. They came and threw the presents into the tomcat's quarters. The bear raised himself up into the fork of a tree, and the wolf scrambled into a bush to see the tomcat. And the tomcat went outside and threw himself upon the ram and went "Meow-meow-meow-meow!"

And the bear said, "There's a problem; the gift is too small, it seems."

And then from the ram the cat jumped onto the bull, and then he said even more loudly, "Meow-meow-meow-meow!"

Well, the wolf wanted to see, but the bear was already in the fork of the tree, so the wolf moved around in the bush, and the cat pounced into the bush, thinking that there was probably something to eat there. The wolf tore out of the bush, and the cat took fright and leaped into the fork of the tree, where the bear was. And the bear backed away, out of the fork of the tree. And he said, "Before he kills me, I'll kill myself!" And he killed himself.

And then the fox and cat stayed on living there. The wolf ran away, and the bear had killed himself, and that's the tale!

A–T 103A

54. The Wolf and the Pig

As the wolves quarreled and fought,
As they praised themselves,
The pig left the yard,
She took with her the soft and the white, *
She thought, "I'll go through the wood, the wood.
And into the heads, the heads of oats."
She had agile little teeth,
And she grabbed the little heads.

---

*That is, her piglets.

A wolf came up close,
She bowed low to him,
"Greetings, wolfie-wolf,
Would you not like
Some of the soft and the white?"
"Oh, you piggy!
I cast my eyes about,
But I can't take them off you."
He grabbed her by the bristles
And slung her over his back.
And he started eating round her bones,
And the tender parts he gathered in a pile.
Then in ran the guiltless fox:
"Oh, cousin, dear cousin of mine!
You've got what you didn't buy, what's cheap.
Won't you divide the meat with me?"
"Oh, you cousin!
You know, Yermak*
Let out a fart on an empty stomach,
And you can't get away with that!"
The fox heard these sorrowful words
And started running back and forth;
She ran to the city of Kozel'sk.
In the city of Kozel'sk
There sits a beautiful child,
A cock in an oak.
"Oh, cock, you cock!
Come down lower,
From lower to the ground.
I shall take your soul
Up to heaven as I go."
The cock, that fool, did
Heed the fox; he came down
Lower to the ground.
The fox began to swing the cock,

---

*Yermak: not identified by the narrator, but perhaps a reference to the cossack who conquered Siberia.

And the cock could no longer last out:
"Oh you, you golden princess!
Just as they're pouring butter
Over the pancakes at our grandfather's,
They're waiting for you!
There it's not like with us—
Pies with porridge,
Remember, oh Lord,
Isidore and Makar,
And the third was Zakhar,
The three matryonas.†
Yes, Luke and Peter,
And the old man in the moon,
Ded Miroyed,‡
And the old granny, white mother,
Tiusha, and Katiusha,
And grandma Matriusha!

A–T 106* + 61A

55. About Vaska Tom

In a certain tsardom and state, and in fact in the very one in which we live, there used to live and dwell a landowner. This landowner had a tomcat, and they called him Vaska Tom. The landowner loved Vaska Tom, and the cat did his cat's work very well—in the grain warehouse he caught rats and mice. Whenever the master would go out for a stroll, Vaska Tom would carry home in his mouth up to a pound of presents from the shop—and the landowner really loved him for that—and he had kept him for about twenty years.

Finally Vaska Tom grew old, his whiskers fell out, and his eyes were poor, his strength ebbed, and he couldn't catch rats or squash mice. Vaska Tom became a burden to the landowner, so he grabbed him by the scruff of the neck, threw him out beyond the yard, and kicked him away with his foot.

---

†Meaning is obscure. Perhaps three deities.
‡Grandfather Miroed: a popular name for the moon.

Vaska Tom ran off and started crying. And he started thinking how he was to live until he died. He decided, "Just let me die there next to the warehouse; the rats and mice will come to drink, and they'll see me there."

So Vaska Tom went there to die. And the rats and mice saw him and were overjoyed that Vaska Tom had died, and the mice began to whistle and the rats to shout, "Our great enemy is dead!"

All the rats and mice came running up to Vaska Tom and decided that they ought to bury Vaska Tom so that he wouldn't come back to life. There were about ten thousand of them. So they stretched out a load of runners and rolled Vaska Tom along on the runners—and he just lay there, he didn't move a whisker! They tied about seven ropes to him, got up on his paws, and took the ropes over his shoulder, and then about two hundred mice and rats brought up the rear with shovels and picks. They all went along rejoicing and whistling away on their little whistles. They dragged Vaska Tom to a sandy spot in a dry pine wood and began to dig with all their might.

But Vaska Tom just lay there, occasionally taking a peep: the mice dug a really deep pit, about three meters deep. The diggers climbed out of the pit. Now they had to push Vaska Tom into the pit. So they grabbed hold of him, some by the neck and some by the tail. When Vaska moved, the mice ran away. When Vaska Tom jumped up and started to catch them, they all dived into the pit! They ran about the sand, but there was no place to hide, neither for the mice nor for the rats. Vaska killed a whole pit full. This was all music to his ears, and he had about a hundred fifty shovels!

And so the cat lives well. He sells the shovels and buys himself fish, whistles a tune, and catches mice in the pit. He lives there, and though you can't tell it in a tale or write it with a pen, he lives better than he did at the landowner's, and he's his own master, is Vaska Tom. And that's how it ended.

A–T 113*

56. (The Louse and the Flea)

A louse met a flea. "Where are you off to?"

"I'm off to spend the night in a gal's snatch."

"Well, I'll crawl up her ass." And they parted.

The next day they met again. "Well, how did you sleep?" asked the louse.

"Don't ask about it! Such a fright I've had! Some bald thing came in where I was and started chasing after me. I jumped and jumped, here and there, and he still came after me; then he sort of spat on me and left."

"That's nothing cousin, there were two knocking at my place, and I hid. They knocked and knocked and then they just went away."

A-T 113C**

57. About a Brave Little Mouse

There lived and dwelt a mouse, Turitsa. Once she came out from under the stove and said, "Where is our Tsar Kuchurim?"

A rat answered her, "In the Stony Caverns. He is about to descend from there and go into battle with you."

Turitsa began to weep and moan, what would her little children do? You see, she had these little mice named Shisha, Episha, Omelka, and Mitrosha, who was the very smallest.

So the tomcat, Tsar Kuchurim, began coming down from the stovetop to do battle with them. But Mitrosha was brave. Kuchurim wanted to catch him but—he leaped away! And he landed right on that cat's back and began to make himself at home. The tomcat ran here and there—he was frightened! Then the little mouse Omelka jumped up, grabbed the cat by the tail, and started nibbling.

And so they ate up the cat's tail, they ate up his ears, and they ate up his eyelids. And so that cat goes around blind. He yowls, "They've insulted me! They've insulted me!"

A–T 113G* (tent.)

58. Doomsday!

Once a peasant was riding through the forest. He rode along, whistling and thinking about how to get where he was going a bit faster. Suddenly he saw that his horse was afraid of something—she snorted and pulled to one side. He glanced up and froze. A bear was chasing him. He whipped the horse, and the horse carried him through the forest at a gallop, but he had lost the way. The bear didn't fall behind, either. Soon they were rushing across the steppe that surrounded their village. The horse sensed the presence of the bear and raced for the village, for home, with all her might.

Along the way they chanced upon a cemetery. The sleigh flew over the graves, over the bushes, and when the bear caught up to them, they started beating him unmercifully, and the bear did a somersault right into the sleigh. The peasant flew out of the sleigh somewhere, and out of fear he fainted. And the bear, who had never been sleigh riding before, took fright. He tried to leap out and grabbed hold of the first cross he met, pulling it up, and he was so frightened that he didn't know what to do. The horse pulled the sleigh on and flew into the village. And everybody saw the bear standing there embracing the cross and riding along in the sleigh. The people all thought: It's Doomsday!

A–T 116

59. The Friendship of the Dog and the Cat

A certain peasant had a dog called Sable. Of course, dogs get old quickly, and this Sable also grew old. The master came to hate it. He started kicking it with his feet, beating it with sticks, and chasing it away from the yard. Sable would curl up in some out-of-the-way place, just so that the master wouldn't notice him.

Once a wolf came running along the road, he saw this old Sable, and he asked him, "Hey, you, Sable, why are you lying about in broad daylight?"

And Sable answered him, "Don't talk of it, brother! I've gotten old. The master has taken a dislike to me and begun chasing me from the yard, so for that reason I have to curl up and lie on the refuse pile."

Then the wolf said to him, "Come with me; I'll feed you."

Sable was overjoyed and ran off after the wolf. They came to the steppe, and there they saw a herd of horses. The wolf fell down and rolled about on the ground, and then he jumped up and asked Sable, "Well, brother, are my eyes red?"

And Sable said, "No."

So once again the wolf fell down onto the ground and began going around. He rolled, jumped up, and asked Sable, "Well, are my eyes red yet?"

And Sable said to him, "Yes, now they're red."

Just at that moment a fat mare took interest and started approaching them. So the wolf jumped up, grabbed the mare by the neck, and brought her down. When he had bitten through her neck, the mare was immobilized. The herd moved away out of fright. The wolf and Sable began to eat the mare. In about three days they had finished the mare. It seemed to Sable a really good thing to live with the wolf, and he thought about how he could repay the wolf. Sable led the wolf into the village and brought him to his house. At Sable's master's a wedding was going on. Sable thought to himself, "It wouldn't be a bad trick to get into the hut and underneath the table."

People were walking to and fro, opening the door, and so Sable and the wolf leaped into the hut among the people, and they went way, way under the table. With all the celebrating, the master was drunk. Sable came out from under the table and started to lick his master's hand, and the master, upon seeing Sable, started stroking his head and bragging, "Sable was with me in his young years, and he found me many good things."

All the guests listened. The master started taking meat from his plate and giving it to his Sable. Sable didn't eat the meat but instead began treating the wolf.

The master kept praising him further, saying that his Sable could even drink vodka. He poured a glass of vodka and put it under the table for Sable. And Sable took the glass and gave it to the wolf. The master, all fired up in his drinking spree, gave Sable about three glasses of vodka. Sable stupefied his friend, the wolf, with that vodka. The wolf got completely drunk. When the guests started singing a song, the wolf in his drunkenness joined in. Then all the guests started shouting, "Wolf! Wolf!" Then Sable dragged the wolf into the yard by his tail.

"Let's get away from here fast, brother, or we'll both come to no good." They both leaped out into the road. What should they do now? They would have to go off into the steppe. So the two friends began to wander about the steppe, or about the woods, and there was nothing to eat, and hungry Sable could scarcely drag his legs after the wolf. Then Sable said to the wolf, "Brother, I have no more strength; I'm going to fall down right now and just lie here."

And the wolf answered him, "Then you stay here, and I'll go get some prey for us."

Sable remained, turning from side to side. He waited and waited, but still no wolf. So Sable thought, "Oh, that scoundrel wolf has no doubt deceived me and won't be coming back. It's better when I move my legs; I need to walk."

Sable got up and set off for the village. He came to the village and saw the cat lying on the refuse pile. And Sable said to the cat, "So, big tom, long tail, what are you lying about here for?"

And the tom said to him, "Don't speak of it, brother! When I was young and good at catching mice, the master fed me well, but now I've grown old and stopped catching mice, so the master beats me and chases me out of the yard."

"Then come on home with me. I'll feed you," said the dog.

The cat got up on his legs and wove off after Sable. At this time Sable, despite being hungry, became very brave. They came to a field where a huge herd of horses was grazing. When they came up near the herd, Sable threw himself down and started rolling around, and when he'd rolled around for a while, he got up and asked the cat, "Well, are my eyes red now?"

And the cat answered him, "No."

So Sable dropped down a second time to the ground and did he roll! And when he had rolled for a while, he jumped up and asked the tom, "Now have my eyes turned red?"

And the cat answered him, "No."

So he rolled around for a third time. He rolled and then jumped up and asked the cat, "Well, have they turned red?"

And for the third time the cat answered, "No, they haven't turned red."

So Sable got angry and said, "It just can't be that they haven't turned red."

He jumped up and threw himself upon a stallion. He tried to catch the stallion by the leg and throw him down, but the stallion let him have one right in the forehead, and Sable fell down, dead. And the cat leaped up to him and thought, "Sable's gone down again," and he looked at him and said, "Why, now your eyes have turned red!"

A–T 101 + 117*

60. The Lion and the Horse

There was a certain good hunter, and this hunter always went out hunting on horseback. He would ride out on his horse because he could take along lots of provisions, and he would ride deep into the forest for a long time. Once the hunter came into the forest to hunt. He started thinking where it would be best to stop, and he found the best place near a hill. He unsaddled his horse, let her loose in the green grass, and went off hunting.

On this hill there lived a lion, or, as they called him, the king of beasts. Just at that time the lion had come down the hill to the bottom, and he fell upon the trail of the horse. The lion was astonished. "Who could be walking around here? Only beasts are supposed to walk around here. This is some very unfamiliar trail."

Soon after that the lion caught up to the horse and started speaking to it: "Why are you walking here? This is my place, and for your trespass I ought to strangle you."

The horse was astonished and said jokingly to the lion, "Well, now, lion, first let's have a test of strength. Whoever wins will be right."

The lion was astonished at the horse's words and said, "Very well, we shall test strengths. Only which strengths?"

And the horse said to him, "I can't say which strengths. You are the tsar of the forests, you ought to know."

The lion answered the horse, "Whichever one of us can leap over that creek will be proved right."

"Very well, let's jump!" said the horse.

The lion jumped, and he jumped over the creek. Then the horse was supposed to jump. The horse jumped only to the middle, and the other half he had to swim across. So the lion said to the horse, "You couldn't jump across it, so I ought to strangle you."

"But it's just that I didn't fulfill your task," said the horse. "Now I'll set the task, and we'll see whether you can fulfill it."

"Very well, set the task!" said the lion.

"We'll both strike this stone. I with my hoof and you with your paw."

The horse was shod, but the lion didn't understand that and agreed. The horse went up to the stone and started striking it with his hoof. Sparks started flying, and the lion's eyes began to squint from those sparks. When the horse stopped striking it, he said, "Now, lion, you strike it!"

The lion went up to the stone. He started striking it with his strong paw, but he couldn't get any fire. The lion tore up his whole right paw. When the blood was flowing, he started striking it with his left paw. The lion tore his left paw into shreds, and the blood was flowing, so the lion thought, "How can I save myself from this horse? Why, now that fire flies out of his hoof, that means he'll strike me and kill me."

The lion asked the horse to wait a bit for him. The lion said that he was going off to his hill to heal his paws so that he could come back again and strike the stone some more. In fact the lion went to his hill not to get healed but only to save himself from the horse.

The horse was left to nibble the green grass, and the lion went away up the hill, scarcely moving because of his sore paws. The lion was going up the hill, and he looked back to see whether perhaps the horse was chasing after him. When the lion got up the hill, a wolf came up to meet him. They greeted each other, and the wolf said to the lion, "Why, oh why, Lev Konstantinovich, are you so greatly agitated?"

So then the lion said to the wolf, "Why should I not be agitated when I scarcely got away alive?"

"From whom?" asked the wolf.

"Well, you see, brother, I came upon this horse. And I scarcely got away from her with my life."

The wolf didn't believe it: "What are you saying, Lev Konstantinovich, that you scarcely got away from a horse with your life?"

"Why, haven't you ever seen a horse?"

And the wolf said, "I've not only seen them, I've eaten them."

"But, brother, that's rubbish that you've eaten them!" said the lion.

"Let me show you," said the wolf. "I'll go out and strangle it."

At the foot of the hill the lion saw the horse and pointed it out to the wolf. But the wolf couldn't make it out very well because he was smaller than the lion. However much the wolf stretched out, he still couldn't see. So the lion said to the wolf, "Turn with your back to me, and I'll take you in my paws, then you'll probably make it out."

The wolf, scarcely thinking, turned his back to the lion, but the lion was still in holy terror and took him in his strong paws and raised him up. He squeezed him ever so tightly and asked whether he could see the horse, but the wolf was silent. The lion repeated his question again, but the wolf was silent. Then the lion let him down onto the ground, but the wolf was dead.

"Oh, you boastful wolf! You said you'd not only seen but eaten them. So then you took one look and died."

A–T 118

61. The Wolf

This business took place in olden times, when Christ still walked the earth with his apostles. Once they were walking along the road, along a very broad road, and a wolf chanced to encounter them and said, "Oh, Lord, I really feel like eating!"

"Go on," Christ said to him. "Go eat a mare."

The wolf ran off to look for a mare. He caught sight of her, walked up and said, "Mare! The Lord has commanded me to eat you."

She answered, "Well, no, you won't eat me; it's not allowed. I have this permit, only it's in back of me."

"Well, show me!"

"Come up closer to my hind legs."

The wolf approached. Then she let him have it in the teeth with her hind hooves, so that the wolf flew at least three yards back! And the mare ran away.

So the wolf went off with a complaint. He came to Christ and said, "Lord, that mare nearly beat me to death!"

"Go then and eat a ram."

The wolf ran off to a ram; he ran up to him and said, "Ram, I will eat you, the Lord has ordered it."

"Perhaps you'll eat me! Stand over there at the foot of the hill and stretch open your mouth."

Then the ram ran down the hill and struck him with his ram's fore-head—bam! He knocked the wolf off his feet, and then he walked away. The wolf got up; he looked all around, but there was no ram.

Again he set off with this complaint. He came to Christ and said, "Lord, the ram deceived me; he very nearly killed me."

"Go then," said Christ, "eat a tailor!"

The wolf ran off. A tailor just happened to encounter him. "Tailor, I'm going to eat you up; the Lord has commanded it."

"Wait, just let me take my leave of my relatives."

"No, I will not let you take your leave of your relatives."

"Oh, well, what's to be done? So be it, eat me! Only just let me measure you first, to see whether I can fit inside you."

"Go on, measure then," said the wolf.

The tailor got behind him, grabbed the wolf by the tail, twisted that tail around his hand, and did he give the old gray one a good ironing out! The wolf fought and fought, he struggled and struggled, he tore off his tail, and did God give him legs! He ran with all his might, and then he met seven other wolves. "Wait," they said, "what are you doing without a tail, oh gray one?"

"The tailor ripped it off."

"And where's the tailor?"

"He's over there, walking down the road."

"Let's go catch him!"

And they set out after the tailor. The tailor heard the pursuit and saw that things looked bad. He took himself up a tree, up to the very top, and sat there. So the wolves came running up and said, "We'll just go up to that tailor, brothers; you, chicken-ass (the tailless one), lie down next to it, and we'll go on top of you; we'll each get on the other one and so get the tailor!"

So chicken-ass lay down on the ground, and a wolf got on him, then another on him, and then a third on him, and so higher and higher. The last one was just climbing on. The tailor saw the inescapable misfortune! They were upon him! So he shouted out from the top, "Well, there's nobody else to be dealt with but chicken-ass!" So chicken-ass jumped out from under the pile and did he run! All seven wolves fell onto the ground and set out after him. When they caught up to him, they ripped him apart, and tufts of hair flew everywhere! And the tailor climbed down from the tree and went home.

A–T 122A + 122M* + 121

62. The Naked Wolf

A tailor set off to a strange village to sew. He was going through the forest when he met a wolf. "Tailor, I shall eat you up!" said he.

"Don't eat me, wolf, I'll sew you a fur coat," answered the tailor.

"Well, alright, sew," agreed the wolf.

"But first I've got to measure you," said the tailor.

The tailor wound the wolf's tail around his hand in such a way that the wolf could not turn his head around. Then the tailor took out his arshin* and started stabbing him in the sides. Then he struck the wolf in the forehead and shouted, "Arshin, measure the lord wolf a little better!"

The wolf lunged, jumped out of his skin, and ran away. He ran through the forest, yelping and howling. All the wolves in the forest gathered at his shouts.

The tailor took fright and climbed up a tree. The wolves gathered around the tree. They wanted to devour the tailor. But how could they get him?

They decided to stand on top of each other. Who would stand first? The naked wolf said, "I'll stand there first!" So the naked wolf took his position, and all the rest piled on top of him. They were about to reach him, but the tailor was sitting in the tree barely alive, and he sneezed: Atchoo!

The naked wolf thought he heard, "Arshin!" And he tore away, and all the other wolves went flying off him. Some were killed, some were trampled, and some expired of fright. So the tailor climbed down the tree, pulled the skins off all the wolves, and sewed himself a fine fur coat.

A–T 121

63. The Tailor

Well, this tailor was walking along to do some sewing in another village. He met up with a hungry wolf. "I'm going to eat you up right now!"

"Very well, I won't stand in your way as you are going to eat me up, but first I ought to measure you."

The wolf turned around with his rear facing the tailor. The tailor wound

---

*Arshin: a measuring stick.

the wolf's tail around his arm. When he had wound the tail around his arm, he started letting that wolf have it in the sides with the measure, and did the hair ever fly! He went right through his sides to his very ribs. And he kept on beating him until he had twisted off his tail.

The wolf tore himself away and lay down under a bush. "Oh, fool that I am, am I not a fool to let him measure me, to let him take the measure of me! Why, he'd never sew me a coat." So the wolf lay there, talking away.

He lay there a whole week, and then he said, "Now I'm going to go and eat up the first thing I meet!" The wolf had gotten really hungry.

A horse came along. He said, "I'm going to eat you up!"

"Well," said the horse, "I won't stand in your way as you are going to eat me up. But I have something stamped on my rear end, and you really must read it out to me."

He raised up her tail to read the stamp. And then she landed one with her hoof, slitting open his belly. The wolf went "pop!" She had half-killed him.

So the wolf lay there and said, "Oh, fool that I am, am I not a fool that I should have to read her stamp? I could have eaten her without a stamp." He lay there, he lay beneath the bush, he rested, but he got hungrier than ever before. "Now, whatever comes by, I'm going to eat up the first thing I meet!"

A ram came along. "I'm going to eat you up, ram!"

"Well then, open up your mouth wide—I'll jump in whole." The ram ran way back and hit him squarely in the snout with his horny forehead, such that the wolf could not get up. And up to that point the wolf had been alive.

A–T 122A

64. The Foolish Wolf

In a certain village there lived a peasant who had a dog. Since his youth the dog had guarded the whole house, but when wretched old age came, he ceased even to bark. His master was fed up with him, so he made ready, took a rope, tied it around the dog's neck, and led him to the woods. He came to an aspen tree and was about to strangle the dog, but seeing the bitter tears rolling down the muzzle of the old cur, his heart was moved, and he took pity on him; he tied the dog to the aspen tree and went home. The poor dog remained in the woods and began to weep and curse his lot.

Suddenly a huge wolf came from behind the bushes, saw the dog, and said, "Good day, spotted cur! I have been waiting a long time for your visit. In times past you drove me out of your house, but now you have come to me, and I can do with you as I please. Now I will pay you back for everything!"

"And what do you want to do with me, little gray wolf?"

"Not much, just eat you up, skin and bones."

"Ah, you foolish gray wolf!" said the dog. "You're so fat that you no longer know what you're doing: after eating savory beef, you wish to eat poor old dog meat? Why should you stupidly break your old teeth on me? My flesh is now like a rotten log. I will give you a better idea: go bring me a hundred pounds or so of excellent horseflesh; let me gain a little weight, then do with me what you please."

The wolf heeded the dog, went away, and came back dragging half a mare. "Here is meat for you!" he said. "Now mind you, shape yourself up!" Having said this, he left. The dog set to eating the meat and ate up all of it. Two days later, the gray wolf came and said to the dog, "Well, brother, have you gained weight or not?"

"Just a little bit; but if you would bring me a sheep, my flesh would become much sweeter!"

The wolf consented to that, too, ran to the open field, lay in a hollow, and waited for the shepherd. When the shepherd came by with his flock, the wolf from behind the bush chose a big fat sheep, jumped on her, seized her by the neck, and dragged her to the dog. "Here is a sheep for you, to help you get fat," he said. The dog set to work, ate up the sheep, and felt his strength coming back to him. The wolf came and asked, "Well, brother, how do you feel now?"

"I am still a little thin. If you would bring me a boar, I would get as fat as a pig."

The wolf got a boar, brought it to the dog, and said, "This is my last service to you. In two days I shall come to see you."

"Very well," thought the dog. "I shall be able to cope with you then."

Two days later the wolf came to the well-fed dog. When the dog saw him, he began to bark.

"Ah, you foul cur," said the gray wolf, "how dare you abuse me?" And he jumped on the dog to tear him to pieces. But the dog had gained strength; he reared up on his hind legs and began to give the gray wolf such a beating that tufts of wolf fur flew out in all directions. The wolf wrested himself free and took to his heels; he ran some distance and wanted to stop, but when he heard the dog's bark he ran again. He came to the woods, lay under a bush, and began to lick the wounds the dog had inflicted upon him. "How that foul cur cheated me," the wolf said to himself. "Just wait! Now if I get hold of something, it won't get out of my teeth so easily."

So the wolf licked his wounds and went to look for new booty. He saw a big billy goat standing on a hill, went to him, and said, "Goat, I have come to eat you."

"Ah, gray wolf," said the goat, "why should you break your old teeth on me? Rather, stand against the hill and open your jaws wide; I will take a run and jump straight into your mouth, then you can swallow me." The wolf stood against the hill and opened his jaws wide, but the goat had his own plan; he flew down the hill like an arrow and hit the wolf with such force that the wolf was knocked off his feet. Then the goat ran out of sight. After about three hours the wolf came to with a splitting headache. He began to wonder whether he had swallowed the goat or not. He thought and thought, and wondered and wondered. "If I had eaten the goat, my belly would be full, but I think the scoundrel deceived me. Well, henceforth I shall know what to do."

Having said this, the wolf ran to the village. He saw a pig with little piglets and wanted to seize one piglet, but the pig would not let him. "Ah, you swinish snout," the wolf said to her, "how dare you be so boorish? I will tear you to pieces and swallow your young in one gulp."

The pig answered, "Well, so far I have not abused you, but now I shall make bold to say that you are a great fool."

"Why?"

"This is why—just judge for yourself, gray one. How can you eat my piglets? They were just born. They have to be washed clean. Let us be friendly, neighbor, and baptize these little children."

The wolf consented—so far so good. They came to a big water mill. The pig said to the wolf, "You dear godfather, stand on this side of the barrier, where there is no water, and I will go to the other side, plunge the piglets in clear water, and hand them over to you one by one."

The wolf was overjoyed, thinking, "Now I'll get the prize in my jaws." The gray wolf went under the bridge, and the pig seized the barrier with her teeth and raised it. The water rushed through, dragging the wolf with it and whirling him around in the eddies. The pig and her piglets went their way; when the pig came home, she ate her fill, fed her children, and lay down on a soft bed.

The gray wolf realized that the pig had cunningly tricked him. He managed somehow to get to the shore and ran about the woods with an empty stomach. He starved for a long time, then could not bear it any longer, so he went back to the village and saw some carrion lying near a barn. "That's fine," he thought. "When night comes I shall at least eat some carrion." For bad times had come upon the wolf; he was glad to have a meal of carrion. Even that was better than to have one's teeth chattering from hunger and to be singing wolfish songs.

Night came; the wolf went to the barn and began to gobble the carrion. But a hunter had long been lying in wait for him with a couple of good bullets readied in advance; he fired his gun, and the gray wolf rolled on the ground with a smashed head. And that was the end of the gray wolf.

A–T 122A + 122M*

65. The Quail and the Killdeer

Once a quail flew and flew, alighted, and fell asleep. A wolf grabbed her and said, "I'm going to eat you."

And she began to beg him, "Don't eat me, and if you don't I'll drive five calves to you. There's little enough good in me, only about a quarter of a pound, counting the feathers."

"You'll deceive me!" he said.

She began to swear to it, "Oh, no, I won't deceive you!"

The wolf was overjoyed. He thought, "Oh, that will be enough for a whole week." He let her go. And he lay down and began to wait. The little quail flew up and away. At the next field boundary there was a killdeer. The quail said, "Cousin, dear cousin, take pity on me for just this one day. The wolf caught me."

"How did you part with him, my dear?"

"Well, I promised to drive five calves to him."

So then the killdeer began to call out, "Tprus, tprus . . . tprus . . ."

And the quail said, "Five calves, fives calves, five calves."

And the wolf waited. "So, they'll be driving them up." He waited and waited, and that's how he died.

A–T 122D

66. The Wolf and the Rams

So once this wolf decided to go out and earn a living. So he was walking along, and a horse was out strolling by with a colt. "Colt, colt! I'll eat you." The colt said, "Before you eat me, take the shoes from my hind legs."

The wolf went up to take off the hind shoes, and the colt gave it to him right under his snout—so that he was backside down and legs up in the air. And the colt was just fine. It ran away with its mother. The wolf howled and howled for a while, and then he continued on.

He was walking along when he saw two rams strolling, a black one and a white one. "Rams, oh rams! I'll eat you!"

"Wait there," they said, "and open your mouth wide. Whoever gets into your throat first, he's the one you'll eat!"

Well, he stood there, he crossed his paws, he waited, and he let his mouth hang open. The rams ran at him on two sides: one of them struck him in the back and the other from the front. They bashed in his sides, and he fell.

Once more he howled and howled for a while, but then he got up and continued on. A donkey was coming from the town, and he was carrying a pitcher of wine and some flat cakes into the village. "Donkey, donkey! I'll eat you!"

And the donkey answered him, "Cousin wolf, I've worn out all my feet, looking for you. All my guests have gathered, you're the only one not there. Sit on my back quickly."

Quickly he sat down on the donkey's back, and he took the pitcher and the flat cakes in his hands. He drank the wine and tasted the flat cakes. But the little donkey sped up and sped more and more quickly toward the village. And the wolf got drunk and started singing his entire wolfish song. He didn't note that the donkey had brought him right into the village.

The peasants spied him and grabbed their pitchforks. But he was drunk and didn't see anything, singing his song in his wolfish way! And so they started beating him from all sides, some with pitchforks, some with other tools. And they beat him up, smashed in his ribs. He tore away scarcely alive and ran through old woman Malanin's garden. He ran to his den and said, "My father did not thieve, and neither did my grandfather. And I, before I die, have no desire to steal!" And that's it.

A–T 122M*/N*

67. The Wolf and the Kids

Once somewhere a pregnant nanny goat was walking along, and she came up to an apple tree and said, "Apple tree, apple tree! Let me give birth beneath you!"

But the apple tree wouldn't let her. It said, "An apple would fall and hurt a kid; that would not be any good for you."

The goat went up to a nut tree and asked to be permitted to deliver her kids. But the nut tree refused, saying, "A nut will fall and hurt a kid."

There was nothing else to be done, so the nanny set off as if she'd been sipping unsalted cabbage soup. She walked and she walked, and then she saw a hut standing with its front to the wood and its rear to her. So the goat said, "Hut, hut! Turn your front toward me and your rear to the forest, and I'll enter into you."

The little hut turned around, and the goat went inside to deliver her babies, and they were born there. So the goat settled down as if she were at home. She often began leaving her kids locked in the hut while she herself went into the wood to eat grass.

Now once when the goat had just left her kids, a wolf came up to the doors of the hut and shouted in a full voice, "Kiddies, children! Unlock the doors, open up! I am your mother, come back; I've brought you some milk; the milk is running out of my udder into a trough and out the trough into the moist earth."

The little kids knew that the voice was not their mother's, and they did not open the door. "Our mother doesn't have a voice like that; hers is sweet and gentle."

Soon after that the wolf went away, and their mother came to the door and shouted, "Oh children! Unlock and open the door. I am your mother;

I've brought some milk. I was in a wood, swallowed a wild onion, and milk is flowing through my udder, from my udder into a trough, from the trough into the moist earth." The little kids opened up for her and began to drink milk.

Meanwhile the wolf went to the blacksmith and said to him, "Blacksmith, blacksmith! Make me a very thin tongue." The smith made it for him.

As soon as the goats had eaten and drunk their fill, the nanny went off to the woods again, having strictly ordered her children to let no one in. As soon as she had gone, the aforementioned wolf came up to the doors and began to shout in a voice similar to their mother's, "Oh kiddies, unlock and open up! I'm your mother; I've brought milk; the milk's running through my udder, out of the udder into a trough, out of the trough into the moist earth."

The kids were not suspicious of the voice and opened the door to the wolf. The wolf ate nearly all of them—only one little kid hid beneath the stove. The wolf ate, left one fleece and the bones, and went away into the wood.

The goat came back, shouted at the door, and the little goat let her in. She collected the fleece, dried it by the stove, and milled it like flour. After a day she ventured to make some pancakes and thought of inviting the wolf to be her guest. She had seen the wolf at the wolf's cousin's, the fox's. Having made up the pancakes, the goat went to the fox's and asked her to be a guest together with the wolf. The fox promised to come, and the goat returned home.

The next morning early, at about five o'clock, the fox and wolf came to the goat's. The wolf had become such a smoothie that the goat didn't recognize him. They sat down at the table; the goat gave them plates, knives and forks, butter and cream, and they started eating pancakes. Meanwhile, the goat pretended to crawl into the cellars for the sour cream, but in fact she had something else on her mind. She took with her a fire lighter and started a fire, and around the fire she stuck some iron palings.

When her guests had eaten the pancakes, the goat asked whether it wouldn't please them to play at her favorite game. They agreed. The goat immediately pulled up one of the floor boards and directed them to go up close. And she said, "Here's my game: you have to jump across this hole quickly and without a pause."

The fox and goat both jumped across. Behind them the fat wolf was getting ready. But he had no sooner jumped than he caught his foot on a floor board and fell into the hole, onto the iron palings and into the fire. The goat and fox covered him over with a board and the wolf burned up. Then the goat and her cousin fox made a wonderful wake for the wolf. They ate and drank their fill and went outside. The goat saw the fox off home, and from then on she herself and her little kid lived and prospered, and she got milk for the little goat.

A–T 123

68. The Frightened Bear and Wolves

An old man lived alone with his old woman, and they had a tomcat and a ram. The old woman collected sour cream and cream, and the tomcat played around.

"Old man," said the old woman, "something's not right in our cellar."

"We'll have to take a look," the old man said to her. "Maybe somebody from outside is messing around there."

So the old woman went into the cellar, and there she caught a glimpse of the tom moving the lid off the cream pot with his paw and licking up some sour cream. She chased the cat out of the cellar and went into the hut, but the cat got there first and hid on the stove in the corner. "Master," said the old woman, "we didn't believe that the cat was the one messing around, but that's who it is, alright. Let's kill him!"

Now the cat heard these words and tore off the stove and raced to the ram in the shed and there started out to deceive him. "Brother ram, they're intending to kill me tomorrow, and slaughter you."

So they agreed to run away that night from their master.

"But how can we?" asked the ram. "I'd be delighted to 'get on my skis' and run off with you, but the shed is locked."

"Never mind!" The cat immediately climbed up on the door, and with his paw he knocked the string off the nail and let the ram out.

So off they went down the wide, wide road, and they found a wolf's head, and they took it with them. They went on and on, and then they saw far off in the forest a little fire burning. So they headed right for it. They came up to it, and around the fire twelve wolves were warming themselves. "God aid you, wolves!"

"Welcome, tomcat and ram!"

"Brother," the ram asked the cat, "what shall we have for supper?"

"Well, there are twelve wolf heads! Go and choose the one that's fattest."

The ram went into the bushes and raised the wolf's head up a bit, the one they had found along the road, and he asked, "Is this the right one, brother tom?"

"No, not that one; choose a better one."

So the ram again raised the same head and once more asked, "Is this the right one?"

The wolves were so frightened that they would have been happy to run away, but they didn't dare to without asking permission. But four of the wolves asked the cat and the ram, "Let us go for some firewood! We'll carry it to you." And they left.

The remaining eight wolves were now even more afraid of the tomcat and the ram: if they could eat twelve, then they'd have no trouble at all with eight. Another four asked to go fetch water. The cat let them go. "Go on then, but hurry right back!"

The last four wolves wanted to set off to fetch the other wolves back: Why hadn't they returned? The cat let them go with a really strict order to hurry right back, but he and the ram were glad that they had gone.

The wolves met up and set off deeper into the forest. They chanced upon a bear, Mikhailo Ivanovich. "Have you heard, Mikhailo Ivanovich, that the tomcat and the ram have eaten twelve wolves each?" they asked.

"No, lads, I haven't heard that."

"But we saw that cat and ram ourselves."

"How could I get a look at them, lads, and see what sort of courage they have?"

"Oh, Mikhailo Ivanovich, that cat is really hot-tempered, there's no way you can get on his good side; he just might tear you to pieces at any moment. We are agile enough with dogs and hares, but you can't do much with this cat. We'd be better off inviting them to dinner."

So they sent a fox off. "Go and invite the cat and the ram."

The fox tried to talk her way out of it. "I'm agile but I'm not slippery enough; they might eat me!"

"Get going!"

There was nothing else she could do but go, so the fox ran off after the cat and ram. She came back and said, "They have promised to come. Oh, Mikhailo Ivanovich, how savage that cat is! He sits there on this stump, tearing it up with his claws: he's sharpening his knives for us! And his eyes bulge!"

The bear was frightened, and he immediately put a wolf as guard on a high stump. He put a rag in his paws and instructed him, "If you see that cat and ram, wave this rag. Then we will all come—and welcome them."

They started getting dinner ready. Four wolves dragged in four cows, and the bear appointed a marmot as cook.

So the cat and ram arrived for their visit. They saw the sentry, got wise to the plot, and made a little plan. The cat said, "I'll creep through the grass quietly and sit near that same stump facing the wolf, and you, brother ram, run back and then hit the wolf with your forehead as hard as you can!"

The ram ran back and struck with all his might and knocked the wolf down. Then the cat pounced right onto his face and dug his claws in and scratched him until the blood ran. When the bear and wolves saw this, they started conversing among themselves. "Well, lads, that's the mettle of the tom and the ram! They cleverly knocked old Eustifeiko the wolf from that high stump and mangled him, so how on earth can we stand up to them? Our preparations will count for nothing with them; they haven't come here to be entertained. They want to besmirch us. Wouldn't it be better, brothers, to hide ourselves?"

So the wolves all ran away through the forest, and the bear clambered up into a spruce tree. The marmot hid in its burrow, and the fox dug herself in under a log. The cat and ram started in on the food prepared for them. The cat ate and purred to himself: "not much, not much . . ." He turned around and saw the marmot's tail sticking out of the burrow. The marmot took fright and leapt into the spruce. The bear was terrified of the cat and plunged out of the spruce onto the ground where he roared off, nearly crushing the fox under the log. The bear started running, and the fox started running.

"So did you hurt yourself?" the fox asked.

"No, cousin, but if I hadn't jumped, that cat would have devoured me long ago."

A–T 125 + 103

69. The Billy Goat and the Ram

A billy goat and a ram went out exploring in the woods. They walked and walked, but wolves were preparing their dinner. The ram munched and munched and woke up one of the wolves. They all started rushing around, spilled everything all over, broke the cups and saucers, and set off in chase. So the billy goat said to the ram, "Ram, where are we going?" So they came up to a snag.† And so they started climbing it. They climbed and climbed, and then the ram slipped and fell; he got caught up on a limb by his horns, but the limb broke, and the ram fell and was killed.

A–T 125

70. Hero Hedgehog

Once a calf in a meadow caught sight of a hedgehog and said to him, "I'm going to eat you up." The hedgehog didn't know the calf, took fright, curled up into a ball, and snorted, "Just you try!" The silly calf, raising its tail, leaped into the air, prepared to butt, and then, spreading wide its feet, licked the hedgehog. "Oh, oh," howled the calf, and it ran to the cow to complain. The hedgehog rolled into its burrow beneath the rowan tree and said to its lady hedgehog, "I have just defeated an enormous beast, most probably a lion." And word of the hedgehog's bravery went even beyond the blue sea, beyond the dark forest.

A–T 125E*

71. (The Ram and the Billy Goat)

There once lived and dwelt in the same yard a billy goat and a ram. They lived peaceably with each other. A wisp of hay—even that they went halves on; but if there was a thorn in their side, it was that tomcat Vaska. He was such a thief and robber, every hour on the prowl, and if there was anything not bolted down, then in an instant he'd have a bellyache from it.

So once this billy and ram were lying there and talking things over between them. Then out of nowhere came this pussy and tomcat, with its gray forehead, and it came up, whining pitifully. Billy and ram asked,

---

†A standing dead tree.

"Cat, puss, oh graybrow! Why are you wandering about here crying, hopping on three legs?"

"Why should I not cry? That old woman has been beating me, she's beaten and beaten me, dragged me by the ears, broken my leg, and readied a choke collar for me!"

"And for what sin are you faced with such a fate?"

"This is my fate for the very simple reason that I forgot myself and lapped up the sour cream." And again the pussy began to cry.

"Cat, puss, graybrow! Now why are you crying?"

"Why should I not cry? As the old woman was beating me, she kept saying, 'My son-in-law is coming to visit, and where will I get any sour cream? I'll be forced to slaughter the billy goat and the ram!' "

The goat and the ram started bleating. "Oh, you graybrow, you dimwit! For what reason have you ruined us? Now we shall butt you!"

So pusskins admitted her fault and asked forgiveness. They forgave her, and the three of them began thinking a little thought: What should they do next?

"Now then, you middle brother ram," asked the cat, "is your forehead really strong? Try it against that gate."

Getting a run at it, the ram smashed into the gate with his forehead. The gate swayed, but it did not open. So then that good-for-nothing elder brother goat got up and ran back. He hit it—and the gates opened.

A column of dust rose up, the grass bent to the earth, and the goat and ram were off running, followed by the cat of the gray brow hopping on three legs. He got tired and pleaded with his adopted brothers, "Either you, elder brother, or you, middle brother! Don't leave your littlest brother to be devoured by beasts!"

The goat took him and put him on his back, and off they flew through the mountains, through the valleys, across the shifting sands. They ran for a long time, a day and a night, as long as they had strength left in their legs.

Then came a steep ravine and a border point. At the bottom of that ravine was a harvested field, and in that field sheaves stood like towns. The goat, the ram, and the cat stopped to rest, and the autumn night was a cold one. "Where can we get some fire?" thought the goat and the ram, but tomcat, who had already got some birch branches, wrapped them around the billy goat's horns and ordered him to knock horns with the ram. So the goat and the ram knocked horns and so soundly that sparks flew from their eyes and the birch branches caught fire.

"Good," purred the gray cat, "now we can warm ourselves." And right after that he added a shock of hay to the fire.

They hadn't yet managed to warm themselves by this means when they looked up and there was an uninvited guest, that peasant-bear Mikhailo Ivanovich. "Let me get warm and rest up," he said. "I am unwell."

"Welcome, you ant-eating little peasant bear! Where are you coming from?"

"I visited the apiary and got in a fight there with the peasants, and then a skunk attacked me. I'm off to the fox for a cure for this pox."

The four of them started out spending the dark night together: the bear beneath the haystack, the cat on the stack, and the goat and ram by the warm fire. Then up came seven gray wolves, and an eighth one that was white, and they made straight for the haystack.

"Fie, fie!" said the white wolf, "it doesn't smell like a Russian here. What sort of folk are there here? Let's test our strength!"

The goat and ram began to bleat from fright, but the tom uttered this speech: "Oh, white wolf, prince above all wolves! Do not anger our senior! God forbid he should become angry, so go your own way, and no ill will come to anyone. Or, perhaps, you don't see that beard of his: there's a force in it; he beats beasts with that beard, and with his horns he merely removes the skin. It would be better for you to approach him with honor and ask him, 'We would like to play "Mother, May I?" with your littlest brother, who's asleep under the haystack.' "

With that the wolves went up and bowed to the goat, then they surrounded Mishka and started quarreling with him. With a great show of force the bear got hold of each wolf by the paw. They screamed bloody murder, somehow got away, and, tails beneath their legs, cleared out of there as fast as their legs could carry them.

Meanwhile the goat and the ram had grabbed the tomcat and run into the forest, and again they collided with those gray wolves. The cat scrambled up to the very top of a fir tree, while the goat and the ram grabbed hold with their front legs onto a fir bough and hung there. The wolves stood round the fir, gnashing their teeth and howling, eyeing the goat and the ram. Old graybrow the cat saw that things were bad, so he began hurling fir cones at the wolves, all the while intoning, "One wolf! two wolves! three wolves! There's one for each and one left over for your brother! I, tomcat, have already devoured two wolves, together with their bones, and I'm pretty well sated. But you, big brother, you went after the bears and didn't get any—take my share of these for yourself."

He had just uttered these words when the goat lost his grip and fell right onto a wolf with his horns. And that puss knew his business: "Hold him, catch him!" Then such a fear overcame the wolves that they set off running as fast as their legs would go and without a glance backward. And so they were gone.

A–T 130D* + 126A*

72. The Tale of a Certain One-Sided Ram

A certain landlord owned many head of livestock. Once he slaughtered five young rams and prepared the sheepskins to make himself a coat. He summoned a tailor. "So sew me a coat," he said.

The tailor measured and measured, and he saw that they were a half-sheepskin short of having enough for a coat. "There's too little sheepskin," he said, "not enough for the pleats."

"We can solve that problem," said the landlord, and he ordered his servant to skin one of the rams just on one side. And the servant did just as the landlord had ordered.

But the ram was now annoyed at the landlord, and he called the billy goat over. He said, "Let's get away from this evil man; one can still live in the woods; there's grass, and we can find some water. We'll be very content." So off they went. They came to the forest and put up a lean-to as a place to spend their nights. They lived there alone and were thriving, eating the grass.

It wasn't just those two who didn't like living at that landlord's place. A cow, a pig, a cock, and a gander all left that yard. And while it was still warm, they lived outside, but when cold, old winter came, they wanted to shelter from the frost. So they walked and walked about the forest, and they came upon the ram's lean-to and started begging him to let them in. "Let us in," they said, "we're cold." But the ram and billy goat didn't want to have anything to do with them, and they didn't let anybody in.

So then the cow came up. "Let me in," she said, "or else I'll turn your lean-to over on its side." The ram saw that things were bad, so he let her in.

Then the pig came up. "Let me in," he said, "or else I'll dig up the dirt and dig right under you. Then you'll see, you'll be even colder." There was nothing else to be done, so they let him in.

Then there was the gander saying, "Let me in, or I'll peck a hole through and you'll be even colder."

And the cockerel said, "Let me in, or I'll shit all over your roof!" There was nothing else to do; they let them in, and they all started living together.

After a short time or a long time, as they lived there, some robbers were walking by one day, and they heard the hue and cry of the animals, and they went up to listen. They didn't know what it was, so they sent one of the robbers: "Go," they said to him, "or else it's a rope around your neck and into the water!" There was nothing else he could do; he had to go. As he entered, the animals set upon him from all sides. So there was nothing else he could do but go back.

"Well, brothers," he said, "do what you like, but I'm not going to return there for anything. I've never in my life seen such a horror. As soon as I got in, some woman appeared out of nowhere and started at me with an oven paddle. Then another woman set at me. Then this cobbler attacked me with an awl, and he got his awl into my rear end; then a tailor was after me with his scissors. And there was a soldier in spurs who threw himself at me with all his hair standing on end. 'I'll get you,' he said. And then there was yet another one, the biggest of them all: 'Let me get at him.' " The robber said, "Brothers, I was a coward."

"Well," said the robbers, "there's nothing else to be done; let's get away from here, or they will probably capture us all." They left.

And so the animals lived there, and they lived in harmony. Suddenly some beastly wolves came to the lean-to, and by the smell they detected who was there. "Well now," the wolves said to one of their number, "you go and be first!" No sooner had he gone in than the other animals began to flail away at him, and he got out of there as fast as his legs would take him.

The wolves didn't know what to do. But there was a hedgehog there with them, and he said, "Wait a little while I try; maybe that will be easier." You see, he knew that the ram was missing one side. So he rolled up and pricked the ram. The ram gave a great leap out over all the rest of the animals and tore off. And all the others went after him; they all ran away. So the wolves moved into the lean-to and stayed there.

A–T 130 + 130B

73. The Bear and the Cock

An old man had a son who was a fool. The fool asked his father to marry him off. "And if you don't marry me off, I'll smash up the whole stove!"

"How shall I marry you? We don't have any money."

"There's no money, but there is the ox. Sell it for slaughter!" The ox heard this and ran away into the forest.

The fool once more appealed to his father: "Marry me off, or I'll smash up the whole stove!" His father said, "I'd be glad to marry you off, but there's no money."

"There's no money, but there's the ram. Sell him for slaughter!"

The ram heard this and ran away into the forest.

The fool wouldn't leave his father alone: "Marry me off!" he said again and again.

"I'm telling you, there's no money!"

"There's no money, but there's the cock; kill him, make a pie, and sell it."

The cock heard this and flew away into the forest.

The ox, the ram, and the cock met up and built themselves a hut in the forest. The bear found out about this and decided to eat them all, so he came to the hut. The cock saw him and started jumping up and down on his roost, waving his wings and shouting, "Cock-a-doodle-doo! Bring him here; I'll trample him with my feet; I'll chop him up with my hatchet. And we have a knife here, and there's a rope, too. We'll kill him and hang him up here!"

The bear took fright and turned back; he ran and ran until he collapsed from fear and died. The fool went into the forest, found the bear, skinned him, and sold the skin. With the money they married off the fool, and the ox, the ram, and the cock came out of the forest and went home.

A–T 130 + 130B + 130A

74. About a Warm Hut

There lived and dwelt a bear. He lived in the forest beneath the roots of a tree. So winter came. He had to save himself from winter. So he set off to build himself a warm hut in a glade. He walked and walked along and met a ram.

"Where are you going, bear?"

"I'm going to save myself from winter."

So they went off, the two of them. And they met a pig. They said, "Come with us, pig."

They went along and met a goose and a cock. "Where are you headed?"

"We're going to save ourselves from winter."

So they set off. They walked and walked. Snow fell, and there was a frost. The bear said, "We have to build a warm hut. Ram, you haul lumber."

But the ram was lazy: "I don't need this hut. I've got my warm coat."

"Pig, you haul the lumber!"

"No, I don't need to. I'll dig myself into the earth and spend the winter there."

So the bear ordered the goose and the cock to haul it, but they didn't want to either: "We'll spread out one wing and cover ourselves with the other, and that's how we'll spend the winter."

"Well, there's nothing else to be done." And the bear began to make his hut alone. He made it warm and moved in.

The winter that came was fierce. The goose and the cock froze and said, "Let us into your hut, bear!"

But the bear was lying on his stove and said, "Br-r-r, I won't let you in; you have wings: spread out one and cover yourselves with the other!"

They said, "If you won't let us in, we'll pull the moss out of the chinking and let the winter in to you." So he was forced to let them in.

And then the ram froze. "Let me in, friend bear, into the hut!"

"No, I won't let you in. You have a warm coat."

And he said, "If you won't let me in, I'll break down your hut; I'll burst it apart with my horns."

And so he was forced to let him in.

It had become fiercely cold. The pig came, and it squealed, "Let me in, friend bear, into the hut to spend the winter."

Again the bear replied, he said, "No, I won't let you in. You didn't want to build the hut; you dug yourself into the earth, so spend the winter there!"

But the pig said, "If you won't let me in, I'll dig under the whole house and let the winter in."

So he was forced to let the pig in.

Thus he had let all of them in. And from then on they lived and prospered through the winter with the bear on the stove, the goose and the cock under the stove, the ram on the bench, and the pig underneath the bench. And that's the whole tale.

A–T 130*

75. The Fox as Carpenter

There lived and dwelt this fox. Now once she went to glean in another village. She came into the village, as it were, to glean. So give her a hen! [Wait, let me collect myself, I'll tell you!]† So they gave her a hen. And she went away from that village into another village with her hen. [You are writing for no good purpose; how stubborn you are! Wait a little, please.] So, she came into another village. "Landlords, let me in to spend the night!"

They said, "But we have no room."

"I only need a little room. I'll get onto the bench, tuck my tail under the bench, turn over, and fall asleep. And then there's my hen; we'll let my hen in with your hens."

So she got up in the middle of the night, ate her hen as it were, and hid her own hen's feathers. In the morning she got up: "Well, give me my hen." [Quit writing there, first we'll draw up a plan, whichever is better; then you can write some more. I'll tell it to you now as I go over the bridge. Why is she writing? Maybe she . . . Who knows what she's writing. And I try to persuade her. . . . And who's it about? What a nuisance! . . . I've already forgotten where I started from and where I finished. A real Podkoliosin, a rut maker. He'd go on like that too. I can't stand it. It's just my luck. Well, that mistress of ours is insistent, a real marvel: when will she stop writing?] So they went to look for the hen. But there was no hen! And the fox said, "Well then, give me a cock for my hen." So they gave her a cock. And then she went to another village with her cock, and she took her time getting there, and it was night.

"Masters, let me in to spend the night."

They say, "We've got no room."

Well, once more she said, "I don't need much space." And that's what

---

†The narrator is interrupting his own narration to comment on the activities of the person taking down his tale. This is not typical of the Russian tales.

she'll say in every house; she has just one line for every house. And then she demanded a lamb for her cock, because she ate the cock in the night, and she went with her lamb to sleep over in the next village, but she took her time getting there, and she asked for a place to spend the night. "Masters, let me in to spend the night."

"But we've got no room."

"I'll get onto the bench, my tail beneath the bench." [She started to write that from the first stupid tale. I could see that coming.] And she just has this one song: "I've got this lamb, and the lamb needs to be put in with the sheep." So she stayed for the night, and in the night she got up and ate the lamb, and in the morning she said, "Well, give me back my lamb." So they went, but there was no lamb! They looked and looked. But no lamb.

"Well then, give me a calf for my lamb." So they gave her a calf. So she set off for the next village with her calf, and she took her time getting there, and it was night. She asked to spend the night, but they wouldn't let her in; they just said, "We've got no room."

"I only need a little space."

And she got up in the middle of the night and ate the calf. Well, in the morning she went and said, "Well, hand it over, give me the calf." But there was no calf!

"Well then, give me a pony for it." [Now what are you writing, wearing yourself out like that; I would tell it to you three times, and you would know it by heart! Why waste the paper on such a stupid tale. She writes with her pen just like a magpie chatters. That's what we say about somebody who talks a lot. Well, well, chatter on, magpie.] So they gave her a pony. She gathered up the tackle, hitched up the pony, and drove off. She rode out of the village, and a cock chanced to meet her: "Give me a ride, cousin fox."

"Come on, get in!"

So they rode on. And a hare was coming along. "Cousin fox, give me a ride!"

"Get in!"

So they let the hare in, and they continued on. And along came a wolf. "Cousin fox, give me a ride!"

"Get in!"

So they continued on, and along came a bear. "Cousin fox, give me a ride!"

"Get in!"

So they rode on. And the fox said to these, well, to these friends of hers, "Let's sing a song." And they rode along, singing songs, each trying to outdo the other. And the bear could drone the notes the longest. And they rode and rode, and then the wagon tongue broke.

The fox said to the cock, "Cock, go fetch a tongue."

So the cock set off with the broken tongue, and he came back carrying a straw for a tongue.

"That's a useless tongue," said the fox. "You go, hare."

The hare brought a thin little twig. It was a poor tongue.

The fox sent the wolf off. "You go, cousin."

The wolf fetched a beam: it won't do!

"You go, cousin bear!"

So the bear uprooted a spruce and brought it back for a tongue.

Once more the fox said, "That's no good for a tongue; I'll go myself."

So off she went herself for the tongue. And while she was gone, the wolf ate the whole innards of the horse and stuffed straw inside.

The fox came back, and she brought a fine tongue. She hitched up the horse. But the horse didn't move! It fell down! Well, they bemoaned it, they wept for the horse, and they decided: "Let's build a hut." But the wolf said, "I don't need a hut; I can get along without a hut."

"Well, cousin bear, let's build a hut."

"Oh, I've got such a warm coat. [Now, you see, I don't know, maybe I forgot a few of the words.] I won't freeze without a hut. [She's wasting her wit writing, stubborn woman: she's a second Podkoliosin!] So the fox said to the hare, "Let's build a hut." And the hare and cock agreed. So they started building the hut. And they built it. And they lived and prospered in their hut. Winter came. The wolf came.

"Cousin, let me in to live here."

"You can get by without a hut, you're so warm."

"Let me in or else I'll climb up on top and smash your hut and crush you all." So they let the wolf in.

The bear came and asked, "Cousin, let me in to live with you."

"You have a fur coat and are so warm that you can live through this without a hut."

"Then I'll climb up on top and smash through your hut and crush you all." So they had to let the bear in, too. And from then on all five of them lived there and lived through the good and got through the bad, too.

A–T 130**

76. The Cock, the Tom, the Pig, the Ram, and the Bull

An old man and an old woman lived together, and they had a lot of livestock: a cock, a tomcat, a pig, a ram, and a bull. One summer they were sitting on the earthwork surrounding their hut, and the old man said, "What do you think, old woman? We've not much use for the cock. We'll soon be having a holiday. Let's butcher him for the holiday!"

"Do as you know best," said the old woman.

But the cock heard and flew away in the night into the woods. The next day the old man searched a long time for the cock but could not find it. He came home in the evening, and the old folks once more were sitting there. "Well, old woman, the cock got lost somewhere; tomorrow I'll butcher the pig."

"Butcher it," said the old woman.

The pig heard this and ran away in the night into the woods.

In the morning the old man went into the barnyard, but there was no pig in the yard. He searched and searched, but he couldn't find it. In the evening the old folks were again sitting there, and the old man said, "Tomorrow I'll butcher the ram."

The ram heard this and ran away into the woods. And the old man couldn't find him either. Again they sat in the evening, and the old woman said, "Only the bull remains in the yard; you'll have to butcher the bull."

"Alright," said the old man.

But the bull heard and ran away into the woods. The old man went to the yard, but there was no bull there. He searched for a long time, but he couldn't find it. He came and said to the old woman, "What a wonder! All our livestock has disappeared. I'll look once more really well, and if I can't find them, then I'll kill the cat, and from its skin I'll make a hat."

The cat heard and ran away in the night into the woods.

Summer in the woods is fine and free, and for the refugees it was also good. For the bull and ram there was as much grass as they wanted; all they had to do was eat it. The cat caught mice and birds, the cock pecked for insects and plant seeds, and the pig ate everything. Things were bad only when a little rain would come, and then they would hide. But summer passed, and autumn came. It became cold, and after autumn winter would come, and it would be even colder. Autumn came, and the bull froze first of all, and he thought of building a winter hut. He found the ram and said, "Let's build a hut together, ram. Winter's coming, and it'll be cold; you'll freeze."

"No, I won't freeze. I have a warm coat. I'll run about, and I'll be warm."

The bull found the pig. "Let's build a hut, pig; it'll be cold this winter, and you'll freeze."

"No, I'm not going to build any hut. I'll dig a deep pit in the earth, I'll get myself into it, then the snow will fall, and I'll be warmer still, and I'll sit there 'til summer."

The bull went to the cock. "Let's build a hut, cock! Winter will come, and it'll be cold."

"No," said the cock, "I'll spread one wing and cover myself with the other. And I'll be warm." The bull found the cat. "Let's build a hut, cat."

"No, I'll be warm; I'll put my nose under my tail and warm myself."

So they all refused to build a hut. The bull chose a dry place, dragged up some logs, ripped out moss, and built a hut. He put in a stove and prepared wood. Autumn came, some days it was cold, but the bull was warm. He heated up his stove and sat inside.

Winter came, it became cold, and the ram ran and ran but could not get warm, so he went to look for the bull. He found him and asked to come into the hut. "What!?" said the bull. "You said you would run and get warm, that you had a warm coat; I won't let you into the hut; why didn't you help me build it?"

"But if you don't let me in, then I'll knock out all the corners in your hut with my horns, and you won't be warm."

"Well, come in then," said the bull. The ram went into the hut and sat down in a corner.

With her snout the pig dug a pit, lay down in it, and the pig got cold. Mistress piggy went looking for the bull. She ran up to the hut and asked the bull to let her in. The bull said to her, "But you wanted to spend the winter lying in your pit, and now you're asking to come in? I won't let you, since you didn't build the hut."

"If you don't let me, I'll dig underneath all the corners of the hut, and it will fall down." So the bull let the pig in; she got into the hut, but it turned out to be hot, so she took herself into the cellar.

The cock spread out one wing and covered himself with the other, but he was still cold. The cold went right through the cock, and he flew off to seek the bull. He barely dragged himself to the hut to ask the bull to let him come in. "But you said that you'd spread one wing and cover yourself with the other and be warm, but now see what you're asking; no, brother, I won't let you in, since you wouldn't help build the hut."

"If you won't let me in, then I'll peck all the moss out of the walls, and you'll be cold yourself."

"Oh, get into the hut, then; you don't need much room." The cock came into the hut and alighted on a perch.

The cat somehow was still managing, but the cold got through to him, too. He went off to look for the bull. He ran up to the hut and shook his paws and asked to come in. The bull said to the cat, "What did you say, that you would put your nose under your tail and be warm? No, I won't let you in; you didn't build the hut."

"If you won't let me in, I'll scratch out all the moss chinking with my claws, and you'll freeze." The bull let in the cat. "Come in," he said. "We've all gotten in here; why should we throw you out alone?" The cat came in and went straight onto the stove and lay there.

Seven gray wolves came along. They saw the hut in the woods, and one young wolf said, "Brothers, I'll go into the hut, and if I don't come back for a long time, come to the rescue." The wolf went up to the hut and fixed his gaze upon the ram. The ram took fright and out of fear bleated. Suddenly the cock shrieked, "Cock-a-doodle-do!" It flew off its perch and began pecking at the wolf's eyes. The cat leaped from the stove, screeched and hissed, and scratched at the wolf's eyes, too. The ram ran from the corner to help and butted the wolf with his horns so much that the wolf did a flip. The bull ran up and punctured the wolf's side with his horns. And in the cellar the pig squealed, "Oink, oink, oink! I'm sharpening my knives, I'm sharpening my axe, I want to eat you alive." The wolf scarcely managed to get out of the hut; it ran and shouted to its comrades, "Oh, brothers, run, run!"

When they had run far away and sat down to rest, the wolf began to talk. "As soon as I went into the hut, I saw something shaggy: it was gazing fixedly at me. Suddenly something started banging and shouting, and something pecked me right in the eyes. Then a small something jumped up from the stove, leaped onto me, and also scratched my eyes. Then the shaggy thing jumped out of the corner and hit me with something, and I couldn't stay on my feet. And something big leaped out next and poked me with something; I saw stars and was overcome by heat. And then something shouted, 'Oink, oink, oink! I'm sharpening the knives, I'm sharpening the axes, I want to eat you alive.' Oh, run, brothers, so that there'll be no chase." And they flew off again. But in the little hut they had all quieted down from their fright, and they lived and prospered.

A–T 130B

77. (The Frightened Bear and the Wolves)

There lived this old man and old woman, and they were all alone in the world, with just a goat and a ram. The old man and old woman died, and the goat and the ram set out along the road. They walked and they walked until they came to a pitch stump. It was already evening, and they needed to spend the night. The ram bleated to the goat, "We need a fire." So the goat butted into the stump, but she couldn't get any fire that way. So the ram ran way back and butted it, and a fire flared up. And they sat warming themselves.

A hare came running up to them: "Goat and ram, let me get warm."

"Warm yourself, get warm, but don't rely on other folk's firewood— supply your own." So the hare dragged up a little twig and sat down to warm himself.

Then a fox came running up to them: "Goat and ram, let me warm myself."

"Warm yourself, get warm, but don't rely on other folk's firewood— supply your own." So the fox dragged up a little branch, threw it on, and sat down to warm herself.

Then a wolf came running up to them: "Goat and ram, let me warm myself."

"Warm yourself, get warm, but don't rely on other folk's firewood— supply your own." So the wolf dragged up a little log and sat down to warm himself.

Then a bear came running up to them: "Goat and ram, let me warm myself."

"Warm yourself, get warm, but don't rely on other folk's firewood— supply your own." So the bear dragged up a stump, threw it on, and sat down to warm himself.

They all fell asleep.

The goat and the ram woke up and spoke: "Two foresters are coming, looking for wolves and bear."

The wolf heard them and woke up the bear: "Bear, bear! The goat and the ram are saying that some foresters are looking for us."

The bear spoke: "Oh, what truth there is in that!"

So they went back to sleep.

The goat and the ram woke up, and they ran off along the road. They ran and ran and came to some drooping spruces. The goat climbed up into the top of a spruce, and the ram went after him. He climbed and climbed, but then he tumbled, caught his horns on a branch, dangled and dangled and then fell. So then the bear and the wolf came running up. From the top of the tree the goat shouted, "Did you have to do that? Did you have to do that?"

A–T 130D*

78. The Fearless Landlord

There lived this fearless landlord, and he absolutely knew no fear. "Servant, hitch up the horses, let us go to look for some fear." The servant hitched up the horses and they rode off.

I don't know whether it was for a long time or for a short time that they rode, but there on the gates was this strangled corpse hanging. "Oh, he still has some fine boots on! Pull on the foot there, servant, take off the boots, and you'll wear them, too." The servant pulled on the leg— but the head came off (because of the noose).

"Landlord," he said, "the boots will not be pulled off."

"Well, then, seat him in the cart with me, and we'll take them off this evening when we stop for the night."

They rode on. Night overtook them. And in the village there lived only this heretic.† He had recently died. Everyone was afraid of him, and they had all run away. He ate up whoever remained. But these two needed to spend the night in the village. So the servant ran into one house and called out, then into another, but there was no answer at all.

---

†In nineteenth-century Russia, the term *heretic* was commonly used to mean *vampire*.

"Servant, run into that house there and ask them!" the landlord said, and the servant ran off.

"No, there's no one there either."

"But is it perhaps warm in the hut?"

"Yes, it's warm, but there's this coffin standing in the middle of the hut."

"Ride on in," he said, "we'll spend the night all the same."

The servant unhitched the horses, and they went into the hut. There was no time to drink tea or have supper, and there was no one to prepare it. The landlord asked the servant, "Where will you lie down to sleep?"

"I'm so frozen," he said, "I'll lie down on the stove. And where will you lie down, landlord?"

"I'll lie down on the drying rack."

They still hadn't fallen asleep, and midnight was coming when the heretic got up out of the coffin. He climbed up onto the drying rack, grabbed the landlord by the legs, and started dragging him down. They grappled there, struggling away, to see who could take whom. This went on for quite a while, but finally the landlord overcame the heretic. He defeated the heretic, put him back in the coffin, and said, "Die!"

The landlord woke up the servant: "Servant, are you alive?"

"I'm alive," he said.

"Well, hitch up the horses. Let's go. There's no need to sleep any longer."

So they hitched up the horses and set off. That village was near a mountain. They rode beyond the rise in the road and stopped. "Servant," the landlord said, "I fought with that heretic in the night, and oh, what strength! If we could get him to join our company, then whatever we met . . . no one could but submit to us! Servant, run back to him and drag him along."

The servant, you understand, was in no position to disobey the landlord, so off the servant went; he went back over the rise in the road, but he was afraid to go into the house, even to go back into the village. He just rumpled up his hair as if the heretic had pulled it and then ran back to the landlord, saying, "Oh, landlord! That heretic almost did me in!"

"Well, then I'll go myself." So the landlord dragged the corpse back and put him in the cart with them.

They rode on to the portage. There they saw a fire to one side, so they went up to this house to spend the night. And in this house there lived a gang of bandits. The landlord requested permission to spend the night. "Let us in to spend the night," he said.

The bandits saw that it was the landlord who had ridden up to spend the night. They spoke among themselves: "A tasty morsel has ridden up, by itself, in a caftan!" They were sitting there eating their supper.

The landlord came right into their hut, prayed to God, and went up to the table. "Bread and salt,"* they said, hospitably.

But the landlord was clever; he saw that things weren't quite right (they'd come to bandits, you see), so he went and helped himself to a little porridge. He tasted it and said, "This porridge is no good!" And he asked, "Which one of you made this porridge?"

They pointed out the one and said, "That one," and the landlord grabbed him and began to whip him. "For real friends you just don't put out such bad food! Over there I've got some real food; you eat it, this real food! Here, servant, bring that thing over here!"

"Which one do you want, landlord?"

"Let's see, the headless one!" he said.

So the servant carried in the strangled corpse on his shoulders and threw it down in the middle of the table. "There," he said, "is some real food for you!" But they all let out a roar, did the bandits, jumped up and ran away, wherever they could.

So the landlord and servant stayed in the hut and spent the night. The next day they got up and rode on most peacefully, wherever their eyes would take them. They rode and they rode until they rode to the capital city. There they saw notices posted at every crossroads: "The lord has this trained bear. Whoever spends the night with it will receive his daughter in marriage." So right then the landlord announced, "I'll spend the night." So they agreed that he would spend that very night there. And they posted notices throughout the city that a certain man had been found to spend the night.

The landlord gave some money to the servant and sent him into the city: "Go, servant, and buy some scissors, a razor, some soap, an iron rod, a bottle of wine, and a violin." The servant went and got them and brought them back and handed them over to him. And he went off to spend the night peacefully. There the royal servants led him into the room and locked it. He uncorked the bottle and poured out a glass of wine. He drank it himself. He poured another and murmured, "Mishka,

---

*The traditional Russian greeting and offering.

take a drink!" Then he poured another and said again, "Mishka, take a drink!" And so he poured out the whole bottle for the bear.

He took the violin and started playing. "Mishka, dance!" he said. And the bear started turning around and around. "Mishka," he said, "now I'm going to shave you." He stuck a wedge into the floor and moved the floor boards apart. Then the landlord said, "Mishka, poke your foot in here!" Mishka poked his paw in. The landlord removed the wedge, and it pinched his paw. Then he soaped him all over and began shaving. He shaved him completely and then walked around with the iron rod saying, "You will not eat any living people." Then he combed out his coat properly and drove the wedge back into the floor. The floor boards moved apart and the bear got out his paw and sat down very quietly in a corner. The landlord said to him, "Sit there, and don't let anybody in!"

So time passed, and it was time to take a look. They opened the door ever so quietly and looked in. The bear threatened them with his paw: "Stop, stop, the landlord is asleep." So the servants got frightened and ran away and told the tsar, "This naked thing is standing there. The bear has torn off his clothes," they said.

So they came to take him out of the room. They came, and the landlord was alive, and the bear was clean shaven. The tsar spoke: "Oh, you, why did you shave him?"

"You have to, so that he won't eat people. So now, give me your daughter." There was nothing else to be done, that was the condition; the tsar ordered her handed over.

The servant hitched up the cart; then he sat the tsarevna in it, and they set off.

Suddenly the tsar thought better of it: he didn't know where they were taking her or to whom she was to be married. A little later he sent off that bear. He ordered him, "Go eat up that landlord and bring back my daughter!" So the bear ran off and caught up to them. The servant saw him, and the landlord ordered the tsarevna to climb out of the cart, and she got down on her hands and knees. [There then follows an indecent episode. The bear took fright at the sight: he thought the landlord had shaved another bear's organs off! So he ran away home!]

A–T 151

79. The Peasant, the Bear, the Fox, and the Gadfly

There lived and dwelt this peasant, and he had this dappled horse. The peasant harnessed it to a cart and set off into the forest for some wood. He had just come into the woods when a large bear came straight toward him. He exchanged greetings with the peasant and asked him, "Tell me, little peasant, who dappled your horse? She's such a dazzling and splendid one."

"Oh, brother Mishka!" said the peasant. "I dappled her myself."

"So you know how to dapple?"

"Who? Me? I'm the past master! If you like, I could probably make you more colorful than my horse."

The bear was overjoyed: "Be so kind, please! For your labor I'll drag over a whole hive for you."

"Well, why not! Fine. Only I'll have to bind you, you old devil, with some ropes; otherwise you won't lie still when I start dappling."

The bear agreed. "Wait," thought the peasant, "I'll swaddle him." He took the reins and ropes and wound them round; he bound the bear so that he began bellowing at the top of his lungs, and the peasant said to him, "Stop, brother Mishka! Don't move; it's time to do the dappling."

"Untie me, peasant!" the bear begged. "I don't want to be dappled anymore; please, release me."

"No, you old devil! You asked for it yourself, and that's how it's going to be." The peasant chopped some wood, laid a big fire, and got a hot, hot fire going; then he took his axe and placed it straight into the fire.

When the axe was red-hot, the peasant dragged it out and started dappling that bear. How it sizzled! The bear started roaring with all his might; he strained and broke all the ropes and reins and headed off running through the woods without a glance backward—and how that forest shook! The bear tore through the forest until his strength gave out. He wanted to lie down, but he couldn't: his belly and sides were scorched, so he bellowed and bellowed. "Oh, let me get my paws on that peasant; I'll give him something to remember me by!"

The next day the peasant's wife went into the fields to cut some rye, and she took a crust of bread and a jug of milk with her. She came to her strip of land and put the jug of milk to one side and began cutting. And the peasant thought, "I'll call in on the wife!" He harnessed his horse and was riding up to their strip when he caught sight of a fox strolling about in the rye. The good-for-nothing crept up to the jug of milk and somehow stuck her head in it, but no way could she pull it out again, so she was wandering about the stubble, shaking her head and saying, "Alright, jug, I was joking, that's enough! That's enough of this playing around. Let me go! Little jug! Little dove! That's enough fooling around, you've had your play and that's enough!" And she just kept on shaking her head.

So while the fox was trying to persuade the jug, the peasant got a chunk of wood, went up to her, and clobbered her legs. The fox rushed off to one side and banged her head against a stone, breaking the jug into tiny pieces. She saw the peasant chasing after her with the chunk of wood, so the fox increased her pace—never mind that she was on three legs, you couldn't have caught her with hounds—and she disappeared into the woods.

The peasant went back and started loading the sheaves onto the cart. Out of nowhere a gadfly appeared, landed on his neck, and bit him fiercely. The peasant grabbed at his neck and caught the gadfly. "Hey," he said, "what shall we do with you? Right! Just you wait, and I'll give you something to remember me by." The peasant took a straw and stuck it up the gadfly's ass. "Fly away now, wherever you know best!"

The poor gadfly flew off, dragging the straw behind it. "Well," it thought to itself, "I fell into his hands! Since the day I was born I've never had such a burden to carry around as I have now!"

On and on it flew, and it flew into the forest until it was quite out of breath. It wanted to land on a tree to rest, and it wanted to fly a little higher, but the straw dragged it down. It struggled and struggled and with great effort managed to sit down, panting, and it started breathing so heavily that the tree shook.

Beneath that very tree the bear was lying down, the very one the peasant had dappled. The bear took fright: What was making that tree shake so? He looked up and saw the gadfly sitting in the tree. So he shouted to it, "Hey, brother! Cousin! Come on down, please, or else you're going to topple this tree."

The gadfly obeyed and flew down. The bear looked at it and asked, "Who pounded that straw into your ass?"

And the gadfly looked at the bear and asked, "And you, brother, who's mutilated you? Look, in some places you've got some fur and in others you can see the bones!"

"Well, brother gadfly, it was that peasant who worked me over."

"Well, brother bear, my straw came from the same peasant."

They looked and saw a fox hopping by on three legs. "Who broke your leg?" asked the bear.

"Oh, cousin! I couldn't see very well myself. It looked like some peasant or other; he was chasing after me with a chunk of wood."

"Brothers, let's all three go after that peasant!" So the three of them got ready and set off for the field where the peasant was gathering in the sheaves. They started creeping up on him; the peasant caught sight of them, took fright, and didn't know what to do.

And so this peasant didn't know what to do. And then he thought of grabbing his wife in an embrace, and he knocked her down onto the ground. She shouted, and the peasant said, "Quiet!" and that was that. He pulled off her pinafore and shirt and raised her legs up as high as possible. The bear saw that the man was hurting some woman, and he said, "No, fox, you and gadfly do as you please, but no way am I going up to that peasant!"

"Why?"

"Because, just look, see how he's treating that person!"

The fox looked and looked: "You're absolutely right. In fact he is breaking someone's leg."

And the gadfly stared and stared and said, "That's not right; he's shoving a straw up somebody's ass."

Everyone, you see, understands his own misfortune his own way. But the gadfly figured it out best of all. The bear and the fox headed for the woods, and the peasant stayed on, in one piece and unharmed.

A–T 152

80. The Bear and the Woman

A peasant woman was plowing in a field. A bear saw her and thought to himself, "Why, I've never ever fought with a woman! Is she stronger than a peasant, or not? I've beaten up on enough peasants, but I've just never happened to have a fight with a woman." He went up to the woman and said, "Let's fight!"

"Well, Mikhail Ivanovich, what if you tear something off me?"

"If I rip you up, then I'll bring you a hive of honey."

"Let's fight." The bear grabbed the woman in his paws and threw her to the ground. She stuck her legs straight up in the air, grabbed at her crotch, and said to him, "Now look what you've done! How can I show myself at home, what will I say to my husband?" The bear looked, and there was this really great hole that he'd ripped! He didn't know what to do. Suddenly out of nowhere a hare came running by.

"Wait a minute, cross-eyes!" the bear shouted at him, "Come here!" The hare came running up. The bear grabbed the woman by the netherlips, pressed them together, and ordered cross-eyes to hold them with his paws. And he ran off into the forest and stripped a whole pile of bast— he could hardly carry it! He wanted to sew the woman up. He brought the bast strips and threw them on the ground. The woman got frightened so much that she farted, and this made the hare jump straight up in the air a yard or two. "Well, Mikhailo Ivanovich! Now you've burst the whole thing!"

"Probably she's going to blow up completely," said the bear, and he rushed off as fast as he could, and so he went away.

A–T 152C

81. About an Old Man, a Wolf, and a Fox

There lived an old man and an old woman. Once the old man set off to plow a field. He started plowing, and a wolf came out of the wood. "Plow," he said, "plow more quickly, old man! Then I shall eat you and your little mare up."

But there was a hunting party in that wood. A fox ran out of the wood and said that hunters were galloping that way. The wolf took fright and said to the old man, "Hide me, old man, from the hunters."

The old man covered him up, and the fox asked, "Why did you do that?"

The old man said, "That's my log."

And the fox asked, "But why isn't your log lying in the cart?"

And the wolf said to the old man, "Old man, put me in the cart." So the old man put the wolf in the cart.

Again the fox came flying up, "God help you, old man. Why is that log lying in the cart untied?" And the fox ran off a little way.

The wolf thought it was the hunters, and he quietly asked the old man, "Tie me to the cart, old man." So the old man took a rope and tied the wolf to the cart.

Again the fox came whirling around and around and ran up to say, "God help you, old man! Why isn't your axe sticking out of that log?"

And the wolf went on, "Stick the axe in, hide me, only don't stick it in me, stick it in my paw."

So the old man stuck it in and chopped the wolf to death. He skinned him and then took the skin and sold it. There's an end to this tale, and I am a fine lad.

A–T 154

82. The Peasant, the Bear, and the Fox

A peasant was plowing a field, and a bear came to him and said, "Peasant, I'm going to break you in two!"

"No, don't touch me: I'm sowing turnips, and I'll take just the roots and leave you the tops."

"Alright," said the bear, "but if you deceive me, don't you ever come back to these woods for wood again." When he had finished saying this, he headed back into the woods. Time passed, and the peasant was digging the turnips when the bear came out of the woods. "Well, peasant, let's share the crop!"

"Fine, little bear. Let me bring you the tops," and he took him a cartload of turnip greens.

The bear was very satisfied with this honest sharing. And then the peasant loaded his turnips into the cart and set off for the town to sell them. Along the way he met the bear. "Peasant, where are you going?"

"Well, little bear, I'm going to town to sell the roots."

"Let me try one, to see what a root tastes like." The peasant gave him a turnip. The bear ate it. "Oh, oh," he howled, "you've deceived me, peasant. Those roots of yours are sweet. Henceforth don't you ever come into my woods after wood or I'll tear you to bits."

The peasant returned to town but was afraid to go into the forest for firewood. He therefore burned up his shelves and his benches and his casks, and finally there was nothing else to burn: he had to go into the woods.

He entered ever so quietly. Suddenly out of nowhere a fox came running. "Why are you being so quiet, peasant?" she asked.

"I'm afraid of the bear; he's angry with me and has promised to rip me to bits."

"Oh, ignore the bear and cut your wood, and I'll be a game beater. If the bear asks, 'What's that shouting?' you say that someone is hunting wolves and bears."

So the peasant started chopping wood. He looked, and there was the bear running up to him, and he shouted at the peasant, "Hey, old man, what is that shouting?"

The peasant said, "Someone's hunting wolves and bears."

"Oh, peasant, put me in your sleigh, throw some wood on me, and tie me with a rope. Then they'll think it's just a log you've got here."

So the peasant put him in his sleigh, tied him with a rope, and then hit him on the head with the butt of his axe until the bear was dead.

The fox came running up and said, "Where's the bear?"

"There he is; I killed him!"

"Well now, peasant, you need to reward me."

"Be so kind, mistress foxy, come along to my house, and I'll reward you."

So the peasant rode along, and the fox ran along in front. The peasant approached the house, and he whistled for his dogs, who pursued the fox. The fox headed for the forest and nipped into a burrow. She hid in the burrow and asked, "Oh you, my dear little eyes, what did you look at while I was running?"

"Oh, foxy, we watched to make sure you didn't stumble."

"And you, little ears, what did you do?"

"We kept listening to see how far away the dogs were."

"And you, tail, what were you doing?"

"I kept on getting under foot so that you would get into a muddle and stumble and fall into the clutches of the dogs."

"Aha! You rascal! Let the dogs eat you!"

And she stuck her tail out of the burrow and shouted, "Go ahead, dogs, and eat the fox's tail." The dogs pulled on the tail and soon throttled the fox. That often happens: on account of the tail, the head perishes.

A–T 1030 + 154

83. The Case of the Beekeeper and the Bear

There was once this case in Smolensk District of a grandfather bee-keeper and a bear. This bear had the habit of going to the beekeeper's apiary and smashing up the beehives. The grandfather pondered what to do with this heathen. Every night the bear would break up one or two hives. The old man took it into his head to get the bear to drink himself to death on wine. So the grandfather took a quarter of a barrel of wine and dragged that wine into his apiary. He poured the wine into a trough and sweetened it with so much honey that the bear would drink the wine with gusto. And then the old man went home, as if to say, "Just let that bear come; he'll get drunk on the wine, and then, when he's dead to the world, I'll get him." That's what grandpa reckoned!

But the bear had another way of reckoning. He went to the apiary, scented that the old man had been there not long before, whistled through his nostrils, smacked his lips, and then set out to drink up the wine. The bear drank his fill of the wine and started considering things to himself: "Oh, what an old man! He's even started treating me to a little wine." But the bear wasn't content to leave things as they were, he wasn't. He took two casks from the apiary, dragged them out and broke them up, and then went away to his bear's lair.

The next morning the old man came after the fact, as it were. He had thought that the bear would be dead drunk. The old man looked in the trough—there was no wine and no bear, and two casks of honey were smashed to boot. So then the old man said that he was "a heathen, and he doesn't drink the way we do; he drank it all, but it didn't finish him off." The old man pondered to himself, "Well now, this next night I'll supply you with half a barrel. You're lying if you say you'll drink that down!" And that's how he reasoned to himself. So then the old grandpa got everything ready for the next night, just as he had the first time, only he added the extra quarter of a barrel of wine. And again the old man left the apiary and went home.

Well, that bear just had to come once more to grandpa's apiary. The bear looked again in the trough—there was more wine supplied than before and sweetened just as much with the honey. The bear thought to himself, "Oh, what a virtuous old man is my grandpa. Today he's given me even more wine."

So the bear drank up every bit of that wine. But that about finished him off. He had just left the apiary when he crashed to the ground with his paws sticking straight up. In the morning the old man came to have a look: the bear was lying there with his paws straight up. "Aha," the old man said with great joy. "You've given in, you heathen. Your paws are already swollen, so you've died." Then the old man ran off home happily to announce to his sons, "Well, my sons, hitch up the horse, fast, the bear has gotten drunk on the wine; he's lying there with swollen paws." The sons hitched the horse to a cart, and they set off to load up the bear. They loaded him onto the cart and tied him down in three places with a rope and carted him home. They put the cart next to the threshing floor gates and discussed among themselves what they should do with him: "There's no time to skin him now; we'll skin him toward evening. Now we've got to go cut the buckwheat." (It was, you know, already the month of September there.)

The old man went with the women to shock the buckwheat. But the bear hadn't really pegged out; he was just in a deep sleep from the booze, and he woke up. He looked here and there to see where he was and saw that he had been brought to the house and tied down. Whatever he did, struggling on the cart, he was tied securely and tightly. Somehow he got his front paws free (he was face down in the cart), and he moved the cart away from its front wheels so that they remained in place, and with the back wheels he set off through the hemp beds in the general direction of the forest! Then that bear went off with the cart and with the back wheels, laying down a road through the hemp with the cart, and that bear disappeared with the cart near the forest.

The old man came back with the women from the field and saw that there was no bear anywhere and no cart anywhere, just the front wheels remained. So the old man figured that somebody had unhitched the front wheels and taken the bear and the cart off somewhere. But then he got to reckoning: Why would they leave the front wheels? "Perhaps I'd better have a good look, see how the track lies." The old man looked. A road led through his hemp; the hemp was torn up. The old man walked along the track until he had passed through all the hemp. But there was no bear, no bear at all. So the old man began mumbling something to himself. "Oh, the very devil! I didn't kill him with drink; I just put him to sleep. He was probably just putting it on so that I wouldn't notice the heathen's breathing! Well, I'll carry on and follow the track."

So grandpa followed the track right up to the forest, and he went through a bit of the forest and then suddenly saw the bear, tangled up in the trees with the cart. The old man started shouting and howling at the bear. And people came running from all around, and from the steppe, and from their various jobs, all in response to his shouting. And they reported it to the old man's sons. The sons came running, and the whole bunch of them killed that bear. Then the old man said, "I thank you for killing this heathen of mine. He has recently drunk three-quarters of a barrel of wine and smashed nine hives of bees, but it's all right now because we've killed him." And then they all said to the old man, "If that bear drank up three-quarters of a barrel, then you can put out a barrel for us; we left our jobs and came running."

"Well, I won't argue with you; I'll put out a barrel for you, too. Here, help me load him up and cart him home, and then we'll have a memorial service for him." So the old man arranged it all, and they brought him home, and he put out the barrel, and the peasants drank it up, and for a whole month they talked about the story of what happened to the old man and the bear. And that's an end to this little tale.

A–T 154**

84. An Old Kindness Is Soon Forgotten

An old man was walking through a little wood carrying a sack. In the woods he met some hunters who were chasing after a wolf. The old man continued on. He met the wolf. "Hide me," said the wolf, "or else the hunters will catch me."

"Well then, climb into the sack!" answered the old man.

The wolf had only just managed to climb into the sack when the hunters were upon them. "You haven't seen a wolf hereabouts, have you, old man?" the hunters asked.

"No, I haven't seen any," the old man answered.

And so the wolf escaped that fate—death. He climbed out of the sack and said to the little peasant, "I'm hungry; I'm going to eat you. You know the saying, 'An old kindness is soon forgotten,' don't you?"

"I don't agree with that saying," said the peasant. And they agreed to summon a court and ask people's opinions.

So they walked and walked along, and they met a horse. The horse was thin; it chewed dry grass. They told the horse about their dispute, and it answered, "Well, that's right; when I was young, they fed me with hay, but now they've driven me out, and I live on whatever comes my way. Yes, an old kindness is soon forgotten."

They continued on. They saw a dog, lying there, just dying. They told him their dispute, and the dog said, "Yes, an old kindness is soon forgotten. When I was young, I was needed. But when I went blind, I was no longer needed."

They continued on and met a fox. The peasant's hair stood on end, because if the fox spoke against him, then there'd be no escaping death. They told her everything. But the fox was sly; she winked at the peasant and said, "I don't believe the wolf was in the sack. Climb in and show me." The wolf climbed in, and the fox winked at the peasant: "Tie it and then with your flail. . ."

The old man tied up the wolf and said, "An old kindness is soon forgotten!" and he hit the fox on the head. And he made out well in this deal: he took two skins.

A–T 155

85. The Russian Bear and the Polar Bear

Now once the Russian bear was walking along the seashore. Suddenly a polar bear crawled out of the water. The Russian bear has black fur, but the polar bear is white. The polar bear is stronger than the Russian bear. He spoke: "Wait for me, I'll just shake myself off!" The Russian bear stopped. The other shook himself off and came up to the Russian bear. "Well," he said, "let's go!"

The polar bear said to him, "Now we'll walk along the shore. We'll not fear anybody; no one will harm us."

And the other said, "No, they will harm us."

"Who can harm us?"

"The Russian man will harm us."

"The Russian man?!" he exclaimed.

"He's the only one we need to fear."

"Show him to me."

"Well, you just come along with me, and I'll show you the sort of man we have to fear."

The Russian bear led the polar bear into the forest. They were walking through the forest, and the polar bear said, "Well, show me this man we ought to fear!"

The Russian bear said, "Wait and I'll show you."

The Russian bear knew the way through the forest, but the polar bear didn't know anything. The polar bear said, "Are you going to show me now, or not?"

"Soon," the other said.

They came out onto the postal road, and he said to the polar bear, "Now we ought to hide ourselves so that people won't see us, and then that man will come whom we ought to fear."

They hid themselves and sat there. Suddenly along came a beggar with his sack. The polar bear asked, "That's obviously the man."

But the Russian bear answered, "That was once a man, but now there's no need to fear him; he'd sooner fear us."

Again they sat. Suddenly along ran a schoolboy with his satchel. He asked, "Is that the man we're supposed to fear?"

The Russian bear answered, "Yes, in about ten years, then we'll fear him."

"Why is it then that you won't show me a Russian man?"

"Just wait a bit, the man will come whom we're supposed to fear."

Then suddenly a hunter appeared, leading two dogs. The Russian bear said, "There goes the man. Be afraid of that one."

"So, you'd say that you have to be afraid of that one?" the polar bear asked.

And the other said, "Go test that man."

The polar bear went and stood in the road. But the hunter had never seen a polar bear before. He stopped and thought, "What sort of wonder is this? I was walking along, my gun loaded for birds. I've no bullet, else I'd let him have it!"

The polar bear stood up on two legs and came up closer to him, then he gathered up some spittle and spat it at the hunter. And the hunter thought, "Only bears do that! Can this be a bear?"

His dogs were straining at the leash, but he wouldn't let them off. Then he thought, "Well, let's try to scare you with this bird shot."

He took his double-barreled shotgun and let him have it right in the mouth. And both shots landed in his mouth; the bear rocked back and forth and then ran from that peasant. He came running up and said, "You spoke the truth when you said we should be afraid of that peasant. No matter how much I spat, that peasant just stood there. Then he spat back at me, and there was even some smoke, and I was shaken."

The peasant went on his way, and they went their own way. And since then the polar bear has believed that there's no one stronger than a peasant.

A–T 157

86. The Sleigh

Once this old woman was walking along alone, and she found a bast shoe with a lining, and then she stopped in a hut to spend the night. She put the bast shoe in the henhouse. So far, so good. In the morning she got up and said, "Well, hosts, give me my hen."

"What hen? You had a bast shoe!"

"No, I had a hen, and if you won't give it to me, I'll go to the boyars' court, and I'll sue you forever."

So they handed over a hen. And she went farther on her way. She walked and walked, and toward night she invited herself into a hut. But she put her hen in with the geese. She spent the night, and in the morning she said, "Give me my goose."

"What goose? Why, you had a hen!"

"If you won't hand it over, I'll go to the courts; I'll go to the boyars."

Well, they took fright and gave her the goose. So she continued on with that goose. She walked and walked, and toward night she came to a hut. She sat down on a bench but put her goose in with the sheep. She spent the night, and then in the morning she said, "Give me my sheep."

"What sheep is that? Why, you had a goose."

"If you won't hand it over peacefully, then I'll go to the courts; I'll go to the boyars; I'll sue you forever."

Well, they gave her the sheep. (Oh, how crafty was that old woman!) So another night she came to a hut and put her sheep in with the bullocks. She spent the night, then took a bullock, but her hosts said, "What is this, woman, are you in your right mind? You had a sheep." But she said, "If you won't give it to me peacefully, I'll take you to court."

So they gave her the bullock. Well, then the old woman went down the road, down the path. She hitched her bullock to a sleigh and sang:

An old woman went walking, she found a bast boot,
For the boot she took a hen,
For the hen a goose,
For the goose a sheep,
For the sheep a bullock,
Giddap, giddap, my bullock,
With your twitching tail!

She rode and rode, and then she met a hare: "Let me ride in the back, good woman!"

"Get in!"

She rode and rode, and then she met a wolf: "Let me sit in the middle, good woman!"

"Get in!" So she rode and rode, and she sang:

Giddap, giddap, my bullock,
I twitch the bullock on the feet,
And the bullock goes down the road.

Then they met a bear. "Let me ride on the front axle, good woman."
"Get in!"

So the bear got in, but the sleigh tongue broke. "Hare, you go into that thicket and bring a tongue."

So the hare went into the thicket and brought back an aspen twig. "Oh, you fool! You go into the thicket, fox, and bring back a tongue." So the fox went into the thicket and brought back an alder twig.

"Oh, you fool! You go into the thicket, wolf, and bring back a tongue." So the wolf went into the thicket and dragged back an old birch.

"Oh, you fool! You go into the thicket, bear, and bring back a tongue." So the bear went into the thicket and dragged back an enormous fir.

So the old woman went into the thicket herself. And the bear devoured the bullock and stuffed its hide with moss. And then all the animals ran away. The old woman came back, sat down in the sleigh, and shouted, "Giddap, giddap, little bullock!"

She whipped her bullock, and down he fell. And that was that!

A–T 158

87. The Pitch-Sided Bullock

There lived this old man with his old woman, and they had a single granddaughter—Alionushka. Everyone in the village had livestock. Some had cows, some had calves, some had sheep, but they had none at all. So once the old man said, "Woman, let's make a bullock for our Alionushka out of straw and smear one side over with pitch."

So they made the bullock from some straw, smeared one side over with pitch, and stood it up in the middle of the yard. In the morning the people all drove their livestock out, and the grandmother and Alionushka drove out their bullock, too. They drove it out into a glade, and then they went away into the forest to gather some sweet wild strawberries. The bullock stood there in the glade, and then suddenly a hare ran up and said, "What sort of marvel is this? For as many years as I've been running around this meadow, I've never seen such a marvel." He ran and ran; he became really curious: he went and touched it with a paw and got his paw stuck in the pitch.

The grandmother and her granddaughter came along and drove the bullock home, but that little hare was still hopping along on three legs. The hare started in asking, "Let me go home, too, and for that I'll fetch Alionushka some beads and ribbons." They felt sorry for the hare, so they let him go home. The hare ran off home.

On the very next day the grandmother and Alionushka once again drove out the bullock. They drove it out into the glade and then took themselves off to look for mushrooms. A fox was running in that glade; she ran and saw the bullock and immediately got interested. She ran round and round it and then just once touched it with a paw. And she got stuck, and no way could that fox get her paw out.

The grandmother and Alionushka came to drive the bullock home, and there was that fox hopping about on three legs. The fox started asking, "Let me go home, too, to my little kits, my little foxies, and in return I'll drive in your geese, your ducks, and your hens. Then you'll have eggs, and meat, and a down pillow, and a featherbed." So they let the fox go.

On the third day, they drove the pitch-sided bullock out into the field. Again they stood him up and went off to pick some flowers. They were gathering the flowers when suddenly a bear came out into the glade and caught sight of the bullock. And Mishka got curious. He walked all around, he walked around again, he went up to it from one side, and then he went up to it from the other. "What sort of marvel is this? In my whole life I've never seen such a bullock!"

"I'll test it out with a paw," he thought. So he touched it with a paw and got his paw stuck. However much Mishka struggled, no way was he able to free his paw. The grandmother and her granddaughter came back to drive the bullock home, and Mishka was hopping about there on three legs. Mishka started in asking, "Let me go to my little ones, my little cubs. In return I'll drive in all your bulls and cows in the autumn."

So they let Mishka go. After that all summer they drove the bullock out into the glade, but no one got caught again. In the autumn the people locked all the livestock up in the yard, and the grandmother and Alionushka also drove in their bullock; they also locked him up in the yard. Suddenly outside there was a noise and a shout, "Honk! Quack! Cluck! Cluck!" Alionushka looked, and there was the fox driving in the hens, ducks, and geese—the down was flying everywhere, along the whole road. She drove them up and shouted, "Alionushka, open the gates!"

Grandmother and Alionushka opened the gates and let in the hens and ducks. So fresh meat appeared at Alionushka's, and a featherbed, and a down pillow, and eggs.

In a short time or long, another shout went through the village—cows lowing and bulls bellowing. Again, the bear shouted, "Open the gates!" So they opened the gates, and Alionushka had fresh milk, and sour cream, and cream, and curds. Only the hare hadn't brought anything. "Well," they thought, "that hare has deceived us." But the hare was waiting for winter. As soon as winter had arrived, the hare came into the village for a spinning bee. The girls were singing songs as they were spinning away. And then the hare started to dance and cut every fancy figure. He danced and danced, and the girls dressed him up—some with beads, some tied on bows. The hare sat down in a corner, he sat and sat there, and then the girls sat down at their distaffs and started singing songs, and he quietly ran away. He brought Alionushka the beads and the bows. Now our Alionushka has everything. And that's the end of the tale.

A–T 159

88. The Ungrateful Rich Man

There lived and dwelt on earth a rich man by the name of Ismagil. Once he went riding over to another place, drank too much mead, and set off for home alone, without anyone accompanying him. He rode along, shaking in the saddle, just about to fall.

He rode up to the forest, pitched forward, and fell into a deep pit. Some hunters had dug it for beasts. Ismagil heard some whispering nearby. He was frightened and started shouting, not in his own voice: "Save me, help!"

A poor man was passing nearby. He heard someone calling for help. He got down from his horse and went up to the pit. The poor man cut a long bough and shouted, "Hold on." Someone was hanging onto the pole. The poor man pulled it out and looked: it was a fox. She darted away into the bushes. The poor man was about to get back on his horse and ride on when he heard from the pit: "It's me, Ismagil, help me!"

The poor man cut a thicker branch and lowered it into the pit. Someone grabbed hold of the branch. He was heavy. Somehow the poor man dragged him out. He looked: it was a bear. The poor man thought, "What amazing things! Somehow a bear and a fox fell into that pit." And again from the pit came a voice: "Help me. I'll give you whatever you want."

The poor man lowered a pole and thought to himself that perhaps he'd come to the village with gold and put on a rich wedding. He began hauling out the pole, but a serpent was wound about it. He was about to throw down the pole and run away from that place when he heard such a pitiful cry: "Pull me out; I'm the rich man Ismagil. I'll reward you." The poor man got the rich man out, but the latter didn't even look at him. He got on his horse and rode off.

The poor man came home and saw near his yard an incredible number of every sort of fowl. And nearby stood a fox, washing one of her paws. "That's for saving me." Nearby there stood a cartload of wood. That was the bear's work. On the roof sat the serpent and next to it a precious stone. The poor man looked at the precious stone; he couldn't tear himself away. The poor man was overjoyed. There was enough wood for the whole winter, he wouldn't be hungry, and now he could go to the bazaar and sell the precious stone.

As soon as the rich Ismagil caught sight of the stone, he started shaking from greed. He started shouting, "Thief! Murderer!" All the people came running. They saw that the poor man had a precious stone. They took the stone away from him and led him off to the judge himself.

"Where did you get this stone?" asked the judge.

"It was given me by the serpent I saved together with that rich man Ismagil." And the poor man told everything all in order.

At that moment in came Ismagil. He shouted, "Thief! He's lying. He didn't get me out of any pit. Where are your witnesses?" Then all the people moved swiftly to one side. They all watched as into the hall walked the bear and the fox and in crawled the serpent. They came up and asked Ismagil, "Were you with us?"

Ismagil took fright, went down on his knees, and confessed to everything. They let the poor man go and gave him back the stone, and people began to say, "Apparently, beasts have more conscience than rich folk."

A–T 160

89. The She-Bear

There lived and dwelt a boy. And he was all alone. And he set off for the field. And there was no one in the field. So then he started to play on his horn. And people popped out of everywhere and said, "Why are you playing on your horn? There's a she-bear around here, and she'll eat you!" But he said, "Oh, then I'll lead her here to you alive!"

But the people said, "What are you thinking? Why, she'll eat you."

And he said, "She won't eat me."

And he set off to find the she-bear. He walked and walked and saw a fox walking along. And he asked the fox, "Fox, you don't know where a she-bear lives, do you?"

The fox said, "Don't go to her; just now she tore up a wolf on the hill, and she'll eat you up." But he didn't listen and asked the fox to show him the way. The fox said, "Go straight, then turn to the left, and there'll be a nut tree there, and in that nut tree is her hut."

So the boy went there and saw a little bear cub running about the hut. And so the boy knocked on the window, and the bear cub asked, "Who's there?"

The boy answered, "Open up!"

The bear cub said, "Why, my mother will come, and she'll eat you up!"

But the boy said, "She won't eat me up! Just you open up!"

The bear cub opened up. Then the boy started to tell him tale after tale. The bear cub liked the boy very much. And he said, "Where shall I put you? Mama will come and eat you up. Well, climb up into the attic."

After a few minutes the she-bear came and asked, "Why ever are you so happy? Or has somebody been here?"

"No, mama," said the cub.

And the she-bear sat down to rest. And then she said, "I have to carry this jar of honey up into the attic."

But the cub said, "Let me carry it." He took the jar and climbed into the attic, and he said to the boy, "Mama has come. I'll ask her now not to eat you up."

And so he said to his mother, "Mama, and if some boy comes to visit me, would you eat him up?"

"And where would he come from, and why would he come here?"

"Well, maybe he'll just come! Give me your word of honor that you won't eat him up."

"I give you my word of honor that I won't eat him up." Then the bear cub climbed up into the loft and said to the boy, "Climb out; mama has given her word of honor that she won't touch you." The boy climbed down and went into the hut. And the bear liked the boy, too. She said, "Will you play with my bear cub?" The boy answered, "I will."

So one day passed and then another, and then the boy said, "Why do you have such a hut? How are we going to live in it?"

And the she-bear said, "But who will build a new one?"

And the boy said, "I will."

And the she-bear answered, "Well, build it."

So he went into the village. He took some nails, rope, and wheels. He knocked together a chest and put it on wheels. The she-bear and cub climbed into it, and the boy slammed shut the lid and closed them in. Then he tied a rope around it. And he brought them like that into the village. As he pulled them around, he shouted, "People, come and see the she-bear!" People jumped up, some with axes and others with shovels, some with rakes and pitchforks, and they shouted, "Kill her, kill her!"

But the boy said, "No, I won't let you kill her! She has given her word of honor that she won't eat anybody. She didn't eat me." And the she-bear had given her word of honor. And the boy took the bear cub and her back to their old place. And the people all began to work in the fields, and the boy began to guard the sheep. And people began to provide him with shoes and clothe him.

A–T 160A*

90. The Bear

There lived and dwelt an old man and an old woman, and they had no children. The old woman said to the old man, "Old man, go get some firewood." So the old man set off after the firewood, and on the way he chanced upon a bear, and the bear said to him, "Old man, let's wrestle!" So the old man went and cut off the bear's paw with his axe, and then he went home with the paw and gave it to the old woman: "Here, old woman, cook this bear paw." So the old woman set about it and tore off the hide, and as she sat on it she began to pluck the fur, and she put the paw on the stove to cook. The bear roared and roared, then fell to thinking, and made himself a limewood paw, and then he went to the old man in the village and sang:

> Squeak, paw
> Squeak, limewood!
> And the water sleeps,
> And the land it sleeps
> And they sleep throughout the hamlets,
> And throughout the villages they sleep.
> Only the woman doesn't sleep.
> She sits on my skin,
> She's spinning my fur,
> She's cooking my flesh,
> She's drying my hide.

At that the old man and old woman took fright. The old man hid in the loft beneath a trough and the old woman on the stove beneath some black clothes. The bear came into the hut. The old man wheezed beneath the trough in fear, and the old woman coughed. The bear found them and caught them and then ate them.

A–T 161A*

91. The Old Woman

An old woman felt like having some bear, so she sent her old man off. "Old man, oh, old man! Would you bring me some bear? You'd know where to get it."

"Wait a minute, old woman! There's a bear sleeping over there; I'll go and bring you a paw." So he chopped off a paw and brought it to her. She fried the paw and fur, sat and spun, ate the meat, and sat on the hide.

Now this bear hopped on his three legs and shouted:

> *In the villages they sleep,*
> *In the countryside they sleep,*
> *Only the woman doesn't sleep,*
> *The troublemaker doesn't sleep,*
> *She sits on my skin,*
> *She eats my meat.*

The bear went into the entrance hall of the old woman's hut and shouted out the same thing again:

> *In the villages they sleep . . .*

The old woman took fright and ran up into the loft. The bear came into the hut, dragged the old woman by her skirts from the rafters into the woods, and then he sat her down on a stump.

Then he went after the old man. The old woman sat on the stump and said, "Stump, stump! Grow higher! Stump, stump! Grow higher!" The stump grew big, bigger than any oak. The bear couldn't find the old man and came back to her. He looked and there she was, sitting up on the oak. He climbed up toward her. She broke off a branch and beat him on his paws—whack! whack! He fell and was impaled. Afterward she said, "Stump, stump! Grow lower! Stump, stump! Grow lower!" The stump again became small; she climbed down and is even now living.

A–T 161A*

92. Sweet and Sour Cousins

There lived and dwelt a "sour" cousin and a "sweet" cousin. The sweet cousin began to look around the sour one's head. The sour cousin said, "I will soon die, and when I die, don't take my ring off my hand."

"Very well," she said, "I won't remove it." It was a gold ring that the sour cousin had on her hand.

So the sour cousin died. The other washed her, dressed her, and laid her out on the bench. And she thought in her mind, "And what if that ring were removed? She's dead, she won't hear." So she tried removing the ring. She tried and tried, but no way could she get it off. So she cut off the finger. Then she buried the sour cousin and put the finger on to boil. She sat there, spinning.

And that sour cousin came out of the grave and walked along singing:

> *All the people in town are sleeping,*
> *All the people in the village are sleeping,*
> *Only my cousin isn't sleeping,*
> *She sits on the stove,*
> *She's spinning with the spindle,*
> *She's cooking my hand,*
> *She removed the golden ring.*

She walked along the street and went into her cousin's entrance hall, and she sang:

> *All the people in the town are sleeping,*
> *All the people in the village are sleeping,*
> *Only my cousin isn't sleeping,*
> *She sits on the stove,*
> *She's spinning with the spindle,*
> *She's cooking my hand,*
> *She removed the golden ring.*

She went into the hut, and she kept on singing the same thing:

> *All the people in the town are sleeping,*
> *All the people in the village are sleeping,*
> *Only my cousin isn't sleeping,*

She sits on the stove,
She's spinning with the spindle,
She's cooking my hand,
She removed the golden ring.

She went up to the oven, up to the stove, and sang the same thing:

All the people in the town are sleeping,
All the people in the village are sleeping,
Only my cousin isn't sleeping,
She sits on the stove,
She's spinning with the spindle,
She's cooking my hand,
She removed the golden ring.

At this the sweet cousin became really frightened; she trembled all over. Suddenly the sour cousin went up to the sweet cousin and said, "Aren't you asleep, cousin?"

"I can't sleep."

"Are you sitting on the stove?"

"That's where I'm sitting."

"Are you spinning the spindle?"

"I'm spinning."

"Are you cooking my hand?"

"I'm cooking it."

" Are you taking off my golden ring?"

"I'm taking it off."

"You lout!" And she ate up her sweet cousin.

A–T 161A*

93. Mumblejumble

There lived an old woman, and she loved to walk in the forest. Once she went to gather berries. She walked along, gathering berries. She bent over, and suddenly something began creeping between her legs. She stamped her foot, thinking it was a gnat, but it was a bear! "Woman!" he said, "I'm going to eat you up!"

"No, don't eat me, and I'll give you a dingaling." So the bear ran off and laughed, "Ho, ho, ho, the woman will give me a dingaling. Ho, ho, ho, the woman will give me a dingaling. Ho, ho, ho, the woman will give me a dingaling."

On the second day the woman again went into the forest to gather berries. She walked along, gathering berries. She bent over, and suddenly between her legs something started creeping. She stamped her foot and thought it was a gnat, but it was the bear. "Woman," he said, "I'm going to eat you up."

"Don't," she said, "I'll give you a warmitup." Again the bear ran off and laughed, "Ho, ho, ho! The woman will give me a warmitup. Ho, ho, ho! The woman will give me a warmitup. Ho, ho, ho! The woman will give me a warmitup."

On the third day she again went into the forest for berries. She bent over, and suddenly something started creeping between her legs. She thought it was a gnat, but it was the bear. "Woman, I'm going to eat you up!"

"No, don't eat me, and I'll give you a neverever." Again the bear ran off and laughed, "Ho, ho, ho! The woman will give me a neverever. Ho, ho, ho! The woman will give me a neverever. Ho, ho, ho! The woman will give me a neverever."

Well, the old woman didn't dare go into the forest to gather berries anymore. She sat at home. The bear saw that the woman wasn't going walking, so he went to her house. He shouted out beneath her window, "Woman, I've come for the dingaling! Woman, I've come for the dingaling! Woman, I've come for the dingaling."

And the woman answered, "The woman doesn't go to the forest and doesn't gather berries any more, and all the woman's gates are firmly locked."

"That's unfortunate. The woman, certainly, has deceived me," said the bear, and he went away.

On the second day he came again. "Woman, I've come for the warmitup. Woman, I've come for the warmitup. Woman, I've come for the warmitup."

And the woman again answered, "The woman doesn't go to the forest and doesn't gather berries, and the woman's gates are firmly locked."

"That's unfortunate! The woman, certainly, has deceived me," said the bear.

The bear went away. On the third day he came again: "Woman, I've come for the neverever. Woman, I've come for the neverever. Woman, I've come for the neverever."

And the woman answered, "The woman doesn't go to the forest and doesn't gather berries, and the woman's gates are firmly locked."

"That's unfortunate. The woman, certainly, has deceived me," said the bear.

On the fourth day he went straight to the woman's house to break down the doors. "If you won't give me something, I'll eat you right now!" He broke down the doors to the entrance hall. The woman didn't know what to do, where to hide herself. She managed to duck into the barn beneath a trough. The bear broke through the doors into the entrance hall, opened the doors into the hut, walked around looking, but nowhere was the old woman to be found. Wasn't she perhaps beneath the trough? He went up to the trough and started opening it. The woman let out an enormous fart. She farted and the trough splintered apart; the bear started running, shitting here and there through the entrance hall, through the hut, he shat over everything. And he never came back to the woman again.

A–T 161A**

94. How the Old Woman Rescued the Old Man

There lived and dwelt an old man and his woman. They lived on the very edge of the village. They had five sheep. Once, toward evening, the woman brewed some beer and treated the old man.

The old man started playing around; he lit a rush light and began to boast: "Even though I'm poor, I'm kind. I'd give away the last thing that I have. That's the sort I am!" Just then a wolf ran up to the window and started listening. "Well, old woman," said the old man, "just ask, what do you need? A warm shawl, I'll buy it. I will not even refuse a wolf; I'd give him my last sheep! That's the sort I am."

Just then the wolf went tap, tap, tap at the window. "Who's there?" asked the old man.

"The wolf."

The old woman sat right down on the floor, she was so afraid. Bravely the old man went up to the window and shouted, "What do you need?"

"A sheep, grandpa," said the wolf.

"Go into the shed and take it, but just one!" The wolf took the sheep and ran off into the forest.

The woman began to curse the old man: "You old fool, why did you give away that sheep? Oh, a fine rich man you have turned out to be! Now you won't be able to show yourself to people, they'll laugh."

"Alright, old woman, we'll live, we'll even prosper! We'd better save the rest. Tomorrow he'll come again." The old man prepared a pitchfork for himself and an axe for the woman. "If he comes tomorrow, we'll give him such a sheep that he'll forget even the smell of sheep."

In the evening the wolf came once more to the window: tap, tap, tap! "Grandfather and grandmother! Give me a sheep!"

The old man and the old woman ran out onto the road. The wolf saw the pitchfork and the axe in their hands; he ran behind the barn and hid. The old man threatened him with the pitchfork and shouted, "Look, wolf, you had better watch out. If I catch you, I'll kill you!"

They shouted, did the old man and the old woman; they shouted and then went back into the hut. The wolf crept into the shed, took a sheep, and was gone.

In the morning the old man and the old woman noticed that one sheep was gone. "Well, old man," said the woman, "think about how to save the sheep. You knew how to teach the wolf to come; now teach him how not to come. Or else he'll ruin us."

The old man thought and thought until he dozed off. "I've thought of it, old lady, I've thought of it," he shouted. "Here's what we'll do: I'll dress one sheep in a housecoat, put some bast shoes on her feet, put a hat on her head, and tie on a club with a sash. Just as if I were guarding the sheep! The wolf will come and ask for a sheep, and then you'll say, 'Go into the yard and ask my old man for a sheep; he's out there.' The wolf will see the sheep in the housecoat and with the club and think that it's me; he'll be frightened and run away. That's what I've thought up, old lady!"

"Oh, you are so clever and sly!" the woman praised the old man.

In the evening they dressed the sheep as they had discussed and tied it to the entrance of the shed. Then, quite pleased with themselves, they lay down to sleep. They hadn't managed to fall asleep yet when the wolf went: tap, tap, tap! "Grandfather and grandmother, give me a sheep!"

"Go into the shed, wolf, that's where grandfather is; go and ask him," answered the woman.

The wolf went to the yard. The sheep was frightened of the wolf and climbed up on the picket fence; she climbed until she came to the end of the rope. Then the wolf stood up on his hind legs and with his front legs leaned against the fence. It appeared to the wolf that the old man was standing next to the fence with a club!

"Grandfather, give me a sheep," asked the wolf. Grandfather stood, silently. "Grandfather, have you gone deaf? Give me a sheep." Grandfather was silent. The wolf sat down and started thinking. Why doesn't grandfather want to talk to me?

The sheep got tired of standing on her hind legs and jumped down to the ground, somehow knocking the club against the fence. It seemed to the wolf that grandfather was creeping up on him with his club. The wolf leaped up and hopped across the fence. From there he took a look: What will grandfather do? But the sheep was frightened by the wolf; she jerked and tore loose her tether. She lurched into a slit in the fence and got stuck: she couldn't pull the club through. The wolf guessed it was a sheep and started laughing: "Wait a minute, grandfather, don't torture yourself! I'll help you crawl through that slit," and he jumped into the yard. The sheep struggled, crawled out of her clothes, and began whirling around in the yard. The wolf grabbed her and was gone.

In the morning the old man and the old woman found the housecoat, the sash, and the club, but the sheep had disappeared along with the bast shoes. "What are we to do, old lady?" asked the old man. "The wolf has dragged off our guardian sheep. You never know, he might drag us off. Couldn't you think up something good?"

The woman started thinking. "Here's what, old man, take the two sheep and put them in the cellar and close the door. We'll hide ourselves in the hut. The wolf will come and knock, but we won't answer him. He'll think: the old man and the old woman have gone away. And he'll go away."

That's what they did: they put the sheep in the cellar; then they waited for the wolf. The wolf knocked: tap, tap, tap! "Grandfather and grandmother, give me a sheep!" There was silence in the hut. He knocked again. Again silence. "Well, I'll just go have a look at the sheep," thought the wolf, and he set off for the shed. The shed was closed; there were no sheep there. "You don't suppose the old man and the old woman have gone away somewhere?" stammered the wolf. "I'll have to have a look in the hut."

He knocked at the door. The old man had crawled onto the rafters; he lay down with his face to the ceiling and was quiet. The old woman had crawled into the stove, where they were drying some tobacco. The door was latched, and she lay down on the tobacco. The wolf came in and began looking around. Then he roared, "Where have you hidden?"

The old man thought, "The wolf has probably found my old lady." He wanted to take a look to see what the wolf would do with the old lady. Very quietly he began to turn over. But the boards were sort of rotten, and they cracked and broke into pieces. The old man fell onto the wolf, the wolf jumped up to the stove. The woman heard the noise and turned around. Tobacco dust got in her nose, and did the old lady sneeze! The hinge flew off the stove door and struck the wolf in the head. Thud! The wolf thought he was dying and rushed to the door, but he hit his head against the door frame with a huge bang and killed himself.

For a long time they lay there, the old man on the floor, the woman in the stove. They listened intently—all was quiet. They got up. Cautiously they poked the wolf. He was dead. "So, bandit, you finally got what was coming to you!" The old man and the old woman rejoiced.

They took the skin off the wolf and sold it. With the money they got, they bought three lambs and a dog. Since then they have been living and prospering and raising lambs. If the old man ever feels like boasting, he first looks out the window and goes into the yard. Then, if there's nobody there, he starts talking. Cautious, that's what the old man's become.

A–T 162A*

95. About an Old Man and a Gray Wolf

An old man lived with his old woman right next to the forest. They had two children, a boy and a girl. In their household there were also five sheep, one colt, a calf, and a bullock.

A hungry gray wolf found out about this, learned of it, and he began pestering the old man, asking him for something to eat. Once the wolf came in the evening, and he started singing under the old man's window:

There dwelt a dweller—his palace in a grove.
He had five ewes,
The sixth was a colt,
The seventh a calf,
The eighth a bullock,
A boy and a girl, the old man and old woman.

"Old man, old man, give me a sheep, or else I'll eat up your old woman." The old man was afraid that the wolf would eat up the old woman, so he gave him a ewe. The wolf ate up the ewe and once more came to the old man and sang:

There dwelt a dweller—his palace in a grove.
He had five ewes,
The sixth was a colt,
The seventh a calf,
The eighth a bullock,
A boy and a girl, the old man and old woman.

"Old man, old man, give me a sheep, or else I'll eat up the old woman." So the old man gave the wolf a second sheep. Then the wolf came for the third, the fourth, and the fifth sheep. The old man calmed down because the wolf wouldn't come any more for anything since he had given him five sheep.

A little time passed, and the wolf got hungry. Again the old man heard the wolf singing beneath his window:

There dwelt a dweller—his palace in a grove.
He had five ewes,
The sixth was a colt,
The seventh a calf,
The eighth a bullock,
A boy and a girl, the old man and old woman.

"Old man, old man, give me the colt, or else I'll eat up the old woman." So the old man gave him the colt and thought that the wolf wouldn't come any more. The wolf ate up the colt and again came to the old man, and under his window he sang:

There dwelt a dweller—his palace in a grove.
He had five ewes,
The sixth was a colt,
The seventh a calf,
The eighth a bullock,
A boy and a girl, the old man and old woman.

"Old man, old man, give me the calf, or else I'll eat up the old woman."
The old man felt pity for the old woman, so he gave his calf to the wolf.
The old man carried on with his life and thought that now, for sure, the
wolf wouldn't come any more. But three days passed, and the wolf was
once again at the old man's house beneath the window, and he sang the
same song:

There dwelt a dweller—his palace in a grove.
He had five ewes,
The sixth was a colt,
The seventh a calf,
The eighth a bullock,
A boy and a girl, the old man and old woman.

"Old man, old man, give me the bullock, or else I'll eat up the old
woman." The old man was more frightened than before and gave his
bullock to the wolf, but then he calmed down because the wolf would
come no more: he had given him everything.

A little time passed, and the old man heard the wolf's song beneath
his window:

There dwelt a dweller—his palace in a grove.
He had five ewes,
The sixth was a colt,
The seventh a calf,
The eighth a bullock,
A boy and a girl, the old man and old woman.

"Old man, old man, give me your boy, or else I'll eat up the old
woman." The old man loved the old woman very much, and he had to
give the boy to the wolf. The wolf took the boy and set off for the forest.

A day or two passed, then the wolf got hungry and again came to the old man to ask for the girl.

> *There dwelt a dweller—his palace in a grove.*
> *He had five ewes,*
> *The sixth was a colt,*
> *The seventh a calf,*
> *The eighth a bullock,*
> *A boy and a girl, the old man and old woman.*

"Old man, old man, give me the girl, or else I'll eat up the old woman." The old man grabbed hold of the old woman; he wouldn't give her to the gray wolf, so he gave up the girl. The wolf was not satisfied; hunger fiercer than before seized him, and he came to the old man for the old woman. Once again just beneath grandfather's window he heard the evil wolf's song:

> *There dwelt a dweller—his palace in a grove.*
> *He had five ewes,*
> *The sixth was a colt,*
> *The seventh a calf,*
> *The eighth a bullock,*
> *A boy and a girl, the old man and old woman.*

"Old man, old man, give me your old woman, or I'll eat you up!" The old man gave the old woman to the wolf, and then he cried for a long time. He obviously wouldn't have long to wait before the greedy wolf came for him. The old man didn't have to wait long before he once again heard the song:

> *There dwelt a dweller—his palace in a grove.*
> *He had five ewes,*
> *The sixth was a colt,*
> *The seventh a calf,*
> *The eighth a bullock,*
> *A boy and a girl, the old man and old woman.*

"Old man, old man, I've come to eat you up!" But out of fear the old man climbed into a basket that was hanging in the corridor beneath the ceiling, and he shook so that he couldn't utter a word.

The wolf waited, but no one came out to him, and he decided to take a look to see whether the old man was at home. He came into the corridor and stood there just beneath the basket in which the old man was sitting. The old man decided that the wolf knew where he had hidden, and he started climbing out of the basket. Suddenly the basket came loose, and with the old man still in it fell down right on the wolf. The wolf tore out of there as fast as he could run and kept on running until he had forgotten where the old man's hut even was.

A–T 163

96. The Wolf

There was this peasant, and he had a sow, and she delivered twelve piglets. He locked them in a shed, and that shed was woven out of brush. Then on the next day the peasant went to look at the piglets. He counted them: one was missing. On the third day again one more was missing. Who was stealing the piglets? So the peasant went to spend the night in the shed. He sat down and waited to see what would happen. A wolf ran out of the wood and straight up to the shed, turned its ass to the door, crammed it in, and stuck its tail through the gap, and then began to feel about the shed with its tail.

The piglets heard the rustling and went from the sow to the door to sniff around the tail. Then the wolf pulled out his tail, turned around, stuck in his muzzle, grabbed a piglet, and took off for the wood. The peasant waited for the next evening, went again into the shed, and sat down right next to the door. It got dark, and the wolf came running. He had just stuck in his tail and begun to feel around from side to side with it when the peasant grabbed the wolf's tail with both hands, braced his legs against the door, and shouted at the top of his lungs, "Ho! Ho! Ho!"

The wolf pulled and pulled and shat and strained so much that his tail pulled off. He ran off, blood dripping. He ran about twenty paces, fell, and expired. The peasant removed his skin and sold it in the market.

A–T 166A*

97. For a Bast Boot a Hen, for a Hen a Goose

There lived and dwelt a widow, but she set off, she went away. She walked and walked and found a bast boot. She came to spend the night and asked, "Let me spend the night! Where can I put my boot?"

"Put it under the bench."

"No, you see, my boot doesn't live beneath a bench but with the chickens."

In the morning she got up: "Where's my cock?"

"What do you mean, you old fool of a woman? You said you had a bast boot."

"No, I had a cock. If you don't give it back, I'll go to the *voevoda** and sue you." Well, they handed it over and off she went.

She walked and walked, and evening came. Again, she went looking for lodging: "Let me in to spend the night."

"Well, spend the night, you're not carrying a bedroll with you, so spend the night."

"Let my chicken spend the night! Where should I put my cock?"

"Put it in with the hens."

"No, my cock lives with the geese."

"Well, put it with the geese."

In the morning she again got up and came outside: "Where's my goose?"

"What do you mean, you old fool of a woman! You had a cock!"

"No, I had a goose; give me my goose, or else I'll go to the voevoda and sue you."

"Oh, be off with you! The forest spirit take you! If you say goose, then goose it is."

So she took a goose and set off, she walked on. So she walked all day until evening, and again she came to an inn. "Let me in to spend the night."

"It's alright to spend the night; you're not carrying a bedroll with you."

"Where should I put my goose?"

"With the geese."

"No, my goose lives with rams."

"Then put it with the rams."

So she put it with the rams. Then she slept through the night and was again going to set off in the morning. "Where's my ram?"

---

*Voevoda: a military governor.

"What do you mean, you old fool of a woman? Why, you had a goose!"

"No, I had a ram. Hand it over! If you don't hand it over, I'll go to the voevoda and sue you."

"Oh, get out of here! The forest spirit take you! The devil take you, be gone!"

So she took a ram and set off. Again she walked on, now with the ram. Evening came, and she needed to spend the night somewhere. She came to an inn. "Let me in to spend the night."

"Well, spend the night, you're carrying no bedroll with you."

"Where should I put my ram?"

"Put it with the rams."

"No, my ram lives with bullocks."

"Well, then, put it with the bullocks."

Well, in the morning she got up and asked for a bullock. "Where's my bullock?"

"What do you mean, old woman? What you had was a ram."

"No, I had a bullock; give me back my bullock."

"Oh, get away from here! The forest spirit take you! What else can we do?" She took a bullock and set off.

Then she found a whole harness for the bullock, a collar, a shaft-bow, a bridle, and everything, and even a little wooden sledge, and she rode off, and she started to sing: "A woman rode through the hills, through the hills in all directions. Let the bullock snort! My little steppe cossack!"

A hare came by. "Let me ride on the runners." So the hare sat down, and they rode off, and the woman began to sing: "A woman was walking along, and that woman found a bast boot. A cock for a boot, for the cock a goose, for the goose a ram, for the ram a bullock, a steppe cossack!"

A fox came along. "Let me ride, if only just there on the runners!"

"Get on, you limp devil!" So he sat down, and off they rode. And she started singing: "A woman was walking along, and the woman found a bast boot. A cock for a boot, for the cock a goose, for the goose a ram, for the ram a bullock, then a steppe cossack, and for the steppe cossack a tail-sporter!

There came a wolf. "Let me get in there somewhere!"

"Well, get in, you limp devil!" And so off they rode.

A bear came. "Let me in there somewhere!"

"Oh, sit down, clay feet." And on they rode. They rode and rode, and then the strap snapped on the sledge, the tongue bar turned back and around, and it broke. "Get down, hare, and go cut another tongue."

Well, the hare got down and went and cut another limb for the sledge tongue, but that was no use. So the old woman said, "Oh, you limp devil! What kind of tongue is that you've brought? Go, fox, you get one."

So the fox went off, but again he brought the wrong thing—it was too thin. "Wolf, now you go and bring one."

So the wolf went and brought back a branch—too thick, it wouldn't do. "Bear, you go."

Well, the bear went and brought a thick one, really thick, torn out by its roots. "That won't do—it's too thick, it's a whole tree torn up by its roots! The devil take the lot of you. Wait here, I'll go myself!" And off she went herself.

She came back, but meanwhile they had driven off the bullock. She rushed about here and there! And so where did they go? Well, they (the bear, the wolf, the fox, and the hare) went and ate the bullock and stretched out his skin on stakes. She just started weeping.

A–T 170 + 158

98. Snow Maiden and the Fox

There once lived an old man with an old woman, and they had a granddaughter, Snow Maiden. Her friends got together to go into the woods for berries, and they came to invite her to go along. For a long time the old folks would not agree, but after many requests they let Snow Maiden go, but they told her not to lag behind her friends. Walking through the forest and gathering berries, tree after tree, bush after bush, Snow Maiden lagged behind her friends. They called and called her, but Snow Maiden did not hear. It was already dark when her friends came home. Snow Maiden, seeing that she remained alone, climbed up a tree and began to weep bitterly, singing: "Oh, oh, Snow Maiden, Oh, oh, little dove, grandfather and grandmother had a granddaughter, Snow Maiden. Her friends lured her into the woods, and then they abandoned her."

A bear came and asked, "What are you weeping about, Snow Maiden?"

"Oh, father bear, why should I not weep? I am my grandfather and grandmother's only granddaughter, Snow Maiden. My girlfriends lured me into the woods, and then they abandoned me."

"Come down, I'll carry you out!"

"No, I am afraid you'll eat me up!" The bear left her. Again she began to weep, singing in her sweet little way: "Oh, oh, Snow Maiden, oh, oh, little dove!"

A wolf came by and asked, "What are you weeping about, Snow Maiden?" And she answered him the same as the bear. "Come down, I'll carry you out!"

"No, I'm afraid you'll eat me up!" The wolf went away, but Snow Maiden again began her lament: "Oh, oh, Snow Maiden! Oh, oh, little dove!"

A fox came by and asked, "Why are you crying, Snow Maiden?"

"Why should I not weep, fox? The girls lured me into the woods, and then they abandoned me."

"Come down, I'll carry you out."

Snow Maiden came down, climbed onto the fox's back, and the fox rushed off with her. She ran to the house and with her tail began to knock at the gate. "Who's there?"

The fox answered that she had brought the old man and old woman their granddaughter, Snow Maiden.

"Oh, you dear little so and so, you unbaptized heathen! Come into our hut! Where should we seat you, and with what should we greet you?" They brought some milk, eggs, and curd and began to do honor to the fox for her service. But the fox asked that as a reward they give her a hen and let her go back into the fields. The old folks said goodbye to the fox, and put a hen in one sack and a dog in another. They carried them behind her to the appointed place. They let out the hen; as soon as the fox had pounced on it, they let out the dog. Seeing the dog, the fox flew off for the woods, and so she got away!

A–T 171

99. Happy

Happy lived and Happy dwelt, all the while wandering everywhere from village to village. If ever anything turned out to be missing, everyone said about Happy that he was always asleep—and knew nothing of it. He would take his fiddle and set off along the highway and byway.

Once he chanced to encounter a wolf: "Where are you going, brother Happy?"

"Well, I'm going along the highway and byway."

"Take me along, brother, for company! Whenever there's a ewe missing, or if anyone steals anything, everyone says that the wolf did it, and it's as if I'm asleep and in fact know nothing of the matter!"

So they set off on their journey along the highway, along the byway, and they played on the fiddle. They chanced to meet up with a bear. So the bear said, "Where are you off to, brothers?"

"Well, you see, whenever anything turns out to be missing, they always say that it was us."

The bear said, "It's the same for me. If any beast turns up missing, they all say that the bear killed it, but it's as if I'm asleep and don't know anything."

So off they went along the highway and the byway, and they played the fiddle. They came to a pond. And the Viatka* men were waiting there with their carts. They were traveling with their oat flour. A storm and wind came up and threw everything from the carts into the pond.

So Happy and his friends sent the bear to drag some hops over to this pond and brew some beer. He dragged over the hops, and they made the beer. They set up a little hut with windows facing the pond for a view. They measured out the beer so that they would know if any went missing.

Now Baba Yaga took to drinking this beer (she would come visiting them). And they started coming up short of beer as they looked at the measure. Little beer remained; a lot was getting away into the pond.

The first night they sent the wolf to stand guard over the beer. The wolf set off and took up his position. Baba Yaga came up with her buckets on her yoke. "Where are you going?"

"For beer. It's none of your business." She threw the buckets off that yoke and did she let the wolf have it with that yoke! Somehow the wolf crawled off back to the hut.

Baba Yaga drank her fill of the beer, put a spell on the buckets, and set off with the beer. In the morning the companions said of the wolf, "Oh, what a pig he was with the beer! He's lying there drunk!"

"Go ahead, go and find out what happened to the beer."

The next night it was the bear's turn to guard the beer. The time came, and the bear set off. He took up his place. Along came Baba Yaga. "What

---

*Viatka: a small town and district northeast of Moscow.

do you want?" She shook, threw off the buckets, took the yoke, and began to beat the bear with her yoke. The bear somehow crawled back into the hut. Baba Yaga drank her fill, filled her buckets, and set off with the beer.

In the morning the companions all arose and said, "Oh, what a pig that bear was with the beer! He's lying there drunk!"

"Go ahead, you go find out what's happening to the beer!"

The third night it was Happy's turn to stand guard. Happy set off with his fiddle and came up to a spruce. Baba Yaga came to Happy. "Well, Happy, what are you doing?"

"I'm playing my fiddle." Baba Yaga threw down her buckets, then her yoke, and let herself go—she was dancing!

"Well, Happy, how about teaching me to play that fiddle?"

"Your fingers are too fat, Baba Yaga."

"What do I have to do, how can I make them a bit thinner?"

"There's a stump standing over there, and there's a wedge in the stump. Pull out the wedge and poke your fingers in the hole. That will make them a bit thinner, and then you'll be able to play with them."

So they pulled out the wedge and poked her fingers in. It trapped her hand, and then he finished her off. And the friends began to drink the beer themselves. And so that was how they found out what had been going on with their business!

A–T 176**

100. The Hound and the Grass Snake

A certain tsar by the name of Pirras had an only baby son whom they had named Izbavel [Saved]. Pirras loved him very much and assigned three nannies to him: the first was to feed him at her breast, the second was to bathe him, and the third was to look after him. Pirras also had a falcon and a hound of which he was very fond, and he loved them immensely.

Once Pirras happened to be absent from the court together with his spouse, who was called Aradiia. At his departure he had entrusted Izbavel to the aforementioned three nannies, whom he asked to keep careful watch over him. The falcon and the hound were also in the same room as Tsarevich Izbavel. When the tsarevich had gone to sleep in his cradle, the nannies went into another room so they would not disturb him with their conversation. At that same time, when no one was left in the room, an enormous grass snake, which no one had previously noted there, crawled out of a corner, approached the cradle, and desired to devour the infant boy. The falcon, catching sight of the serpent, became agitated and then poked the hound with its beak to let him know so that he might defend the tsarevich, who was lying in the cradle. The hound, when he saw the serpent, rushed at it immediately, and they began biting each other. The serpent bit the hound in many places, but finally the hound overcame it and ate the serpent up and it died. At the same time that the hound and the serpent were biting each other, they knocked the little tsarevich out of his cradle, and he was covered up by that cradle, and the whole room was bespattered by the blood of the serpent and hound. The hound, having killed the serpent, lay down in the tsarevich's cradle.

Soon after, the nannies came into the room, and, seeing the blood and the hound lying there in the cradle, they imagined that the hound had eaten the little tsarevich. They took fright in a most extraordinary manner and wept with bitter tears. One of the three nannies ran to the Tsaritsa Aradiia and told her that the hound had eaten up her beloved son, whose blood had been spilled all over the room. The tsaritsa, hearing this sad news, shouted out at the top of her lungs, "Oh!" Pirras, when he heard this and consequently saw his spouse in a faint, tried in every possible way to be of aid. And when she regained consciousness, he asked the cause of all this. When Pirras was informed about everything, he immediately returned to his house, where the tsaritsa begged him to kill his favorite hound. Pirras then went into the room in which the little tsarevich was located, and the hound, seeing him, went up to him and crawled at his feet and showed his joy with his tail. The tsaritsa said to the tsar, "Kill that cursed hound, for he is the cause of our misfortune." Pirras, grabbing his sword, cut the hound in two, and then they began to notice where the blood was coming from. Finally they saw the serpent, which was lying on the floor near the cradle. The tsar examined it very carefully and saw the many wounds on it and then he noted several others on the hound where he had been bitten. Then Pirras discovered that he had killed his favorite hound without reason, for when they lifted up the cradle, they found the little tsarevich beneath it, alive.

A–T 178A

101. Masha and the Bear

Well, there lived and dwelt an old man and an old woman, and they had this granddaughter. The granddaughter set off into the woods with her friends for some berries. Well, they all went their separate ways in the forest, and then the friends decided to leave, so they called and they called but the girl strayed farther and farther. The girl's friends went home without her. She walked and walked and went into a dwelling. She saw that nothing was tidied up there, so she cleaned it up, all of it.

Then a bear came: "Who has tidied up my house?"

And she said, "I have."

"Well, now," he said, "I'll bring a hammock, and you will rock me."

So he brought a hammock and lay down, and she rocked him and sang softly, and he closed one eye, but with the other he looked at her. Then afterward she said, "Let me go outside and play tag."

"Go ahead, go ahead, go play, but don't go far away."

So, off she ran outside. Some sheep ran up to her: "Get on, miss. Mashenka, get on, we'll take you to your grandmother and grandfather."

Mashenka got up onto the very largest sheep, and the sheep set off carrying her. But the bear heard this, came running up, grabbed Mashenka, and carried her back. And once more he made Mashenka rock him. So Mashenka again rocked him and sang softly. Well, she rocked him, and she rocked him, and he was falling asleep, so that meant that she could ask him, "Can I go outside and play tag?"

"Go ahead, but don't be gone for long."

Well, off she went. Some cows came running up. And a cow said, "Get on me, Mashenka, and I'll take you to your grandmother."

She got on, grabbed hold by the horns, and the cow ran off, and then, you see, that bear heard it and grabbed her, just so. Again he dragged Mashenka home, made her rock him, and she, the poor thing, again rocked him and sat, her head hanging down, and he dozed and dreamt. But then she spoke: "Let me go outside and run around, to play tag."

"Oh, go ahead, but don't be gone for long, and don't go away again, you hear?"

"No, today I won't go away."

So she just went outside, and some horses came running up, including one really swift one. He said, "Get on, Masha, the bear won't catch me."

Masha got on, and did she grab hold of that mane! The bear jumped out, but there was nothing there. He couldn't catch Mashenka, and Mashenka was off home.

Her grandfather and grandmother were overjoyed: "Oh, our little doll! How we cried and grieved for you; glory be unto you, oh Lord, that she has appeared. Never will we ever let you go into the woods again." And so it was.

A–T 179A*

102. The Beasts at the Trough

There was once a poor peasant and a rich one. And so the poor old man made a beautiful trough. The rich one saw the trough at the poor one's house and asked him to make another, similar one for him. The other went into the forest to make the trough for the landowning peasant. He grew tired and took a rest. He went and turned the trough upside down and crawled under it.

A hare ran by, sat down at the table. "Oh," he said, "What a fine little table you have, but there's nothing on the table!" The hare sat a while, then ran off. And he carried back a head of cabbage from the forest and put it there on the trough.

Then he saw a fox run up. "What a good table! But there's nothing on the table." And so the fox brought a duck.

And then they all noticed a wolf running up. He ran to the trough and said, "Oh, what a fine table, but there's nothing on the table!" And so he brought a whole ram.

They saw that a bear was approaching them, and he said, "Oh, what a good table, but there's nothing on the table." He went and brought some honey.

They had just sat down at the table when the peasant woke up and heard them making noise on the trough. He began to stand up, and the beasts all took fright and ran away and abandoned everything, leaving it all to the old man. He carried the trough off to the landowning peasant and received some money; then the peasant became rich.

A–T 179B*

103. How the Wolf, the Dog, the Cat, and the Mouse Became Enemies

The wolf, the dog, and the cat were like true brothers. The wolf was the senior, the dog was more junior, and the cat was more junior still.

And the wolf said to God, "Oh Lord, why was I born such an unfortunate one? In the forest what I can get I eat; if I can't get anything, then I sit hungry; but the dog lives with the master in warmth, in comfort; they feed him and give him water, and he sleeps under a roof. And that's how the cat lives with the master; but here I am, always beneath the open heavens, even in frost, even in the rains there's no place to hide. Everybody shouts at me; whoever shoots, shoots at me; they terrify me. Well, sometimes I do them damage because I want to live. And that seems to be how I have to exist!"

And then God said to him, "You can go live in the village for about three years. Here's a pass for you. When the three years are up, then come back to me with this pass; then you can live in the village like the dog and the cat."

The wolf took the pass. He went around with that pass for a year. The second year he brought it to his junior brother and said to him, "Brother, you live beneath a roof, so here, take this pass and guard it." The dog took the pass, and the wolf went off. But then the master called the dog, and the dog said, "I'll give this pass to the most junior brother; he'll just be sleeping on the stove anyway, so he can guard the pass better." So the cat took it and tucked the pass into a crevice.

And then when the three years had passed, the wolf came to the dog: "Please, brother, give me the pass."

The dog said, "I gave it to our brother, the cat."

So they went to the cat. "Cat, give us the pass immediately."

The cat climbed up for the pass, but some mice had eaten it up so that it was impossible to read it. And the dog told the wolf, "A mouse ate your pass."

The wolf was furious and rushed at the dog, the dog at the cat, and the cat at the mouse. And since then they have all been each other's enemies. The wolf doesn't like dogs, the dog doesn't like cats, and the cat doesn't like the mouse.

A–T 200

104. Verlioka

There lived and dwelt this old man and old woman, and they had two granddaughters who were orphans. They were so cute and so happy that the grandfather and grandmother just couldn't enjoy them enough! Then once the grandfather got it into his head to sow some peas. He sowed them, and they grew and flowered. The grandfather looked at them and thought, "Now I will be able to eat pea pie all winter long."

Just to spite the old man, some sparrows attacked the peas. The old man saw that things were going badly, so he sent the younger granddaughter to chase away the sparrows. The granddaughter sat down alongside the peas and waved a little switch, all the while saying, "Shoo, shoo, sparrows! Don't you eat my grandpa's peas."

But then she heard a cracking noise in the forest: Verlioka was coming. He was really tall, with but one eye, and his nose was like a hook, and his beard a tuft. His moustache was a half-yard long. On his head was a brush and on one foot a wooden boot. He was propped up on a crutch, and he smirked hideously. There was this strange feature of Verlioka's nature: if he ever caught sight of a person, and especially a peaceful one, he just had to start up a friendship and pound him on the back. And he gave no quarter to the old or the small, nor to the quiet or the brave.

Now Verlioka caught sight of grandfather's granddaughter, and she was so cute, well, how could he not just touch her a bit! But she, apparently, didn't like his antics—maybe she cursed him, I don't know. But anyway, Verlioka immediately killed her with his crutch.

The grandfather waited and waited, but there was no granddaughter. He sent the older one after her. Verlioka also took that one. Grandfather waited and waited, but that one was gone, too! And so he said to his wife, "Why are they so late? They've probably gotten waylaid by some boys, chattering away while the sparrows are shelling the peas. You go, old woman, and drag them back here by the ear!" The old woman climbed down off the stove, took the stick that was in the corner, crossed over the threshold, and never came back. It seems she saw the granddaughters, and then she saw Verlioka and guessed that it was his work: in a rage she grabbed him by the hair. But for our troublemaker it was but one more event.

The grandfather was waiting for the granddaughters and for the old woman. He waited and waited, but there was no sign of them. So the grandfather said to himself, "Some crafty devil . . . Probably some dark-eyed youth has been eyeing my wife. It is well said: 'There's little good to come from one's own rib! And a woman's still just a woman, even if she's old!' "* And after thinking thus wisely on the matter, he got up from the table, put on his heavy coat, lit his pipe, prayed to God, and wove off down the road. He came to the pea patch and looked. There were his beloved granddaughters lying there, just as if they were asleep, except that on one of them blood like a crimson ribbon stripe was visible on her forehead, and on one white cheek of the other five blue fingers had left their mark. But the old woman was so disfigured that you couldn't recognize her at all. The grandfather broke down in tears, kissed them, caressed them, and tearfully spoke to himself.

He would probably have cried for a long time, but he heard something. In the forest there was a crackling noise as Verlioka approached. He was really tall, with but one eye, and his nose was like a hook, and his beard a tuft. His moustache was a half-yard long. On his head was a brush and on one foot a wooden boot. He was propped up on a crutch, and he smirked hideously. He grabbed the grandfather and started beating him. The poor old man struggled free with all his might and ran off home. He ran in and sat down on the bench, rested, and said, "Aha, so he'd do such nasty deeds to us! Just you wait, brother, we've got hands ... Even if you go on arguing with your tongue, don't give free rein to your hands. We ourselves have moustaches, we're adults. Lay a hand on us and pay with your head. It is clear that you, Verlioka, weren't taught from childhood the proverb 'Do good and you won't have to repent; do ill and you'll pay dearly.' 'You've taken the bast, now give back the bag.' "** The old man talked it over with himself for a long time, but finally, having talked himself up for it, he took an iron crutch and set off to fight Verlioka.

He walked and walked, and he saw a pond, and on that pond there sat a drake with a docked tail. The drake saw the old man and shouted, "Quack, quack, quack! I guess I expected you to come here. Good health, old man, for a hundred years!"

"Good health, drake! And why have you been expecting me?"

"Oh, I knew that you'd go out to take revenge on Verlioka for your granddaughters and the old woman."

"And who told you that?"

---

*A well-known Russian saying.
**Another Russian proverb.

"My cousin told me."

"And how does your cousin know?"

"My cousin knows everything that takes place on earth, and if sometimes something hasn't turned out right, then one cousin will whisper it to another cousin in the ear, and when two cousins have done whispering, the whole world will know."*

"Look at that, what an extraordinary thing!" said the old man.

"It's not extraordinary, it's the truth! And it's such a truth that it's so not just with you and me but it's the case even with the elders."

"So that's it," the old man spoke, and his mouth gaped open. But then, collecting himself, he took off his cap, bowed to the drake with the docked tail, and said, "You, my good sir, do you know Verlioka?"

"Quack, quack, quack! How could I not? I know him, the crooked . . ."

The drake turned his head to the side (they see better from the side); he screwed up his eyes, looked at the grandfather, and said, "Oho! And who never has misfortune? 'Live your whole life, learn your whole life, but you'll still die a fool.'* Quack, quack, quack!" He straightened his wings, turned his rear around, and began instructing grandfather. "Listen, old man, learn how to live on earth! Once somehow over there on that bank Verlioka started beating up on some poor unfortunate. And at that time I had a good saying for every occasion. Oh, oh, oh. Verlioka was amusing himself, and I was sitting on the water, shouting to myself: ah, ah, ah! So then when he had finished dealing with the unfortunate one in his own way, he ran up to me, and, without saying a nasty word, he grabbed me by the tail. But it wasn't as if he'd attacked just anybody. . . . Anyway, just my tail remained in his hands. And even though that tail wasn't so very large, still I was sorry to part with it. Who doesn't like his own things best? As they say 'a bird's own tail is closest to his body!'* Verlioka went off home and said along the way, 'Just you wait, I'll teach you to stand up for others.' So I took that to heart, and since then, no matter who's done what, I've shouted out "ah, ah, ah!" and then "quack, quack, quack!" So what's the difference? Life has gotten better, and there's a little more respect from people. They all say, 'That drake, even if he is dock-tailed, he's really clever.'"

"But then couldn't you, my good philanthropist, show me where that Verlioka lives?"

---

*Yet another proverb.

"Quack, quack, quack!" The drake climbed out of the water and, shifting from side to side just like a merchant's wife, he set off along the bank with the old man after him.

They walked and they walked, and on the road there lay a rope, and it said, "Greetings, grandfather, clever old man!"

"Greetings, rope."

"How are things? Where are you going?"

"I'm alive and so forth. I am going to Verlioka to take revenge. Just think. He strangled my old wife, and he killed my two granddaughters, and those granddaughters were really prizes!"

"I knew your granddaughters, and I respected your wife; take me along to help you!"

The old man thought, "Perhaps it would help to tie up Verlioka." So he answered, "Crawl along if you know the way." So the rope started crawling along after them, just like a snake.

They went on and on, and there in the road lay a maul, which said, "Greetings, grandfather, clever old man!"

"Greetings, maul!"

"How are things? Where are you going?"

"I'm alive and so forth. I'm going to Verlioka to take revenge. Just think. He strangled my old wife, and he killed my two granddaughters, and those granddaughters were really prizes!"

"Take me along to help."

"Come along if you know the way." And he thought to himself, "A maul might just come in handy." So the maul got up, leaned with its handle on the earth, and hopped along.

Off they went again. They walked and they walked, and there on the road lay an acorn, and it squeaked, "Greetings, oh long-legged grandfather!"

"Greetings, oaken acorn!"

"Where are you off to?"

"I'm going to fight Verlioka, if you know him."

"How could I not know him? It's time for him to get his due. Take me along to help you."

"And what might you do to help?"

"Don't spit in the well, old man, you might have to drink of the water! The finch is not a very big bird, but nonetheless it burned up a whole field. And besides, as they say, 'A gold sovereign may be small, but it's valuable, while a penny is larger but useless.' "†

---

†More proverbs.

The old man thought about it. "Oh, let him come! The more, the merrier." And he said, "Fall in behind." Regardless, the acorn hopped along in front of everyone.

So finally they came to a deep, drowsy forest, and in that forest there stood this little hut. They looked, and in that hut there wasn't a soul. The fire had long since gone out. On a peg hung some wheat porridge. The acorn was no fool. It hopped right into the porridge, the rope stretched out on the threshold, and the grandfather put the maul up on a shelf, while the drake settled down on the stove, and the old man stood behind the door. Verlioka came and threw some wood down on the ground and began stirring up the cinders in the stove. The acorn hiding in the porridge started humming a song: "Pee, pee, pee . . . We've come to fight Verlioka!"

"Shut up, porridge. I'll pour you out into a bucket," shouted Verlioka. But the acorn paid no attention to him and just kept on squeaking. Verlioka got mad and grabbed the pot and dumped the porridge into a bucket. But the acorn jumped out of the bucket, flew right into Verlioka's eye, and knocked it out. Verlioka was about to run away, but there was no way he could. The rope caught him, and Verlioka fell. The maul came down from the shelf, and the old man came out from behind the door, and did they give him what for! And from behind the stove the drake sat and went "quack, quack, quack!" His strength was of no use to Verlioka, nor was his courage. Now there's a tale for you, but as for me, I'll take biscuits—quite a few!

A–T 210*

105. The Goat Tarata

A priest lived and dwelt, and he had many goats and kept a worker. Spring came, and the priest said, "Worker! Drive the goats out to pasture and feed them well!"

So the worker drove them out. All day he herded them among the hills and dales and through the dark woods. The time came to drive them home. The goats came up to the gates, and the priest came out onto the porch and asked:

> *Oh, you little goats, my little nannies,*
> *Are you sated, have you drunk your fill?*
> *Have you walked over all the hills,*
> *Nibbled on the feathergrass?*
> *Have you lain beneath the birches?*

The goats answered the priest:

> *We are sated, we've drunk our fill;*
> *We have walked over all the hills,*
> *Nibbled on the feathergrass,*
> *We ate of the aspens*
> *And have lain beneath the birches.*

But one goat said:

> *I'm not sated, I've not drunk enough.*
> *I haven't walked over all the hills,*
> *I haven't nibbled the feathergrass,*
> *Nor did I eat any aspen,*
> *Nor have I lain beneath the birch.*

The priest aimed his gun, and, bang, he killed the worker.

Now the priest had one son. In the morning he sent out the son. The son drove the goats all day; he herded them among the hills and dales and through the dark forests. The time came to drive them home.

The goats came up to the gates, and the priest asked:

> *Oh, you little goats, my little nannies,*
> *Are you sated, have you drunk your fill?*
> *Have you walked over all the hills,*
> *Nibbled on the feathergrass?*
> *Have you lain beneath the birches?*

And the goats answered:

We are sated, we've drunk our fill;
We have walked over all the hills,
Nibbled on the feathergrass,
We ate of the aspens
And have lain beneath the birches.

But one goat said:

I am not sated, I've not drunk enough.
I haven't walked over all the hills,
I haven't nibbled the feathergrass,
Nor did I eat any aspen,
Nor have I lain beneath the birch.

And the priest killed his son.

Now he had one daughter. On the third day he sent her to herd the goats. So she drove them out and herded them all day among the hills and dales and through the dark forests. The time came to drive them home. The goats came up to the gates, and the priest asked:

Oh, you little goats, my little nannies,
Are you sated, have you drunk your fill?
Have you walked over all the hills,
Nibbled on the feathergrass?
Have you lain beneath the birches?

And the goats answered:

We are sated, we've drunk our fill;
We have walked over all the hills,
Nibbled on the feathergrass,
We ate of the aspens
And have lain beneath the birches.

But one goat said:

I'm not sated, I've not drunk enough.
I haven't walked over all the hills,

I haven't nibbled the feathergrass,
Nor did I eat any aspen,
Nor have I lain beneath the birch.

So the priest killed his daughter.

On the fourth day he sent his wife. She herded the goats all day among the hills and among the dales and through the dark forests. The time came to drive them home. The goats came up to the gates, and the priest asked:

Oh, you little goats, my little nannies,
Are you sated, have you drunk your fill?
Have you walked over all the hills,
Nibbled on the feathergrass?
Have you lain beneath the birches?

And the goats answered:

We are sated, we've drunk our fill;
We have walked over all the hills,
Nibbled on the feathergrass,
We ate of the aspens
And have lain beneath the birches.

But one goat said:

I'm not sated, I've not drunk enough.
I haven't walked over all the hills,
I haven't nibbled the feathergrass,
Nor did I eat any aspen,
Nor have I lain beneath the birch.

So the priest's wife met the same end.

On the fifth day the priest himself drove them. He herded them all day through hills and through dales and through the dark forests. He came in first and asked:

Oh, you little goats, my little nannies,
Are you sated, have you drunk your fill?

Have you walked over all the hills,
Nibbled on the feathergrass?
Have you lain beneath the birches?

And the goats answered:

We are sated, we've drunk our fill;
We have walked over all the hills,
Nibbled on the feathergrass,
We ate of the aspens
And have lain beneath the birches.

But the one goat repeated the same as before:

I'm not sated, I've not drunk enough.
I haven't walked over all the hills,
I haven't nibbled the feathergrass,
Nor did I eat any aspen,
Nor have I lain beneath the birch.

The priest caught the goat and ripped off half a side. She tore herself away and ran into a field into a marmot's burrow. The marmot was startled and ran away from the burrow. It spent the night lying outside. It sat and wept. Along came a cross-eyed hare. "Why are you weeping, marmot?"

"Someone's in my burrow."

The hare went up to the burrow. "Who's in the marmot's burrow?"

"I am, the goat Tarata, with half a side ripped off; I'll jump out, you cross-eyed hare, and tear out your other eye."

And with that the hare fled straightaway into the forest.

Then came a wolf. "Why are you weeping, marmot?"

"Someone's in my burrow."

The wolf went up to the burrow. "Who's in the marmot's burrow?"

"I am, the goat Tarata, with half a side ripped off; I'll jump out and tear out your eyes."

The wolf took to the woods, frightened.

A bear came by. "Why are you weeping, marmot?"

"Someone's in my burrow."

The bear went up to the burrow and asked, "Who's there?"

"I am, the goat Tarata. Half my side is torn away. I'll jump out now and tear out your eyes."

The bear was frightened and ran away into the woods.

A hedgehog crawled up. "Why are you weeping, marmot?"

"Well, someone's in my burrow."

The hedgehog crawled up to the burrow and asked, "Who's there?"

"I am, the goat Tarata, half a side torn away. I'll jump out and tear out your eyes!"

The hedgehog curled up like a stone and tucked himself in. And he just hit the goat with all his prickles right in the bare side! The goat crawled out of the burrow and ran away into the woods.

A–T 212

106. About a Goat

There lived an old man and an old woman. The old man and old woman had a son and a daughter. The old man and the old woman died. They left behind only a glass full of peas. [The children] sat on the trunk eating the peas, and they dropped a pea into the cellar. It sprouted and came up there and started to grow. It grew and grew; it grew up to the trunk. They broke up the trunk, and it grew up to the ceiling. They broke open the ceiling, and it grew up to the roof.

After some time the sister and brother wanted to eat, but they had nothing to eat. The sister climbed up the vine. She climbed and climbed and caught sight of a hut that turned about on cock's legs. She said, "Hut, little hut! With your rear to the woods and your front to me!" The hut turned with its rear to the wood and its front to her. She went into the hut.

A billy goat was living there. The goat lay on the sleeping benches, its feet on the rafters, its teeth on a peg, its eyes fixed straight ahead, its beard on the icon shelf. And in one corner of his room stood the millstones.

She went up to the millstones, farted, then turned them, and out came a pancake and a biscuit, a piece of gingerbread, and, yes, a little tart. The goat saw her and began to bawl: "Feet, come to me! Hands, come to me! Head, come to me! Eyes, come to me! Beard, come to me!" Meanwhile, she ran away.

After a little while they wanted to eat again. The sister said, "Brother, you sit here a while, and I'll climb up there and bring you something again." So the sister climbed up the vine, but her brother was stealing along behind her. When they had climbed up to the hut, the sister glanced around and saw her brother. "What are you doing, brother? Go back!"

But her brother said, "No, I won't. I won't be left behind." (He wasn't terribly clever and really resembled a fool.)

"Now look here, brother, when you go into the hut, don't laugh."

They had just stepped into the hut when the brother saw the goat and started laughing: "Ha, ha, ha! Look at that, sister! What ever is it?"

The goat woke up and began calling out: "Feet, come to me! Hands, come to me! Head, come to me! Eyes, come to me! Beard, come to me!" They all came to him, and he jumped up and said, "Hut, little hut! Make yourself into three corners." It did so, and he began chasing the brother and sister. When he had caught them, he put them in his cellar and began feeding them.

About two days passed, and then he gave them a knife and said, "Cut one finger from each of your hands—I'll taste you!" They found a lime sapling and cut off one joint each from it and gave them to the goat. The goat threw them onto the stove but the lime sapling didn't sizzle. The goat thought, "No, they're still not fat. It's not time to roast them."

About two days later he again gave them the knife. "Cut off one toe from each foot." They found a braided strip of birch bark, cut through it, and gave it to the goat. The goat threw it into the stove. The birch bark smoked, and the goat thought, "Now there's a lot of fat; it's time to roast!" He heated up the oven and led the sister and brother out of the cellar, brought a bread paddle, and said: "Sit on the paddle. I'll set you in the oven and roast you." The sister sat on the paddle, put one foot on the floor, the other on the stoking hole, her arms on the oven sides. The goat shoved, shoved her toward the oven, but couldn't shove her in.

Then he said, "You're not sitting right!"

"Then how? I don't know how!"

"Wait! I'll teach you!" He himself sat down on the paddle, tucked his feet in, tucked in his arms, tucked in his beard. But the sister was not timid; she popped him into the oven! She closed the latch and locked it. Then she went outside, but she instructed her brother, "When the goat is roasted, and the juice is running out of the oven, don't lick it or else you'll be made into a kid-goat!" (He still wasn't very big.)

"Very well, sister, very well."

When the sister had gone away, the goat began to sizzle and the juices ran. The brother wet his finger and licked it. When his sister returned to the hut, her brother ran to meet her and said, "Baa, little sister! Baa, baa, my dear!" He was already a little goat!

After some time the sister grew up and became very beautiful. Passing through the village there (it turned out that there was a village there) was one Ivan Torgovoi [Ivan the Trader], and he took note of her. She was very pleasing to him, and he began to court her. She agreed to marry him, and she took her little brother along with her.

Now not far away from there lived Baba Yaga. And she had three daughters. Once Ivanushko set off to do some trading and lost a mitten. Baba Yaga was walking along, and she found it. She came to Ivan the Trader's house and said, "Maria Ivanovna (this was his wife), let me in!"

"No, I won't let you in."

"But Ivanushko has sent his mitten and commanded that you let me in!" She looked and recognized her husband's mitten. She took it and let Baba Yaga in.

Baba Yaga removed Maria Ivanovna's dress and put it on her daughter, then she carried Maria away to the river, tied her to a gray rock, a burning stone, and threw her under a bridge. And she put two serpents to her breasts to suck her.

When Ivanushko returned home, Baba Yaga's daughter leaped out to meet him: one leg was of shit, the other of dirt. Now his own wife had one silver leg, and the other was gold (maybe slippers?). Ivanushko guessed right then what had happened, but there was nothing to be done. Still he ceased going trading.

After a few days the Yaga's daughter, Egibisna, said, "Ivan the Trader, Ivan the Trader, slaughter the goat: I'm feeling like some fresh goat meat!"

Ivan the Trader said to her, "What are you going on about, fool? That goat is some sort of human!"

But Egibisna kept on at him (she was Baba Yaga's daughter). Ivan the Trader couldn't stand torture. He whetted his knife and went to the shed (since Egibisna had locked the goat up in the shed). When Ivanushko got to the shed, the kid-goat said, "Ivan the Trader, Ivan the Trader, let me out to the stream to wash and whiten myself so that it won't be dismal for you to eat me." Ivanushko let him out.

The little goat ran to the stream. "Baa, little sister! Baa, my dear! They're sharpening their knives; they want to slaughter me! Shouldn't it make me ill? Shouldn't I be bitter?" And he flung himself in the sand and wept.

But his sister answered him, "Oh, little brother! Oh, my dear! The gray stone is drawing me to the bottom, the burning stone is drawing me upward, and two serpents are sucking my breasts. Shouldn't it make me ill; should I not be bitter?" The kid-goat wept and ran away home. There was no time left to butcher, it was already late.

The next day Egibisna again pestered Ivanushko, "Ivan the Trader, Ivan the Trader! Slaughter the goat! I have a taste for fresh goat meat."

Ivan couldn't stand to be tormented, and again he went to butcher the goat. But the little goat said, "Ivan the Trader, let me go to the stream to wash and whiten myself so that it won't be sad for you to eat me."

Ivanushko let him go and thought to himself, "What is this? Where does that goat go? His sister went off somewhere. . . ." Then the little goat ran off and Ivanushko ran after him.

He came to the stream and saw his wife, thrown beneath the bridge. He took an iron hook, pulled her out, untied whatever was around her, brought her a dress. She dressed and washed, and they went home. When the Yaga's daughter saw her, she said to Ivanushko, "Why did you bring that bitch, that scab, back here?" Ivanushko became angry at Egibisna, put her on the gates, and shot her.

Where her head fell, a tussock grew out; where her arms fell, a rake grew out;, where her legs fell, there grew walking sticks; and where her topknot fell, there grew an impenetrable swamp and in the midst of the swamp a river.

A–T 218B*

107. How the Cock Took Away the Tsar's Money

There lived an old man, and he had no old woman. He lived, and every day he went fishing. His fate was bound up in the sea: if he caught a fish, he was satisfied; if he didn't catch one, he'd go to bed hungry. This old man had nothing but a cock. Now next door there lived a lonely grandmother. And she had a hen. So once the old man came to her: "Neighbor, give me just one egg!"

"Take one, old man, my hen has laid enough." So she gave him an egg. The old man went home, cooked it, and ate it.

The next day the old man had no catch, and he went back to the grandmother. "Neighbor, give me an egg!" The grandmother gave him an egg. He went home, cooked it, and ate it.

On the third day he again caught nothing in the sea. So he came to the grandmother and asked her, "Neighbor, rescue me! Give me an egg!"

"Oh, old man! You keep on asking because you catch no fish. Your back doesn't ache; I gave you one egg, I gave you a second, and you want a third? I won't give it to you! Go home and chop off your useless cock's leg. He'll bring you an egg!"

The old man thought carefully, "If I chop off the cock's leg, he'll bring me an egg; otherwise I feed him, and there's no profit from him at all."

He went home, caught the cock, and was just about to chop off his leg when the cock hopped and skipped away from the old man. He ran and ran, and so he got away. One day passed, and the cock was not at home, then a second and a third. On the fourth, the old man went to the old woman: "So, old one! You taught me to cut a leg off my cock so it would bring eggs to me, but he has completely disappeared! Three days he hasn't been home."

But the cock was walking down the road, just walking along. He walked and walked, and then he met up with a jackal. The jackal asked, "Cock, where are you going?"

He answered, "I'm going to fight a war against the tsar and take half the tsar's kingdom and his money."

The jackal said, "I'll go with you."

"Come along."

So they walked and walked along the road, and the jackal said, "I'm exhausted, cock."

"Well then, crawl into me." The jackal crawled into the cock and sat there, while the cock walked on. He walked and walked, and then he met up with a wolf.

The wolf asked him, "Cock, where are you going?"

The cock answered, "I'm going to fight a war against the tsar and take away from that tsar half his kingdom and his money."

The wolf said, "With that tongue, cock, you could clean up a Turk!"

"If you don't believe it, then don't come," answered the cock.

The wolf thought and thought and then stated, "Cock, for such a cause, I'll join with you."

"Come along."

So they walked down the road. They walked and walked, and the wolf grew tired. "Cock, I'm exhausted."

"Well, if you're exhausted, climb into me." In the wolf climbed, and he sat there, and the cock walked on. He walked and walked, and some bees came flying toward him. They saw the cock and asked, "Cock, where are you going?"

"I'm going to fight a war against the tsar and take from the tsar half his kingdom and his money."

The bees began to discuss it: "And we'll fly with you for such a cause."

"Come along, come fly with me!"

So the cock walked on, and the bees flew behind him. They flew and they flew and they stated, "Cock, oh cock, we're exhausted from this flying!"

"Then crawl into me." So the bees crawled into the cock and sat there, but the cock, you know, he just walked on.

He walked and walked until he came to a stream. The stream was large, and he couldn't walk across it, nor could he fly across. He became sad. He paced and paced on the bank and thought, "What should I do now?" He thought and thought, then turned his rear end to the stream and said, "Water, oh water, come into me!" So the water went into the cock. The stream dried up, and the cock continued on. He came to the outpost where the tsar was living. He went up to the tsar's house, climbed onto the wattle lattice, and shouted:

Cock-a-doodle-doo, cock-a-doodle doo!
I, the cock, have come to fight the tsar!
On my shoulder I'm carrying my sabre,
I'll take the tsar's treasure!

And from within the cock the wolf and jackal made a noise: "The tsar has no money! The tsar has no money! The tsar has no money!"

The tsar heard these words and was taken aback at this strange thing: "What is this that I have no money! Put that cock, servants, with my hens in the chicken house! Let them peck him!"

So the tsar's servants ran and caught the cock and put him in with the hens for the night. They put him in with the hens and went away themselves. Then the cock stated, "Well, now, jackal, climb out and slaughter the royal hens!" The jackal climbed out and slaughtered all the hens. In the morning the servants came, opened the henhouse, and the cock jumped out, sat down on the wattle lattice, and shouted:

> *Cock-a-doodle-doo, cock-a-doodle doo!*
> *I, the cock, have come to fight the tsar!*
> *On my shoulder I'm carrying my sabre,*
> *I'll take the tsar's treasure!*

And then the wolf made a noise from within the cock: "The tsar has no money! The tsar has no money! The tsar has no money!" The tsar heard these words and was taken aback by this strange thing. So he gave his servants an order: "Catch that damned cock and put him down at the livestock pen with the cattle. Let them trample him." So the servants went, caught the cock, and put him with the cattle for the night. The cock sat in the livestock pen and stated, "Well now, wolf, climb out and slaughter the royal livestock or else the cows and bulls will crush me."

Out climbed the wolf, and he slaughtered all the royal livestock. In the morning the royal servants came, and all the royal livestock were slaughtered. The cock jumped away from the depot, sat on the wattle lattice, and crowed:

> *Cock-a-doodle-doo, cock-a-doodle doo!*
> *I, the cock, have come to fight the tsar!*
> *On my shoulder I'm carrying my sabre,*
> *I'll take the tsar's treasure!*

And from within the cock the bees made a noise: "The tsar has no money, the tsar has no money, the tsar has no money." The servants came to the tsar and said to him, "All the livestock is slaughtered, and the cock has leaped out and fled." The tsar listened to the servants, and then the cock began to crow:

> *Cock-a-doodle-doo, cock-a-doodle doo!*
> *I, the cock, have come to fight the tsar!*
> *On my shoulder I'm carrying my sabre,*
> *I'll take the tsar's treasure!*

And from within the cock the bees made a noise: "The tsar has no money, the tsar has no money, the tsar has no money!"

For a whole day the cock shouted away. The tsar was angered, and he gave his servants an order: "Catch that cock, put him in the oven, and let him roast!"

The servants came and heated up the oven; they caught the cock, put him in the oven, and closed it. The cock sat in the oven and stated, "Water, water! Pour out over the oven!" The water poured over the oven. In the morning the royal servants opened the latch, the cock jumped out, and in the oven only water remained. The servants ran to the tsar and reported to him, "We didn't even get the latch opened, and the cock jumped out. In the oven just water remained." The cock perched on the wattle lattice and shouted out to himself:

Cock-a-doodle-doo, cock-a-doodle doo!
I, the cock, have come to fight the tsar!
On my shoulder I'm carrying my sabre,
I'll take the tsar's treasure!

And from within the bees made a noise: "The tsar has no money! The tsar has no money! The tsar has no money!" The tsar listened and listened and grew angry at the cock: "What is this, I have no money?! Catch that cock and bring him here to me in my chambers."

The servants ran, and they caught the cock and brought him to the tsar in his chambers. The tsar had devised a way to offend the cock. So he stated, "Put that cock in my trousers!" So the cock perched in the tsar's trousers and stated, "Bees, bees! Fly out and sting Tsar Yerokha!" Out flew the bees and began to sting the tsar. They stung Yerokha so much that he swelled up. The tsar's trousers fell off him, and that cock flew out!

In the morning the servants came and opened the doors to the palace, and the bees flew away as the cock jumped outside. So the cock jumped outside and perched on the wattle lattice, and then he shouted:

Cock-a-doodle-doo, cock-a-doodle doo!
I, the cock, have come to fight the tsar!
On my shoulder I'm carrying my sabre,
I'll take the tsar's treasure!

And then the wolf and jackal ran around the royal hut and made this noise: "The tsar has no money, the tsar has no money, the tsar has no money!" All day long they shouted, then another, and then a third. On the third day the tsar stated to his servants, "Catch him, that damned thing, put him in a trunk full of money and let him see whether or not I have money."

The servants caught the cock and placed him in the trunk full of money, and the cock took and pecked up all the gold sovereigns. In the morning the servants came and opened the trunk, and the cock flew out, but there was no money in the trunk. They went to the tsar and reported to him, "Oh, father tsar! There's no money in the trunk!"

"How is it that there's no money?"

"There just isn't," the servants stated.

But the cock perched on the wattle lattice and shouted:

Cock-a-doodle-doo, cock-a-doodle doo!
Tsar Yerokha has no money!
Tsar Yerokha has no money!

The cock shouted and then ran home to the grandfather, the wolf and jackal ran into the woods, and the bees flew away to the steppe. When the cock got home, he shouted:

Old man, old man, old man!
Open the gates wide!
Lay down new carpets!
Receive the cock, I've brought some money!

The old man heard the cock, opened the gates, and spread out new carpets. The cock sat on a carpet and poured out all the sovereigns. The old man went off to the neighbor woman's and praised him: "That cock of mine has brought me a whole pile of money." The old woman ran to the old man's to look at the money. She saw a heap of money and began to ask for some. The old man gave her two sovereigns. The next day she came back and asked, "Old man, give me a coin!"

And on that next day the old man gave her two sovereigns.

On the third day she also came to ask: "Old man, give me a coin."

And how many times did you give me an egg?"

"Twice," answered the old woman.

"And I have twice given money to you, but now I won't. Go chop off your hen's leg, and she will also bring you some money."

The stupid old woman went home and chopped off her hen's leg. But the hen wriggled and shuddered, wriggled and shuddered, and died. The woman was left without a hen, and the old man lived on with his cock. From then on they lived and prospered and accumulated wealth.

I was there with them; I drank mead and beer; I ate little cakes. They lived well and received their guests politely. Whoever dropped by would be fed and offered a drink.

A–T 219E*

108. The Old Man, the Old Woman, and the Cock

There lived an old man and an old woman. They lived on and on to the point where all they had left were a cock and a hen. Once the old woman said to her old man, "I don't want to live with you any more; let's divide things up! You take the cock for yourself, and I'll take the hen." And so the old folks divided things up and began to live in different huts: the old man with his cock and the old woman with her hen.

Once they started quarreling about who was living better. "So, old man," said the old woman, "however you interpret it, my life is incomparably better than yours. Judge for yourself: I have a hen, and you have a cock. The hen brings me eggs, and what does your cock do?"

Anger overcame the old man because he had been deceived by the old woman. He grabbed a knife and was about to butcher the cock. The cock said to him, "Don't touch me, master. We will not live worse than the old woman; just let me fly over to a certain place and back," he said, and he flew away. The cock flew to the house of a rich merchant, sat down on his painted gate, and started crowing: "Cock-a-doodle-do! Cock-a-doodle-do!" The merchant saw the cock and said to his workmen, "Catch him. See how full-throated he is!" The workers caught the cock and gave him to the merchant, but the merchant left him for the night in his shop. "In the morning," he thought, "I'll put him out with my hens." In the morning the merchant had just barely opened the door into his shop when the cock—whirrrr!—and flew away. He flew home, sat down on the old man's picket fence, and started crowing right beneath his window: "Cock-a-doodle-do! Cock-a-doodle-do! Bring the mats, grandfather, spread them out on the courtyard and see what I've brought you." The old man ran out of his hut and spread out the mats. The cock dropped a whole pile of money on them—gold and silver!

The old woman was furious that such fortune had come to the old man, and she said, "Anyway, old man, I still live better. If you like, let's divide things up again. You take the hen for yourself and let me have the cock." And so once again the old people divided things up: the old man took the hen for himself, and he gave the cock to the old woman.

The old woman again started arguing that she was living better: with the cock she could obtain anything, but the old man might make his way through all the money and be left with just the hen. "Now I won't have to get quite so many goods myself," the old woman said. "My cock will get them all for me." So the old woman grabbed a knife and started chasing round the yard after the cock. "I'll get you, you so-and-so, I'll kill you!" But she didn't really mean to kill him, only to frighten him a little. "Fly away and quickly bring back whatever you can so that there'll be twice as much as the old man has."

The cock didn't say a thing; he just moved off and flew away. The old woman sat down at the window and waited. She just couldn't wait for her cock to come back! And so here came the cock flying in. He alighted on the old woman's picket fence and started crowing beneath the window: "Cock-a-doodle-doo! Cock-a-doodle-doo!"

The old woman ran out of her hut quite out of her mind, and she spread her very largest cloth in the courtyard, and then she scattered out some grain and waited for the cock to put out all the treasure onto the cloth. The old woman waited and waited, but there was nothing. "Very well, my dearest, if you don't want to give it up honestly, I'll take it myself!" The old woman was angry, and she grabbed the cock by the legs, put him belly side up, and slit open his stomach. She looked, but it was empty. The old woman was even more angry, and she ran to her old man's. She wanted to scold him properly for the cock and by the way grab a handful of money from him. She looked and saw the old man sitting there on a bench in his hut, his clothes all in patches. And he had nothing at all: all had disappeared the moment the cock was no more.

A–T 219E**

109. A Legend About a Cuckoo

Once this peasant, in anticipation of next year's harvest, set out for his fields and began to sow rye. Crows and jackdaws found out that they'd have a feast there and flew up in clouds from all sides. The peasant would cast a handful of rye, then look and all his uninvited guests would be there tax free and without tariff pecking his wealth as if he were obliged to feed them according to some written agreement, and they pecked away and did not fear his shouts. From time to time a startled crow would fly away, one that, as they say, was afraid of a shadow, but the brave ones never batted an eye. An enormous sadness overcame the little peasant when he thought all his labors were in vain and his wealth would be lost, and he was thinking of abandoning his unsuccessful sowing and just waiting until the crows should take off again and fly back to the forests, the threshing floors, the towns, and the villages. But then a gray cuckoo chanced to fly by, and she took pity on the poor plowman and said to him, "Do not weep, little peasant, do not grieve. I shall fly with your complaint to falcon, the falcon's son. These crows shall repay you dearly for your loss; they will serve as messengers for you and bring you white wheat and grapes* from over the seas." The cuckoo appeared before the falcon's gaze and with great sadness related of the evil the crows had done to the peasant. The falcon became furious, and when he had heard the cuckoo's words he sent a little bird, a tit, to fly off to the crow, Karp's daughter, to summon her to judgment and sentencing. The crow came flying in fright, and she responded to the falcon's threatening speech with saccharine humility: "The cuckoo's complaint, oh falcon falcon's son, is pure falsehood. To the contrary, we help the peasants. The plowman throws a handful of rye seeds onto the ground, and one will fall upon a stone and another on the road, and we collect those seeds and bring them to the fertile soil so that the seed can put down its roots where it should, find nourishment, and be cared for properly. The next year the little peasant is amazed and cannot get over his amazement and in his heart he praises God that so much grain has sprouted in his field, that the stalks of grain are bowing their heads in their fullness, and just note: rather than the two measures he has cast into the ground, he will mill a full twelve. We help the peasants, and, poor things, we are slandered. In fact, all the poverty and scarcity in the peasant's life are due to the cuckoo. If the peasant ever goes into the forest to strip some bast for boots or cut some branches for sifting his grain, the cuckoo sits there in a fir tree and cuckoos away. The peasant stops his work and thinks to

---

*Apparently, luxury items.

himself: Why should I work and labor? I have only this year to live in the wide world; I'll go lie on the stove, and with what remains of my life I'll just lie there and enjoy it.* And another peasant might fall into drunkenness and other filthy amusements, and to hell with plow and harrow and his whole household. But the peasant errs if he believes that the cuckoo's cooing means death. The year will pass, he eats enough and rests enough, and it's just idleness that overcomes him in his work. The peasant becomes utterly impoverished, he hasn't a crust of bread, his children are going around nearly naked, and even if he takes up his begging bowl and goes throughout the whole Orthodox world, that cuckoo's cuckooing is still at fault."

"It is true, crow, all the fault should fall upon the cuckoo. Cuckoo, you shall be neither sated nor hungry, and you shall live your days in sadness and boredom, and from now on you shall not cherish your fledglings." And since then the cuckoo has been mournful, and her cuckoo, as the crow put it, is still in people's minds an ill omen for numbering the years of their lives.

A–T 220

110. The Eagle and the Crow

There lived and dwelt in Rus this crow with her nannies and her grannies and all her little children and all the neighbors, too. The swan-geese came and laid some eggs, and the crow started mistreating them and started carrying off their eggs.

Once an elf owl happened to fly by, and he saw how the crows were mistreating those big eggs, and he flew right up to a gray eagle. He flew up and said, "Father gray eagle! Give us a proper judgment against that rascally crow!" The gray eagle sent that light-footed envoy, the sparrow, after the crow. The sparrow immediately flew off and grabbed the crow. The crow was about to get away, but the sparrow let her have a few kicks and hauled her up before the gray eagle.

The eagle opened court. "Oh, you rascally crow, you stupid fool, you useless nose and shitty tail! It is said of you that you are sticking other

---

*The Russian peasant believed that the cuckoo's call heralded an imminent death.

people's goods into your own mouth, that you are hauling off the eggs of big birds."

"That's all slander, father gray eagle, slander!"

"And it is also said about you that when a little peasant goes out to sow, you hop out with all your hell-raising and peck up his seed."

"Slander, father gray eagle, slander!"

"And they also say that when the women are reaping the crops, they cut and stack the sheaves in the fields, and you go about with your hell-raising and peck them all over and mess them up."

"Slander, father gray eagle, slander!"

But they sentenced the crow to prison.

A–T 220A

111. The Crow Karabut (About a Mistrial of the Birds)

In a certain tsardom,
In a certain state,
They gathered, they flocked
To a green, to a meadow,
All in a single circle.
And they selected their leaders:
As tsar, the white swan,
As governor, the eagle owl,
The crane as steward,
The tit as page,
The sparrow as jailer,
The jackdaw carried a rod,
The magpie was centurion.
Only the crow Karabut had no rank.
She flew off from that council,
She flew to a pub,
She got drunk and boozy.
She flew by the cuckoo's home:
The cuckoo had a new home,
With a tent-shaped top.
The crow broke that top,

She knocked out the doors,
She cooled off the house,
And bound up the children,
And threw them in the cellar.
Then she flew off to a snag,
To the very tip-top.
The cuckoo came flying home,
She didn't recognize her home.
"I had a brand-new house,
A tent-shaped top;
Now there's no top,
And the doors are knocked out,
And my hut is cold!"
Her children responded:
"Crow Karabut came flying from the council.
She broke the top,
She knocked out the doors,
She cooled off the house,
She bound us up
And threw us into the cellar."
So they made a search:
They sent the centurion magpie,
The jackdaw with the rod,
The sparrow as jailer.
They all flew off to search,
And the crow sat on the snag,
On the very tip-top.
The jackdaw with the rod went tap, tap, tap!
The crow Karabut went rap, rap, rap!
The crow Karabut flew off
To the tsar, the white swan,
To the governor, the eagle owl,
To the steward, the crane.
They deliberated and discussed,
Then they let the crow go free.
So the crow flew off
To a young soldier's widow,
And that soldier's widow was weaving muslin,
And then a hawk flew up for that muslin.

And the crow Karabut bought up that muslin for some trousers and shirts for the leaders, and these she presented to them.

> *Then they accused the crow,*
> *They gave her a sentence:*
> *To make a little hatchet*
> *From the eye of a needle*
> *And with that little hatchet to cut*
> *Three cartloads of dry wood.*
> *And the judges said, "Tap, tap tap!"*
> *And the crow Karabut said, "Rap, rap, rap!"*

A–T 221*

112. The Bone Palace

There was this prince Kirbit. This prince, this Kirbit, had a palace built: in all our realm there was no palace cleaner than his. The mistress had been brought in from other lands.

She had a conversation with this prince, with Kirbit: "Oh, Prince Kirbit! Your palace is fine, but it will rot out. You should build a palace, Prince Kirbit, one that won't rot out!"

"What palace, what should it be made of so that it won't rot out?"

"Oh, Prince Kirbit, you have an estate. On these estates live various birds, and they eat various dead victims. They take off the meat and leave the bones. Build a bone palace!"

The prince spoke: "How does one do that? How does one collect the bones?"

"Each bird, after it has eaten carrion, leaves the bones; it alone knows where."

"Which bird should be chosen to inform all the others?"

And his house mistress said, "There's none better than the titmouse."

The titmouse informed all the birds, "The prince demands of you that every bird bring bones, those whose meat she has used." All the birds flew and brought the bones.

The prince asked the titmouse, "Are all the birds in the gathering?"

"No, prince, the elf owl alone is not here."

"Go ask the elf owl why he hasn't appeared. If he does not wish to live on my estates, then let him take himself away from them!"

The elf owl flew up. The prince asked, "Why did you not appear?"
"Forgive me, prince, I was looking over the laws."
"Which laws were you looking over?"
"Whoever heeds a woman is nine times worse than that woman."†

The prince thought it over to himself: "I have listened to a woman tell
me to build a bone palace, thus I am nine times worse than that woman."
He ordered the birds to carry away the bones, dump them in a ravine,
and bury them with earth so that they could not be seen (for he had been
shamed).

A–T 220 + 221B*

113. The Mouse and the Sparrow

In no certain tsardom, in no certain state, there lived and dwelt a mouse
and a sparrow. Now this mouse and this sparrow lived in a single burrow
for a long time and fed themselves, as it were, on various grains.

So one time they had hauled up some of these grains and were divid-
ing them between them. They divided and divided, and then they saw
that it turned out there was a single extra grain. The sparrow said, "How
should we divide this single grain?" And the mouse answered him, "Let's
try biting through this little grain. Let me try biting through it." But the
sparrow said, "No, let me try." So they quarreled and quarreled, and
finally the sparrow took the little grain, started biting on it, and swallowed it!

The mouse was furious with the sparrow and started fighting with
him. So they fought and fought, but neither could overcome the other.
So they decided to invite others to help them in their bout. The mouse
invited various beasts and called on the bear. The sparrow invited various birds—eagles, falcons, and all sorts of other birds, and the firebird
flew in for an appearance.

So then all these birds began fighting the bear. They fought and fought,
but the bear would not give in to them. Then the firebird herself began to
fight with the bear. She fought and fought. She fought to the point where
she broke off her wing.

---

†A Russian proverb.

So, she had broken off her wing, and off she flew into the forest. She flew into the forest and alighted on a certain snag and just sat there. Now, just then Ivan the peasant's son was walking through that forest. He caught sight of that firebird on the snag, and he desired to shoot her. But the firebird said to him, "Ivan the peasant's son, please don't shoot me! I can do much good for you. Better take me down from this snag and carry me home."

So Ivan the peasant's son took her and brought her home, and they started living there. Well, they lived a day and then another, and then they lived there a whole week. And the firebird began to get well. In what was not a long time, in a short time, she was completely well. And as she got well—her wing completely healed, that means—she began to ask to be set free to go home.

And the firebird said to Ivan the peasant's son, "Come, let's visit my sisters; I'll carry you there on my back!" So Ivan the peasant's son got on the firebird, and they flew off to visit the eldest sister.

So they flew to this eldest sister, and this sister rejoiced to see them. She immediately set out to be hospitable to them, and she offered them so much, more or less everything, and it was time to go home. So the firebird said to her elder sister, "Sister, give me our father's blessing, that chest there."

"And what do you mean, sister? No, I won't give you that for anything."

"Well, if you won't give it, then keep it, and God be with you!"

So the firebird was angry, and she and Ivan the peasant's son flew off to a second sister, which is to say the middle one. So they flew and they flew, and then the firebird said to Ivan the peasant's son, "Glance back there, look back there at what's happening!" So Ivan the peasant's son looked back and saw that back there was a fire, something was burning. And he asked the firebird, "What's that burning there?" And the firebird answered, "That's my sister's town burning! I've burned it down because she wouldn't give me that chest."

So on they flew and flew, and they flew to the middle sister. And she, this middle sister, also rejoiced to see them but just didn't know how to entertain them. And so they stayed there for a long time. But then once again they were forced to set off on their way, on their journey, and the firebird said to that middle sister of hers, "Give me," she said, "father's blessing, that chest there."

"What do you mean, sister? How could I give up that chest!" And so she didn't give it up.

So the firebird got angry at her middle sister, and she and Ivan the peasant's son flew off to her third sister. So again they flew so much, or a little, or a lot, but then again the firebird said to Ivan the peasant's son, "Now look, will you," she said, "what's going on back there." And so then Ivan the peasant's son took a look, and once more he saw a fire, something was burning. And again he asked the firebird, "What is that burning?"

"That is my middle sister's town burning. I burned it down because she wouldn't give me the chest."

So now they flew up to the very youngest sister. This sister rejoiced even more than the others, but she didn't know how to entertain them. But they stayed there, and when they had stayed a long time, they began to get ready for the road, the journey home, so to speak. So when they had gotten ready, the firebird said to that sister, "Give me," she said, "that chest, father's blessing!" And she started asking her. And that sister wasn't very willing to give up that chest, but she gave it up anyway.

So now the firebird took that chest, took her leave of her sister, and she and Ivan the peasant's son flew off back home. So they arrived, they flew up to that very place where the firebird had her home. And she began to treat Ivan the peasant's son to various and sundry dishes. They began to feast, to make merry. And so Ivan the peasant's son was hosted there most marvelously, and yet the time came to get ready to go home. So he started gathering up his things.

So as he had begun getting ready to go home, the firebird said to him, "Well, Ivan the peasant's son, you have done me a favor, now I have to do something for you. Take this chest," she said, "I'm making a gift of it to you. But watch out, don't open the chest along the road; you should only open it when you get home." So Ivan the peasant's son took the chest, they said their farewells, and he set off along the way, on the journey, back to where he had come from.

So he walked along. He walked and walked, but it was still a long way home. And he was very tempted to look in the chest. He couldn't stand it any more, so he went and opened it up. As soon as he opened the chest, he saw immediately that he was in an enormous palace. When he looked through the window, he saw he was in a city, with all the people in enormous numbers simply strolling around.

So somehow he became the tsar and started to rule the country. And when he became the tsar, he brought over his mother and father. And from then on they lived and prospered there, and they live there even now.

A–T 222B*

114. The Hen, the Mouse, and the Grouse

In times long ago there lived a hen, a mouse, and a grouse. Once the hen found a barley corn and began to cackle from joy: "I've found a grain, a grain I've found! I'll have to grind it. Who will carry it to the mill?"

"Not I," said the mouse. "Not I," said the grouse.

There was nothing else she could do, so the hen took the grain and set off with it. She came to the mill and ground the grain. "Who will carry the flour home?" she asked.

"Not I," said the mouse. "Not I," said the grouse.

There was nothing else she could do. The hen took the flour and carried it home.

"Who will mix the bread?" asked the hen.

"Not I," said the mouse. "Not I," they both said.

The hen mixed the dough, and heated the oven, and put the bread into the stove herself. Out came a loaf for a splendid feast, fancy and shiny. The hen put it on the table and asked, "Who will eat it?"

"I will" and "I will," said the mouse and the grouse, and both climbed up to the table.

A–T 222C*

115. The Fox, the Cock, and the Crane

A good tale, a good story, is begun and commenced not from the russet one, nor from the dappled gray, nor even from the raven black. Not from a youth's whistle nor a wench's fart. An old, old woman returned, and she took seven bricks from her stove. But this is no tale, it's a prelude to a tale, and the tale will be on Saturday in the evening.

Mother fox was walking along, toward the noble's home. She wanted to eat a calf from the calf shed, a hen from the henhouse, a child from the woman, a pup from the bitch, a lamb from the ewe, a colt from the mare. Thief-cock saw her, and he began to flutter about with his feathers and wings. He began to crow, and everybody heard him and came running: the old women with their spades and with their oven paddles, the old men with their axes and with their yoke beams, the youngsters with whisks and with rattles—they all wanted to beat that fox and kill her. The fox took offense, set off for the forest like a hunchbacked devil, collapsed beneath an alder bush, and fell asleep for three full days. Thief-cock flew out into the empty steppe and alighted on a fine tree. Mother fox had her little lie-down, and then she, too, set out into the empty steppe. She walked along near the fine tree. She noted with her bright eyes that the thief-cock was sitting there.

"Well, now, thief-cock, are you flying from your hunt, or are you looking for us wild beasts?"

"Oh, mother fox, I'm flying back from my hunt; I'm not looking for you beasts!"

"Well, thief-cock, come on down and confess, the final time is near, the end of your life is nigh. People are living with and keeping just one wife, but you maintain many wives, and you're quarrelsome, and you scratch them until they have bloody wounds!"

The cock started going from branch to branch, from bough to bough, lower and lower, and then he hopped even lower. Mother fox ran up, grabbed that cock in her claws, put the wings and feathers to one side, began shaking him, and she pronounced, "Well, now, thief-cock, when I was in dire need, starving to death, and I went to a rich merchant or boyar so as to get a bit of something to eat, how did he find out I was there? Then somehow the devil brought you into it all."

The cock said to this, "Oh, mother fox and princess, my lady! Everyone knows you. The lords esteem you, they make wraps and skirts of you, they wear them on holidays. They live for just one master; they never serve two. That's how I'll live for you, and I'll serve you, too!"

"Thief-cock! Stop weaving webs and spouting rot!" She shook him more than ever before as she pronounced her words.

"Oh, mother fox, princess, my lady! Everyone knows you, the lords esteem you, they make wraps and skirts of you, they wear them on holidays. They live for just one master; they never serve two. That's how I'll live for you, and I'll serve you, too! We shall live together by the shore of the sea, we'll make a little hut, and you'll live there baking communion bread, and I'll eat it, and I'll sing you little songs!"

Mother fox weakened her grip. The cock flew away and alighted again in the fine tree. "Oh, mother fox, I wish to congratulate you on your new rank, eat special fish and ham, and do have some walnuts, but don't break your teeth!"*

Mother fox went off through the open steppe, sadder than ever, and then she met a crane. "Well, thief-crane, why are you walking along smirking?"

"And why, mother fox, are you walking along so sad and cursing?"

"Why should I not curse when every last bird's in the harness and even that one laughs at me!"

"Whatever do you mean?"

"That thief-cock!"

"Well, mother fox, do you know how to fly?"

"No, I don't know how to fly."

"Get on, I'll teach you how."

So she got on the crane. And the crane carried her high up. "Mother fox, can you see the earth?"

"Just barely; we're near the sheep run."

The crane shook her off, and mother fox fell in a soft place, onto a haystack. The crane came flying up: "Mother fox, don't you know how to fly?"

"I can sort of fly, but the landing's difficult."

"Get on, I'll teach you."

So she got on the crane. The crane carried the fox off still higher. She shook her off. Mother fox fell in a hard place, into a spruce swamp. Her bones sank three yards into the ground—all that was left of that fox was her name!

But then the merchant's hens started losing their eggs; they wouldn't leave them in their nests. "What's the matter with you hens? Where are you hiding those eggs, where are you losing them?"

"Why, we're losing our eggs because we no longer have that caressing master, our cock is no more!"

---

*The cock sneers at the fox, referring to delicacies that would never have been served on the average peasant's table.

"And where has the cock gone?"

"Why, our cock's sitting out there in the open steppe, in a fine tree."

Now the merchant had a tom turkey. He had flown in one holiday for dinner. The cock returned to the merchant, and the merchant asked him, "Well, thief-cock, where have you been, where have you been fooling about, and where have you traveled?"

"Oh, I'm not a local, I'm just passing through, I'm from Barracks Street, I'm with a legless hen."†

A–T 225A + 61A

116. The Raven and the Lobster

A raven flew above the sea, looked down, and saw a lobster crawling along. She grabbed him and carried him off to the woods, intending to perch somewhere on a branch and enjoy a good meal. The lobster saw that his end was coming and said to the raven, "Oh, raven, raven, I knew your father and mother; they were fine people!"

"Humph!" answered the raven, without opening her mouth.

"And I know your brothers and sisters, too; what fine people they are!"

"Humph!"

"But although they are all fine people, they are not equal to you. It seems to me that in the whole world there is no one wiser than you."

"Aha!" cawed the raven, opening her mouth wide and dropping the lobster into the sea.

A–T 227*

117. The Magpie and the Raven

A magpie and a raven were flying, and they got together. "Where are you flying to, raven?"

---

†A number of tales either begin or end with "nonsense," deriving from the tradition of the medieval storytellers.

"Oh, I wanted to relocate." (But the magpie knew that she had been sitting in the same tree for seven years.)

The magpie said to the raven, "You were well off sitting there: no winds knocked you off, no sun or moon."

"Well yes, but I got a little filthy sitting there."

"But do you not carry with you that habit of making a mess?" asked the magpie.

"I do take it with me."

"Well then, you'll just make a mess in your new place."

A–T 227**

118. The Great Horned Owl and the Little Tiny Screech Owl

There lived a horned owl in the woods. She was flying once and saw that a bird had frozen, so she flew up and looked at it and said, "Why, it's of our breed, a little tiny owlet." And she dragged it to her nest and started feeding it. She kept it there for a week. She brought it food, and it sat in the nest ever so quietly.

Once the owl flew back, took it under her wing, and was warming it, and she said, "My, what a fierce frost we are having today!"

And it answered from under her wing, "This is no frost, the frost is yet to come. Just wait for the Christmas frosts, then you can say 'this is a frost.' "

So the horned owl asked, "How do you know this?"

"How would I not know?! I've been living on earth for seven years already."

"Who are you, anyway?" she asked.

"Why, I'm a screech owl."

"But I thought you were a little horned owl. So I took pity on you and nourished you, and you're older than I am, you know more than I do. So, go on, my dearie, get out of my nest!"

And she went and threw it out. The screech owl flew off to search for a new place for itself.

A–T 230

119. The Sparrow and the Mare

There was this bunch of sparrows sitting in this peasant's yard. One sparrow began boasting in front of the others, his buddies.

"This gray mare has fallen in love with me, she's always gazing at me. Do you want me to have her right here before this honorable company?"

"We'll watch," said his friends.

So the sparrow flew up to the mare and said, "Greetings, my dear little mare!"

"Greetings, songster! What do you need?"

"Well, this is my need, I'd like to ask you . . ."

The mare said, "That's a fine idea. According to our country custom, when a lad begins wooing a girl, he buys her some trade goods: some nuts and spice cookies. And what are you going to present to me?"

"Just tell me what you want!"

"Now then, you just bring a quarter of oats over here, grain by grain, and then let our lovemaking begin!"

And so with all his might the sparrow began fussing about; he labored long and finally managed to bring up the whole quarter of oats. He flew up and said, "Well, my dear little mare! The oats are ready!" But in fact his heart could hardly take it; he was glad but also scared to death.

"Well," said the mare, "there's no point in putting off the matter, denying pleasure is worse than death, and I'll never get through life a virgin. In any case, there's no shame in getting it from such a fine young lad. Bring some oats and call your friends. And you settle down on my tail just alongside the asshole, and wait until I raise my tail."

The mare began eating the oats, and the sparrow sat there on her tail, and his buddies watched to see what would happen. The mare ate and ate and farted; she raised her tail, and the sparrow got to her ass. The mare trapped him with her tail. Things were bad for him right then, he might die!

So she ate and ate, and again she farted. The sparrow hopped out of there and began boasting in front of his friends: "So that's how! Most likely the mare couldn't handle it all from 'my brother' here, so she just farted!"

A–T 233D*

120. The Cock and the Hen

There lived and dwelt a cock and a hen. They ran to the priest to peck beneath his window, and the cock choked. The hen ran to the river. "River, river, give some water to bring the cock around; he's choked!"

The river said, "Go to the lime tree, ask for some leaves."

Then the hen ran to the lime: "Lime, lime! Give some leaves. I'll carry the leaves to the river, and the river will give some water to bring the cock around."

But the lime said, "Go to the threadmaker, ask for some thread!'

And off she ran. "Threadmaker, threadmaker, give me some thread. I'll carry the threads to the lime, the lime will give leaves, I'll take the leaves to the river, and the river will give some water to bring the cock around, for the cock has choked."

But the threadmaker sent her to the pastry baker: "Go to the pastry baker, ask for a kolach*."

The hen ran to the pastry baker. "Pastry baker, pastry baker, give me a kolach. I'll take it to the threadmaker, the threadmaker will give me some threads, I'll carry the threads to the lime tree, the lime tree will give me some leaves, I'll take the leaves to the river, and the river will give me some water to bring the cock around, for the cock has choked."

The pastry baker sent her to the cowherd. "Go to the cowherd, ask for some milk."

The hen ran to the cowherd. "Cowherd, cowherd, give me some milk. I'll take it to the pastry baker, the pastry baker will give me a kolach, I'll take it to the threadmaker, the threadmaker will give me some threads, I'll carry the threads to the lime tree, the lime tree will give me some leaves, I'll take the leaves to the river, and the river will give me some water to bring the cock around, for the cock has choked."

The cowherd sent her to the haymowers. "Go to the haymowers, ask for some grass."

So the hen ran to the haymowers. "Haymowers, haymowers, give me some grass. I'll take it to the cowherd, the cowherd will give me some milk, I'll take it to the pastry baker, the pastry baker will give me a kolach,

---

*Sweet pastry

I'll take it to the threadmaker, the threadmaker will give me some threads, I'll carry the threads to the lime tree, the lime tree will give me some leaves, I'll take the leaves to the river, and the river will give me some water to bring the cock around, for the cock has choked."

But the haymowers sent her to the blacksmith for a scythe. "Go, ask for a scythe."

The hen ran to the blacksmith. "Blacksmith, blacksmith, give me a scythe. I'll take it to the haymowers, the haymowers will give me some grass, I'll take it to the cowherd, the cowherd will give me some milk, I'll take it to the pastry baker, the pastry baker will give me a kolach, I'll take it to the threadmaker, the threadmaker will give me some threads, I'll carry the threads to the lime tree, the lime tree will give me some leaves, I'll take the leaves to the river, and the river will give me some water to bring the cock around, for the cock has choked."

But the blacksmith sent her to the charcoal maker.

"Charcoal maker, charcoal maker, give me some coal. I'll take it to the blacksmith, the blacksmith will give me a scythe, I'll take it to the haymowers, the haymowers will give me some grass, I'll take it to the cowherd, the cowherd will give me some milk, I'll take it to the pastry baker, the pastry baker will give me a kolach, I'll take it to the threadmaker, the threadmaker will give me some threads, I'll carry the threads to the lime tree, the lime tree will give me some leaves, I'll take the leaves to the river, and the river will give me some water to bring the cock around, for the cock has choked."

But the charcoal maker sent her to the wood merchants.

"Wood merchants, wood merchants, give me some wood! I'll take it to the charcoal maker, the charcoal maker will give me some coal, I'll take it to the blacksmith, the blacksmith with give me a scythe, I'll take it to the haymowers, the haymowers will give me some grass, I'll take it to the cowherd, the cowherd will give me some milk, I'll take it to the pastry baker, the pastry baker will give me a kolach, I'll take it to the threadmaker, the threadmaker will give me some threads, I'll carry the threads to the lime tree, the lime tree will give me some leaves, I'll take the leaves to the river, and the river will give me some water to bring the cock around, for the cock has choked."

The wood merchants gave her some wood. She grabbed the wood, ran to the charcoal maker, the charcoal maker gave her the coal, she carried the coal to the blacksmith, the blacksmith gave her the scythe, she carried the scythe to the haymowers, the haymowers gave her some grass, she took the grass to the cowherd, the cowherd gave her some milk, she carried the milk to the pastry baker, the pastry baker gave her a kolach, she carried the kolach to the threadmaker, the threadmaker gave her threads, the threads she carried to the lime tree, and the lime gave her some leaves, the leaves she carried to the river, and the river gave some water to bring the cock around.

She took the water and ran to the cock, but the cock lay there dead. She rolled the cock over, and the cock jumped up and sang out, "Cock-a-doodle-do!"

A–T 241A (2021A)

121. The Birds' Courting (A Song)

All the guests had come, gathered together,
They were just waiting for the owl.
Then the owl arrived, Elizar's godmother.
And the owl sat down on the stove rack.
The little barn owl strode across the floor,
He poured out a glass and gave it to the owl.
"So drink, oh owl, Elizar's own daughter!"
"Don't wait on me, barn owl, son of Afanasii!
Why is it, little barn owl, that you don't marry?"
"I'd be glad to marry, but there's no bride.
I'd take the crow, but she's an old aunt,
I'd take the jackdaw, but she's much too pious.
I'd take the magpie—she's a coquettish bitch!"
"Well, oh barn owl, would you not take me?"
"Well, owl, can you spin and weave?"
"I can neither spin nor weave, but I don't go around naked.

And you, little barn owl, do you know how to plow?
To plow and plant grain in the field?"
"In the city they don't plow, and they eat only pastries,
But in the countryside they all plow and chew chaff!"

A–T 243*

122. The Crane and the Heron

There once was an owl flying around, a merry bird was she. She flew and flew, perched on a tree, wiggled her tail, looked from side to side, and took wing again. She flew and flew, perched on a tree, wiggled her tail, and rolled her eyes. . . . But that's the pre-tale flourish, just for fun; the real tale has not yet begun!

Once upon a time a crane and a heron lived in a bog; they had built themselves little huts, one at each end of it. The crane grew weary of living alone and decided to marry: "I will go court the heron!"

The crane set out—flap, flap!—and he flapped over the bog for seven versts. Finally he arrived and asked, "Is the heron at home?"

"She is."

"Heron, be my wife."

"No, crane, I will not be your wife; your legs are too long, your clothes are too short, you fly very poorly, and you cannot support me. Go away, you gangleshanks!"

The crane returned home with a bad taste in his mouth. Later the heron changed her mind and thought to herself, "Why should I live alone? It would be better to marry the crane!"

She came to him and said, "Crane, marry me."

"No, heron, I don't need you. I don't want to get married, and I won't take you as my wife. Get out of here!"

The heron wept for shame and went home. The crane changed his mind and thought to himself, "I was wrong not to marry the heron; it is tiresome to live alone. I will go now and take her as my wife." He came and said, "Heron, I have decided to marry you; be my wife."

"No, crane, I won't be your wife!"

So the crane went home. Then the heron changed her mind and thought, "Why did I refuse him? What good is it to live alone? I'd rather marry the crane!" So she came to propose, and this time the crane refused. And to this very day they go courting each other, but they never get married.

A–T 244A*

123. The Silly Magpie

In a certain tsardom, in a certain country, there lived a tsar with a tsaritsa. The tsaritsa had a magpie, and that magpie could talk! Whatever she overheard, she would tell the tsaritsa.

The tsar's servants did not like the tsaritsa. And one servant girl especially disliked her. She thought about removing the tsaritsa from the earth. And she reported everything bad about the tsaritsa to the tsar.

Once the tsaritsa fell in love with a fisherman. She began to visit him, and the servant girl saw her and told the tsar. The tsar found out about the affair and decided to execute the tsaritsa for treason. The magpie had overheard the servant girl telling the tsar about the fisherman and the tsaritsa, and she related it all to the tsaritsa: "Tsaritsa!"

"What is it, magpie?"

"Your servant girl has told the tsar about your love affair."

The tsaritsa called in the servant girl and said to her in the magpie's presence, "Why are you going around with the fisherman?"

The magpie heard these words and flew off to the tsar in his palace and said, "Tsar!"

"What do you want?"

"The tsaritsa's servant girl is going around with the fisherman." The tsar heard these words and thought, "What a wicked servant girl! She wanted me to execute the tsaritsa. Oh well! . . ."

He thought and thought and concluded, "I will execute the servant girl for her evil deed and pardon the tsaritsa!" That's what the tsar concluded, and that is what he did.

The servants found out about these doings of the magpie, that she had tattled to the tsar about everything, and they got together and said, "The magpie tells everything to the tsaritsa, and she tattles on us. Let's catch her, and we'll sew up her mouth."

So the servants caught the magpie and sewed up her mouth. And after they had sewn it up, they said, "Now we'll poison the tsaritsa." The magpie flew to the tsaritsa. She sat on her window and muttered:

> *The servants sewed and sewed,*
> *And they sewed up my mouth.*
> *They sewed up my mouth,*
> *They've destroyed the tsaritsa,*
> *They've destroyed the tsaritsa,*
> *And they'll destroy the tsar.*

The tsaritsa didn't understand what the magpie was chattering, and once again the magpie began muttering:

The servants were sewing,
They sewed up the magpie's mouth.
They sewed up my mouth,
And they've poisoned you, tsaritsa,
They've poisoned you, tsaritsa.
And they will kill the tsar.

Just then the tsaritsa understood it, but it was too late. She began to be tortured [by the poison]. She was tortured, and then she died. What the servants had thought up was what they did. And the magpie flew to the hens. One hen ran up to the magpie and pecked through the threads on the magpie's beak. The magpie flew off to the tsar; she flew up and said, "Tsar, the servants have poisoned the tsaritsa and will destroy you."

The tsar grew angry at the servants and hanged them all. So the tsar lived alone with the magpie. They lived thus and fell into poverty. There were no servants, no one to feed the tsar. Somehow the tsar took exception to the magpie and said to her, "I have executed all the servants, and you are the one guilty of everything, stupid magpie. How shall I live now? No one prepares food for me to eat. What shall I do now?"

The magpie answered the tsar, "If I were you, tsar, and just a bit wise, I wouldn't listen to servants."

The tsar took offense at such words and thrust a stick at the magpie, and she was knocked off her feet. She was tortured and tortured until she died.

Where the tsar went I don't know!

A–T 245B**

124. The Kite and His Wife

There lived this kite and his wife. They had a single child. And then once they began to quarrel: Who should have the child? They quarreled and quarreled, but no way could they resolve their dispute. So they went to the tsar. How should he settle the matter? The tsar called a council of his whole tsardom. There were generals there, but no one could resolve the matter. And then a certain little peasant turned up. "I will resolve the matter," he said.

"Resolve it," said the tsar.

The little peasant said, "You, kite and mother kite, fly over here!" The kites flew over to him.

"You, kite," said the peasant, "you fly around everywhere, therefore, you can have another child, but where should mother kite get one?"

That's how the peasant resolved this case. And so the little kite stayed with its mother.

A–T 246**

125. The Eagle and the Old Crow

An eagle was flying toward the forest, thinking to himself, "Where will I find some food?"

He flew up to the forest and saw an old crow sitting on a bough, so old and dried up she was just feathers. He thought and thought and flew on by. And the crow sitting there on the tree asked him, "Where are you flying, father eagle?"

"I feel like eating, crow. I will fly into the forest. Perhaps I'll find some little crows there and eat them."

The crow spoke to him: "Look, father eagle, don't eat my children."

The eagle asked the crow, "And which are yours, crow?"

"My children are fine, handsome, and proud. In the whole world, father eagle, you'll find no finer. Even if you should fly from east to west or from south to north, you'll never find any as wonderful."

The eagle listened to the crow and then spoke: "Very well, crow, I won't touch your babies. I'll look in the forest for sickly and puny crow babies."

So the eagle flew off, and the crow stayed sitting in the tree. She sat there, looking at the ground. But the eagle flew round and round the forest, and he found the crow's nest. He looked into the nest, and in it were sitting some really mangy little crows. The eagle ate them. He ate his fill and then flew back, and the crow saw him and asked, "Well, did you find any little crows, father eagle?"

"I found some."

"And did you eat your fill, father eagle?"

"I ate my fill."

"And which did you eat, father eagle; were they perhaps mine?"

"No, crow."

"Well, which did you eat?"

"Oh, some mangy ones."

"Oh, father eagle, those were mine!"

"But you said to me that yours were handsome, the very best," answered the eagle.

"But, those were my babies, father eagle, there were no better on earth."

"Well, crow, I was looking for worse ones. Forgive me and farewell!"

The old crow was left sitting in the tree. Since that time she has crowed. She'll crow, fly off a little, then perch on the tree and look at the ground.

A–T 247

126. The Dog and the Woodpecker

There lived this peasant and his woman, and they had never worked a day in their lives. They had this dog, and she fed them and brought them drink. But the time came when the dog was old. How could she feed the peasant and his woman? She nearly died of hunger herself. "Listen, old man," said the woman. "Take that dog, lead her out beyond the village, and chase her away. Let her go where she likes. She's of no use to us anymore! There was a time when she fed us, and then we looked after her." So the peasant took the dog, led her out beyond the village, and chased her away.

So the dog started wandering around in the unplowed steppe, afraid to go home because the old man and the old woman would start beating and hurting her. She walked and walked; then she sat down on the ground and started howling in a loud voice. A woodpecker was flying by and asked, "Why are you howling?"

"Why should I not howl, woodpecker! When I was young, I fed and brought drink to the old man and the old woman; then I got old, and they chased me away. I don't know where I will live out my old age."

"Come with me; you can stand guard over my babies, and I will feed you." So the dog agreed and ran off after the woodpecker.

The woodpecker flew into the forest to an old oak, and in that oak there was a hollow, and in the hollow was the woodpecker's nest. "Sit down there next to the oak," said the woodpecker, "and don't let anybody in, and I'll fly off and look for some fodder."

The dog settled down alongside the oak, and the woodpecker flew off. She flew and flew, and then she saw some women coming along the road with pots, carrying dinner to their husbands in the field. She went back to the oak, flew up, and said, "Now, dog, follow me. Some women are coming along the road with pots, they're taking dinner to their husbands in the field. You stand behind a bush; I'll throw myself into the water, then roll about in the sand, and get in front of these women along the road, fluttering low, as if I can't fly any higher. They will start trying to catch me, put their pots down on the ground, and come after me. Then you quickly rush to the pots and eat your fill."

So the dog ran off after the woodpecker and, as agreed, got down behind a bush. And the woodpecker rolled around in the sand and began fluttering about in front of the woman on the road. "Look," said the women, "that woodpecker is all wet; let's catch her." They threw their pots onto the ground and went after the woodpecker, and she went on and on; she led them off to one side, and then she flew up and away. And the dog meanwhile had run out from behind the bush, eaten up everything that was in the pots, and gone away.

The women came back, looked, and saw their pots lying about empty. There was nothing they could do, so they gathered them up and went home.

The woodpecker caught up to the dog and asked, "Well, are you satisfied?"

"I am satisfied," answered the dog. "Let's go home."

So the woodpecker flew and the dog ran, and along the way they met a fox. "Catch the fox," said the woodpecker.

The dog rushed after the fox, and the fox set off with all possible speed. Just at that moment a peasant was riding along with a barrel of tar. So the fox darted across the road, right toward the cart, and jumped through the wheel spokes. The dog was right after her but got caught in the wheel, and right there her spirit departed.

"Well, peasant," said the woodpecker, "now that you've strangled my dog, I will cause you great misfortune!" She sat down in the cart and began drilling a hole in the barrel, tapping away at the very bottom.

When the peasant chased her away from the barrel, the woodpecker threw herself at the horse, sat down between his ears, and drilled into his head. The peasant chased her off the horse, so she went back to the barrel. Finally she drilled a hole in the barrel and let out all the tar. And she said, "That's still not quite enough for you." So she went back to drilling the horse's head.

The peasant took a big plank, sat in the cart and bided his time, and then struck with all his strength. Only instead of hitting the woodpecker, with his mighty swing he hit the horse on the head and clobbered it to death. The woodpecker flew to the peasant's hut and flew right in the window. The peasant's wife was just then lighting the stove, and their small child was sitting on a bench. The woodpecker landed on the child's head and started pecking. So the mother grabbed a stick and hit out, but she missed the woodpecker and struck the child. . . .

So the woman set about trying to catch the woodpecker, and finally she caught him and put him under a sieve. The peasant came home and was met by his wife. "Well, wife," he said, "I had an accident on the road."

"Why, husband," she said, "I had an accident, too." So they told each other what had happened.

"Where's that woodpecker now? Did she fly away?" asked the peasant.

"I caught her and put her under a sieve."

"Very well then, I'll deal with her: we'll eat her alive!"

He lifted up the sieve and was about to take the woodpecker into his teeth. But she flew right into his mouth alive and jumped headfirst right down to his ass. She stuck her head out of the peasant's ass and shouted, "I'm alive, I'm alive!"

The peasant saw his misfortune and said to his wife, "You take a log, and I'll get down on all fours. When that woodpecker sticks his head out, you warm him up with that log!"

He got down on his hands and knees; his wife took the log, and just when that woodpecker stuck her head out, she whacked him with the log, but she missed the woodpecker and struck the peasant's ass. What could the peasant do? There was no way he could get that woodpecker out of him. She kept on sticking her head out of his ass and shouting, "I'm alive, alive!"

So he said to his wife, "Take this sharp scythe, and I'll get down on my hands and knees again, and then just as that woodpecker sticks his head out, you whack it off with the scythe."

So his wife took the sharp scythe, and the peasant got down on all fours. As soon as the bird stuck her head out, the woman struck with the scythe, but she didn't cut off the woodpecker's head: she sliced the peasant's ass. The woodpecker flew off, but the peasant was all covered in blood, and he died.

A–T 248

127. The Fox and the Thrush

There lived by themselves this old man and this old woman, and they had no possessions at all except this boar. The boar went off into the woods to eat acorns. He met up with a wolf. "Boar, boar, where are you going?"

"To the woods, to eat acorns."

"Take me with you."

"I'd take you," he said, "but you see there's this deep, wide pit, and you'd never jump over it."

"Never mind," he said, "I'll jump it."

So off they went. They walked and walked through the forest, and they came to that very pit. "Well," said the wolf, "Jump!" The boar jumped, and he jumped across it. The wolf jumped, and he jumped right into the pit. Well, then the boar ate his fill of the acorns and set off home.

The next day the boar again went into the forest. He met up with a bear. "Boar, boar, where are you going?"

"To the woods, to eat acorns."

"Take me with you," said the bear.

"I'd take you, but there's this deep, wide pit, and you'd never jump over it."

"Not to worry," he said, "I'll jump it."

So they came up to this pit. The boar jumped, and he jumped right over it. The bear jumped, and he got himself right into the pit. The boar ate his fill of acorns and then set off home.

On the third day the boar again went into the forest to eat some acorns. He met up with a cross-eyed hare. "Greetings, boar!"

"Greetings, cross-eyed hare!"

"Where are you going?"

"To the forest, to eat acorns."

"Take me with you."

"No, cross-eyes, there's this pit, and it's deep and wide. You'd never jump over it."

"What do you mean, 'never jump over it'? I'll jump right over it!"

So they set off, and they came to the pit. And the boar jumped, and he jumped right over it. The hare jumped, and he fell into the pit. Well, the boar ate his fill of acorns and set off home.

On the fourth day the boar set off again into the forest to eat some acorns. He met up with a fox, and she also asked the boar to take her with him. "No," said the boar, "there's this deep, wide pit. You'd not be able to jump over it."

"Ha, ha, ha!" said the fox. "I'll jump over it!"

Well, she fell into the pit. So now there were four of them in the pit, and they began to worry about how to get something to eat.

So the fox said, "Let's drone with our voices; whoever can't draw his out, we'll eat!"

So they began to drone. First the hare fell behind, and the fox outlasted all the others. They took the hare, tore him to bits, and ate him up.

But they soon got hungry and again began talking about droning, and they decided that whoever quit first would be eaten. "If I quit first," said the fox, "then eat me! It's all the same!"

So they began drawing out their voices, but this time the wolf quit—he couldn't draw out his voice any more. So the fox and the bear took him, tore him to bits, and ate him up.

So now the fox fooled the bear: she gave him a little meat and hid the rest from him to eat on the quiet. So the bear got hungry again and said, "Cousin, cousin, where are you getting that food?"

"Oh, my dear cousin! Here, stick your paw in your ribs, grab hold of a rib, and then you'll find out how to eat!" So the bear did just that, and with one of his paws he grabbed hold of a rib and punctured himself. So the fox remained alone. Afterward, having polished off the bear, the fox began to get hungry.

A tree stood over the pit, and in that tree a thrush was weaving a nest. The fox sat; she sat in the pit and kept watching the thrush, and she said to her, "Thrush, thrush, what are you doing?"

"I'm weaving a nest."

"Why are you doing that?"

"To hatch some babies."

"Thrush, feed me, and if you don't feed me, I'll eat your babies."

The thrush grieved, the thrush fretted about feeding the fox. She flew into the village and brought her a hen. The fox put that hen away and said again, "Thrush, thrush, did you feed me?"

"I fed you."

"Then give me a drink!"

She flew to the village and brought some water. The fox drank her fill and said, "Thrush, thrush, did you give me a drink?"

"I gave you a drink."

"Then pull me out of this pit."

The thrush grieved, the thrush fretted about how to pull the fox out. So she began throwing sticks into the pit. She threw in so many that the fox crawled out on the sticks to freedom and lay down next to the tree and stretched out. "Well," she said, "did you feed me, thrush?"

"I fed you."

"Did you give me a drink?"

"I gave you a drink."

"Did you pull me out of the pit?"

"I pulled you out of the pit."

"Now amuse me."

The thrush grieved, the thrush fretted about amusing the fox. "I'll fly off," she said, "and you, fox, come after me."

Alright then. The thrush flew off to the village and sat on a rich peasant's gate, and the fox lay down beneath the gate. The thrush began calling out, "Woman, woman, bring me a piece of suet! Woman, woman, bring me a piece of suet!" The dogs jumped out and tore up the fox.

I was there, I drank wine and beer, it flowed over my lips, but not into my mouth. They gave me a blue caftan. I set off, and crows flew around and shouted, "Blue caftan, blue caftan!" I thought they were saying, "Remove the caftan, remove the caftan," so I removed it. So they gave me a red cap. The crows flew around and shouted, "Red cap, red cap," and I thought they were saying, "Wrong cap, wrong cap!" so I took it off and am left with nothing.

A–T 20A + 21 + 248A*

128. The Old Man and the Old Woman

There lived and dwelt an old man, and he had much grain. This old man wove bast shoes. He went to cut some strips. He brought the bast strips home, trimmed them, and put them on the stove to steam overnight. In the morning when they had got up, the old woman went to the stove, and on the stove instead of strips there was a pot of pancakes. The old woman stood up and looked: "Old man! There aren't any strips there, only pancakes."

"Well," he said, "heat up the stove and make the pancakes." They ate their fill of pancakes.

Again the old man went for some bast strips, brought them back, trimmed them, and put them on the stove. And in the morning once more there were pancakes instead of bast strips.

Now this old man had lots of grain, and he lived alongside a stream. So now he said, "Old woman! Why do we need these sheaves of grain? We'll live on pancakes and push the grain into the river." So they went and pushed it in. Then the old man went and took the bast strips and put them on the stove. In the morning he woke up: on the stove were bast strips, not pancakes. And they had neither grain nor pancakes. Once more he went and collected strips and then put them on the stove. In the morning they got up. There were just bast strips, nothing but bast strips. And on the third day the same thing happened.

So the old man said, "We'll have to go by boat and catch the grain sheaves!" So they set off in their boat, and all day they tried to catch the grain, but they caught just one head, and in that head was a single kernel. Then they dried the grain, dried and dried it, until it was dried out, and then they milled it. The old woman made a pudding with the flour and put it on a shelf. A fly came and was eating a bit of it. The old man saw the fly and grabbed hand scales.† The old woman was sitting next to the pudding. The old man wanted to hit the fly with the scales, but instead he struck the old woman and killed her. And he cried, "Oh, my dear wife! I wanted that fly, not my old woman, to die!"

A–T 248B*

---

†*Bezmen:* a notoriously inaccurate hand-held scale that was not legally employed in business transactions.

129. About the Ruff

In Lake Vodlo* a ruff was born: a bristly ruff, a complaining ruff. Spittle-mouthed, bullet-nosed, needlelike tail, a sharp bristle, and an evil countenance.

Now this ruff had come to suffer complete boredom in his Lake Vodlo, so he said to his wife, "Well, wife, all around Lake Vodlo these foolish peasants, these ferocious hunters catch fish; they fish with nets and flail with flails and cross over fords—they give us no rest. Although I've never seen it, I've heard from people that there's this really peaceful lake called Lake Pan. Some really lazy peasants live there; they don't fish, they just boil water—that's where we should go. This lake is really to be recommended. As the old folks used to say, those are a really peaceful people. They live on one side of the lake, on the second side is a mountain, on the third moss, and on the fourth the God Dmitrii.** Now they pray to Dmitrii the One Pleasing God, and they don't care about anything else."

They thought and thought and decided to leave Lake Vodlo and go for the quiet life in their old age. So the ruff, his wife, and their children came together with all their children and swam out of Lake Vodlo into the River Chuyala. In the Chuyala rapids they encountered many difficulties. The ruff went through and led his wife and children from the River Chuyala into the mother River Vodla. They swam along the Vodla and up to the River Panega. The Panega is a quiet, dark river. And the ruff said, "Here we will have a carefree life."

From the River Panega they came to Lake Pan. (Formerly they hadn't known this lake; only recently had it become so renowned.) There the ruff stopped with his followers. He settled down. The children grew up, he married off his sons and daughters, and he left nothing for the bream and perch in Lake Pan to live on.

The bream went away to lesser places; they didn't dare show their noses in the lake; they didn't have enough to eat, not enough to drink,

---

*A lake just east of Lake Onega, in Karelia.

**Peasants often referred to their most popular saints as gods. St. Dmitrii the One Pleasing God was especially popular in the north of Russia. He was a martyr from Saloniki (Thessaloniki) whose saint's day, 8 November, was celebrated in Moscow by the patriarch in the presence of the sovereign. The day itself was dedicated to the souls of the dead, probably because of the aid the Russian armies received from St. Dmitrii at the Battle of Kulikovo Field in 1380.

and some of them died of hunger. They came together to take counsel about what to do with this interloper, how to deal with the ruff. They thought, they wondered, and they wrote a request to the ruff. They got a piece of paper, wrote out the complaint against the ruff, and sent it to the turbot in the White Sea. "Mother fish, turbot, deliberate for us with the ruff; how are we to live, how shall we feed our ourselves?"

The turbot received the complaint and gathered together various fishes for counsel. How should the ruff be brought to court? They chose the salmon. "Salmon fish, swim into Lake Pan and bring the interloper ruff to the court."

The salmon took some minnows, understanding folk, and set off into Lake Pan. Along the path, along the way, they encountered many difficulties, but they searched Lake Pan anyway and stood face to face with the ruff. The salmon said, "Oh, you bristly ruff! The turbot has summoned you to the court in the White Sea."

The ruff spread out his fins and said to the salmon, "So now, salmon fish, your flesh is very pink, your sides are salty, but your head is empty. They transport you five hundred, six hundred, even a thousand versts, but not every man will eat you. The salmon fish is eaten only by high officials, the chiliarchs,* and the like. But I, the poor ruff, am eaten by every poor peasant. He buys and sells me, gives me as alms, carries me home, and gives me to his wife. And his wife will bake oatcakes and make a fish soup. They'll start eating it and praise me: 'Even if it's bony, it's a good soup.' "

The ruff turned his tail toward the salmon and said, "I won't go with you and don't even want to talk with you, and if you want the ruff, then eat me tail first!"

The salmon thought, "How shall I eat the ruff tail first? With his spiny fins, he'll tear out my throat." He turned around and swam back into the White Sea to mother turbot.

The turbot spoke: "Well, salmon fish, did you bring the ruff?"

The salmon answered, "It is difficult to speak with the ruff but even more difficult to swallow him."

They thought, and they made suggestions about whom to send after the ruff. They chose the burbot and instructed him, "Swim swiftly, speak with the ruff intelligently, don't be too long on the way, and bring the ruff back to trial."

---

*Chiliarch: obsolete term for a commander over a thousand men.

The burbot took twenty minnows, understanding folk, and set off from the White Sea to Lake Pan. Along the way, along the road, they encountered many difficulties, but they got to Lake Pan and searched out the bristly ruff. And the burbot said to the ruff, "Now then, bristly ruff, ruff the stoolie, why do you cause so much trouble for so many people and not appear at court before mother turbot?"

The ruff did not like this speech; he became furious; he bristled and said to the burbot, "Fat-bellied burbot, you are soft in the lips, sparse of tooth, and your head is useless. I will not go with you and do not wish to talk with you." He turned his tail around, spread out his fins, and said, "If you want the ruff, eat him tail first."

The burbot took fright. He returned to the White Sea in his own traces. He came up to the turbot and bowed low to her: "Mother turbot, the bristly ruff has cursed me out. My head was spinning with shame. Then he turned tail first to me and spread out his fins and said, 'If you want the ruff, then eat him tail first.' And I feared death and came back here."

The turbot thought deeply. "Whom should we choose to send after the ruff?" They thought, they made suggestions, and then they chose the grayling.

The turbot said, "Grayling, take at least twenty minnows, understanding folk, only bring the ruff to court."

The grayling said, "I don't need anyone; I'll go alone."

So the grayling swam from the White Sea to Lake Pan. Along the way, along the road, he tarried little, he encountered no difficulties, and immediately he sought out the way into Lake Pan. He stood before the ruff and spoke amicably, kindly: "Now, ruff, kind fish, mother turbot fish has sent me. She wants to visit with you and ask you to remain in the White Sea."

The bristly ruff said, "Now then, mother turbot knew whom to send for me. You, fine grayling, have pleased me greatly: You have fine lips, frequent teeth, and white clothing. I shall go with you!"

He took leave of his wife and children and set out on the road with the grayling. They went along the Panega River and were about to enter into the Vodla, but at its very mouth there was a net, and there was no way they could get by that net. They swam and swam, they followed and followed it round, but it was impossible to pass. They stopped to rest, to wait until they took in the net. They waited and waited, and the grayling dozed and fell into the net. The ruff said, "No way do I dare doze here!"

He stuck his nose into the bank and remained quiet. He stayed there a day and a night, and still they did not raise the net, but in the early morning dawn the ruff dozed and fell into the net.

In the morning Bogdan came: "God's brought us a ruff." Foka came and killed the ruff. Savva came and took out a pood† and a half of lard; Rodion came and brought the pot. Nenila came and washed the ruff. Akulina came and cooked him. Vavila came and brought large forks. They raised the ruff up out of the pot, put him out on the plates, and called the collective-farm workers to eat. Vakhrusha came and ate some ruff, and Antropka came and gobbled some (while the collective-farm workers were gathering), and Elizar came, but he just licked some plates, and the priest came, and he got some broth in the face. And with that the tale is finished.

A–T 254A**

130. The Fox and the Crayfish

A fox and a crayfish were standing together and talking.

The fox said to the crayfish, "Let's have a race!"

The crayfish said, "Why not? Let's!"

They began to race. As soon as the fox started, the crayfish grabbed hold of his tail. The fox ran to the goal, and still the crayfish did not let go. The fox turned around to see where the crayfish was. He shook his tail, and the crayfish let himself go and said, "I've been waiting here for you for a long time."

A–T 275

131. The Little Shepherd and the Gadfly

There lived and there dwelt a grandfather and a grandmother. They lived very poorly. And sometimes there was nothing to eat, not a morsel. They

---

†Pood: forty pounds dry weight.

had a son. They decided to send him out to be a shepherd in order some-how to make a living. Once he herded his goats by a rye field, and the goats climbed through the fence into the rye, and there was no way the little shepherd boy could drive them out.

The little shepherd boy sat down on a stone and began to weep about his misfortune. A hare was walking by; he saw the little shepherd boy and asked, "Why are you crying?"

"I can't chase the goats out of the rye."

"I will help you," said the hare and hopped into the field. He ran and nearly wore himself out, but he couldn't drive them out. He sat down next to the little shepherd boy and began to weep.

A fox ran up and asked, "Why are you crying?"

"We can't drive the goats out of the rye."

"I'll drive them out in a flash," said the fox. She ran around the field and nearly wore herself out, but she couldn't drive them out. She re-turned with nothing. They sat down, all three, and began to weep.

A bear came out of the forest, saw them, and asked, "Why are you crying?"

"We simply can't drive the goats out of the rye."

"I'll drive them out for you." The bear ran and exhausted himself, but he couldn't drive them out. He returned with nothing. They sat down, and all four cried.

A gadfly flew by and thought, "They're so big, yet they are crying." "Who has insulted you?"

"We can't drive the goats out of the rye."

"I'll assist you in your misfortune," said the gadfly.

But the little shepherd boy didn't believe it. "Go away. I chased them but couldn't chase them out. The hare chased them but couldn't chase them out, the fox chased them but couldn't chase them out, and the bear chased them but couldn't chase them out."

But the gadfly began to buzz and fly into the field. When the goats saw the gadfly hovering over them, they ran out onto the road. And the little shepherd boy was happy that the goats had been chased out, and he ran after them. He even forgot to say "thank you" to his helpers!

A–T 281A*

132. The Flea and the Fly

It was the month of May, and this flea was living in the village. In the month of June, she set off for the city. A fly met the flea and said, "Well, my lady flea, where have you spent your whole life?"

"Oh, you wicked fly, in those unfortunate parts, in the village."

"And what, my lady, did living in the village not show you?"

"Oh, time passed, you wicked thing!"

"But what time, my lady?"

"Oh, beautiful springtime passed. In the springtime I could find pleasure, but now I've gotten sick."

"And what has made you sick, tell me?"

"When it was splendid spring, I would tickle everyone in a row; but now warm summer has come, and in the warm summer the peasants are tired. One lay down and squashed me."

The fly said, "And what will you find in the city? I've just come from the city."

"Oh, fly, you naughty thing! I'll go to the landlord's, I'll lie down on a soft bed, and there I'll be fed! But oh how awful it was in the village, that peasant squashing me that day, and then pinning me, a little flea, to that board."

And the fly spoke, "Why ever did he pin you down?"

"He, my little father, was just exhausted, so I'll go to the landlord's to a soft bed. Well, now, fly, tell me of your circumstances. Why are you going to the village?"

"I would have died in the city, my lady, having eaten nothing!"

"Why's that, you wild one? It's obvious they don't let you survive there, is that it?"

"Have mercy. You folks in the village, both young and old, stay in the house. The old women look after the little children, and there it'll be just fine for me: she'll put out some porridge with milk, and I, my lady, will be a lodger!"

"You are quite right," said the flea. "Go with God!"

A–T 282A*

133. A Conversation Between a Mosquito and a Gadfly

Once a gadfly asked a mosquito, "Why don't you fly around at midday?"

"Why, it's too hot for me," said the mosquito. "I'm very fat. And why don't you fly around in the rain?"

"Why, I'm so very well dressed," said the gadfly. "I'm afraid I'll get all messed up."

A–T 282B*

134. A Tale About How and With the Aid of What Each Saint Could Most Help Ordinary People

Ilia the Prophet came to Ivan the Faster, for Ivan the Faster had a lot of every sort of amusement: at his place every sort of insect hummed and whirred, and bumblebees buzzed.

And Ilia said to Ivan, "Oh, Ivan, you have so much fun, save a little of this music for my nameday.† Lock them up in a dungeon. Bring them to my nameday celebration, and you'll be bringing a fine gift."

So one by one Ivan the Faster locked up all the insects, and when he was ready to go to the nameday, he unlocked his dungeon, but they had all perished.

He was very sad. Some guests and others were gathered at Ilia's. (Ilia is called the prophet because at his nameday celebration all the guests prophesy as to who can help out the world in what way.) Ilia was waiting for Ivan with his happy music, but he arrived with dead music—they were all in the dungeon, and all had perished.

Then Ivan started out to tell a story about his insects. "Oh, you don't know how sad I am. The gadfly, he was fooling around with the mosquito, and the gadfly said, 'I, mosquito, cannot fly in the rain because I'll shed my dress.' And in answer the mosquito said to him, 'Oh, gadfly,

---

†The nameday, or saint's day, was usually celebrated rather than the birthday.

gadfly, if I had a fur coat and felt boots, I would go with the hunter into the forest in autumn, but in the summer in the heat I cannot fly because I'm very plump. I fly only in cloudy weather or on rainy days.' And then a midge piped up: 'If I weren't afraid of thunder, then I would bite man all over.'

"And then the blackfly said, 'But in the cold I go like an old man or with the slow gait of women. I drink human blood and that makes them melancholy, but the frost breaks my wings, and then I perish.' And then in answer a gnat said, 'All night long I keep people from sleeping, swarming about them, but I don't know how to bite.' And then the fly popped up and said, 'When I drop into the shed in winter, then I give the stock no peace; in summer I eat both man and beast, and I probably have more human blood than you, in the summer from people, and in winter it's from the stock, and I am very satisfied.' "

Then they all moaned that all the insects had perished in the dungeon. "Oh, Ivan, Ivan! You locked them up and didn't look, didn't take care of them. Obviously you killed them by starvation. Otherwise, you'd have given them some bread and water. You didn't tell us earlier, or we would have sent you several people, and they would have brought them bread and water."

Then Ilia the Prophet began to boast: "When I was visiting, Ivan, I grabbed a few mosquitoes, a fly, and a blackfly. They will live with me until deep, dark autumn. If I'd known that the rest would perish at your place, I'd have grabbed a gadfly and every other sort."

Ivan said to him, "Ilia, you don't have to pity me. These insects would all have been very crafty. The gadfly, the gnat, and the mosquito would have devoured both man and beast so that they would have died of melancholy."

So Ilia asked Ivan, "Tell me, Ivan, why are these bugs born? Why do they appear on your nameday and not on mine?"

And Ivan answered him, "The gadfly is born when the alder flowers, it's from the alder flower itself. And if the alder doesn't flower, then there are no gadflies. And the mosquito is born when the willow flowers; and the midge is born when the wild rose flowers; and the gnat is born of the birch, the shaking birch. The blackfly is born from the fir bark when the sap is running; the fly is born when leaves are falling from the aspen. The aspen is very bitter, but the fly is very brazen. There's no peace anywhere from it, not for people in their huts nor for beasts in the sheds."

They finished their conversation and began to boast about the harvest. Ivan pointed out the color of the rye, and Ilia responded to him: "No, Ivan, for three days while you fasted, the color was coming into the rye, but I've outdone you; I knocked all the color from the rye, and for my nameday I've brought all the grain to head and the flax to fiber. I have saved many people from severe hunger, from winter's cold, because on my nameday they start harvesting the rye and threshing it. Families can be fed, and by the new year they can start plowing, and they can pick the flax and soak and ret it. And then the peasants come with the flax, and the women begin to spin and weave. They spin the thread and weave canvas; they cover their naked bodies so they can live without shame or disgrace."

Then St. Frol and St. Lavr began to boast: "We will save men from everything. Whatever the peasants plant in their ground, we shall bring forth strong and vigorous. Potatoes, oats, and grain and all sorts of berries will ripen, and we shall tell people, 'Hurry and gather in what you have sown in the earth; don't let your radishes and turnips be buried beneath the snow, and gather in the mushrooms, the cloudberries, and the lingonberries; then in winter you will know no need for drink, and you will not live in hunger. If you don't take heed in autumn, then you won't get through winter, for note that winter is long and cold, winter has long teeth, and there is much need for many things. If you don't prepare, then just remember: autumn was for that, but we let it slip by.' "

Christmas is known for its snow, and St. Michael's Day for its frost. St. Michael said, "I freeze the ground so that Christmas will have snow and thus bring much good to the peasants. They will put manure on their lands from which the grain will grow in the coming year. They can advantageously go together if they don't have enough of the summer's crop to last the whole year."

The other saints who were guests at Ivan's, but who had nothing much to boast about, answered, "If there were no world, there would be no snow. Both light and snow upon the earth are from the Lord, indeed, by the command of the Lord. The snow will melt and all will grow, just as the Lord has ordered it. The Lord created clever people, and he created the ways and strength for them to farm the earth. If the Lord had not ordained this, then there would be nothing at all for us to do, my friends!"

Then Mikola, St. Nicholas, decided to do some boasting himself: "I cause the leaves to grow on the trees and the roots of the grass to grow."

And St. George said, "I put the water beneath the ice."

And St. Peter said that he showed men the ways to cut the grass and dry it, to rake and turn it, and thus to make hay for the horses and the cows, the sheep and the calves, so that the stock can have food in the winter.

The Dormition, the Most Pure Virgin's holiday, had nothing of which to boast. And Saints Frol and Lavr jumped up with speeches for themselves and for their deeds. The day of the Protective Veil of the Mother of God boasted thus: "I shall cover the house with shining white [snow], the big man and his wife with wealth."

And the army's holiday, autumn Kazan, said, "I give much aid to the tsar and lord, and I send many people into the army who serve the tsar with faith and truth, so they can go to war."

The days of the Presentation and the Annunciation did not boast at all, for few people know those holidays. But the peasants wait all year just for the holiday of the joyful Resurrection of Christ: "The cheese and butter of St. Peter's Day are fine, but the egg of Christ's Day is more beautiful!"

A–T 282B***

135. The Spider

In the olden days, in times very, very long past, during one lovely spring and one hot summer, a great shame was done, a great burden was placed on the world: mosquitoes and midges in great swarms began to bite people and suck their hot blood. Then a spider came, a brave and good knight, and he began to twist his legs and weave his webs in the paths of the mosquitoes and the midges. A dirty fly, in fact a nasty yellow jacket, fell into the spider's web, and the spider began to beat her, torment her, strangle her by the throat. The fly implored the spider, "Little father spider, do not beat me, do not kill me; I would leave behind many orphans who would fly into all the yards and tease the dogs." The spider let her go. She flew away buzzing and announced to all the mosquitoes and midges, "Hey, you mosquitoes and midges, hide under the aspen-tree root; a spider has come who twists his legs and weaves his webs in the paths of mosquitoes and midges; he'll catch you all."

They flew away, hid under the aspen-tree root, and lay as though dead. The spider came and found a cricket, a roach, and a bedbug: "You, cricket, sit on that tuffet and smoke your hookah pipe; you, roach, beat the drum; and you, bedbug, go to the aspen-tree root and spread the news that the valiant spider, the brave knight, is no longer among the living. Say that I was sent to Kazan, that in Kazan my head was cut off on the block, and the block was cleft asunder."

The cricket sat on the tuffet and smoked his hookah pipe; the roach beat the drum, and the bedbug went under the aspen-tree root and said, "Why do you hide, why do you lie as though dead? The valiant spider, the brave knight, is no longer among the living: he was sent to Kazan, and in Kazan his head was cut off on the block, and the block was cleft asunder."

They cheered and rejoiced and made the sign of the cross three times each; they flew off, almost stumbled, and then all fell into the spider's web. He said, "You're nice little things! You should visit me more often, drink beer and wine, and bring me presents."

A–T 283A*

136. About a Spider

A certain man had endured forty mishaps. He had been burned out and become a widower, and he had about decided to quit living. "I'll quit living," he said. He simply couldn't go on living anymore.

He lay down next to a shed and saw a spider spinning its web, and forty times the wind tore it loose. Then on the forty-first try the spider succeeded. On account of that spider the man started to live, and he set off to say prayers for his parents.

A–T 283A***

137. The Louse House

In a certain city there lived a louse in her own hut. Well, along came a flea, Miss Hider. "Who lives in this city, who lives in this Kiev?"

And the louse answered, "In this city, in this Kiev, lives a louse, Miss Creeper. Who are you?"

"I am the flea, Miss Hider. Let me in."

"Come in!"

Well, almost immediately up came Beauty, the bedbug. "Who lives in this city, who lives in this Kiev?"

"In this city, in this Kiev, live the louse, Miss Creeper, and the flea, Miss Hider. Who are you?"

"Beauty, the bedbug. Let me in!"

"Come in!"

Then came a fly, Lady Buzzer. "Who lives in this city, who lives in this Kiev?"

"The louse, Miss Creeper; the flea, Miss Hider; and the bedbug, Beauty. Who are you?"

"I'm the fly, Lady Buzzer. Let me in!"

"Come in!"

Then came a little gray mouse. "Who lives in this city, who lives in this Kiev?"

"The louse, Miss Creeper; the flea, Miss Hider; the bedbug, Beauty; and the fly, Lady Buzzer. Who are you?"

"The gray mouse. Let me in!"

"Come in!"

Then there came a pigeon-toed hare. "Who lives in this city, who lives in this Kiev?"

"The louse, Miss Creeper; the flea, Miss Hider; the bedbug, Beauty; the fly, Lady Buzzer; and the gray mouse. Who are you?"

"I am the hare with the pigeon toes. Let me in!"

"Come in!"

Out from under a bush came a hisser, with warts for legs. "Who lives in this city, who lives in this Kiev?"

"The louse, Miss Creeper; the flea, Miss Hider; the bedbug, Beauty; the fly, Lady Buzzer; the gray mouse; and the hare with the pigeon toes. Who are you?"

"I'm the hisser from under the bush with warts for legs. Let me come in!"

"Come in!"

Then there came a sly fox. "Who lives in this city, who lives in this Kiev?"

"The louse, Miss Creeper; the flea, Miss Hider; the bedbug, Beauty; the fly, Lady Buzzer; the gray mouse; the hare with the pigeon toes; and the hisser with warts for legs. Who are you?"

"I am the sly fox. Let me in!"

"Come in!"

Then came the gray wolf. "Who lives in this city, who lives in this Kiev?"

"The louse, Miss Creeper; the flea, Miss Hider; the bedbug, Beauty; the fly, Lady Buzzer; the gray mouse; the hare with the pigeon toes; the hisser with warts for legs; and the sly fox. Who are you?"

"I am the gray wolf. Let me in!"

"Come in!"

Then a bear came. "Who lives in this city, who lives in this Kiev?"

"The louse, Miss Creeper; the flea, Miss Hider; the bedbug, Beauty; the fly, Lady Buzzer; the gray mouse; the hare with the pigeon toes; the hisser with warts for legs; the sly fox; and the gray wolf. Who are you?"

"I am the bumbling, stumbling bear, oppressor of all. Let me in!"

But when he got in, he crushed them all to death! And there's no more to the tale than that!

A–T 283B*

138. A Conversation in the Swamp

Two frogs lived in a swamp: one at one end, and the other at the other. They met once in the very middle of the swamp and stared at each other, their eyes bulging out. One puffed herself up and puffed herself up and with much importance pronounced, "Monster."

The other was offended and answered, "And who do you think you are?"

The puffed-up frog became angry and shouted to the whole swamp, "Monster! Monster! Monster!"

And the other did not just sit and take it but repeated, "Who do you think you are? And who do you think you are? And who do you think you are?"

Since then whenever they meet, they curse each other roundly. One intones, "MOn-n-nSTer! MOn-n-nSTer!" And the other, "And who do you think you are? And who do you think you are?"

A–T 284*

139. (The Barley and the Wheat)

The barley called out to the wheat, "Let's go to where the gold is born; there you and I will play our games!"

The wheat answered, "You know, barley, your beard is long, but your mind is short. Why should you and I go to play there with the gold? It will come to us soon enough!"

A–T 293E*

140. The Landlord and the Hedgehog

A hedgehog was running along a road and found a coin. At that same time a landowner was riding by. The hedgehog saw him, clutched his coin in his little paws, and said, as if speaking to himself, "I have one, but the landlord has none. I have one, but the landlord has none!"

The landlord found this very displeasing. He ordered his coachman to stop the coach, and he asked the hedgehog, "What is it that you have and I haven't?"

"This coin," said the hedgehog. And he showed the landlord his copper coin.

The landlord became angry and ordered his coachman to take the coin away from the hedgehog.

"So, you really haven't got a single coin," said the hedgehog. "Otherwise, you wouldn't have taken mine."

The landlord in his rage completely lost control of himself. He flung the coin down on the road. "Take it," he shouted, "take your coin, it's no damn use to me."

And the hedgehog laughed. "You're afraid, afraid. That's why you threw the coin, because you're afraid of me. I'll go and tell everyone what a brave one our landlord is!"

Then the landlord jumped out of his coach and went straight to the hedgehog. "Now you'll just find out how afraid I am of you." He stretched out his hand, wanting to grab the hedgehog, but the hedgehog wasn't there. He had made himself into a ball and stuck out all his needles. Just try to touch him! "Alright," threatened the landlord. "I'll still teach you one!"

He got back into his coach and ordered the coachman to drive on, faster. And the hedgehog danced and said to himself, "Our landlord is rich, but he has only a little mind! Our landlord is rich, but he has only a little mind!" That is how the hedgehog had a laugh at a greedy landlord.

A–T 293G*

141. Why There Are Frosts in May

Once March and April met. They talked and discussed the weather. And then March invited April to visit. So on the next day April set off by sleigh. March saw April coming on the sleigh and started raining and blowing, and the roads were washed away. April had to return to his own lands.

After a little time March again invited April to visit. This time April set off by cart. March saw April coming in a cart and started blowing and snowing, and the roads were blocked. It was impossible to ride through the snow or walk through it! Again April was forced to return where he'd come from with nothing.

Then once April met with another neighbor, May. They bowed to each other, as neighbors do, and talked a bit about life and things. April said that he was just then busy with distributing nesting space to the thrushes, and May said that he was busy growing flowers.

After this natural conversation, May invited his guest to visit. April said, "March already invited me once. I set off by cart, and it started snowing; I started out on a sleigh, and it started raining. How will I get there?"

May said, "What a son-of-a-bitch you're mixed up with! With him, first it's rain, then it's snow, and there's just no hospitality."

The next year as their proximity approached, the invitations began again. May said to April, "When you go visiting, take your cart and your sleigh and a boat."

So that's what April did. He got into his cart, and on his cart he put his sleigh and a boat. Having done all this, he arrived to visit March. March was astonished at the arrival of his neighbor. They were enjoying their visit. "But how did you get here? The weather's so awful," March asked with interest.

"Why May taught me how. He ordered me to take a boat and a sleigh." Since then March has been furious with May: from time to time he lets a frost slip through.

A–T 294

142. Why the Moon Has No Clothes

The moon looked down on people from above and thought, "Why are people on earth all dressed and shod, and only I am naked and unclad."

And he thought of sewing himself some clothes. Somehow in the heavens he searched out a tailor, went to him, and asked him to sew him some clothing. The tailor measured him and began sewing the clothes. A long time or a short time, much time or little time passed, but then the moon came for the clothing. The tailor tried it on him, but the clothing was too narrow and short.

The tailor thought and thought, then he shook his head and said, "Apparently, I've made an error. I've gotten old, I don't see well, and I didn't see things properly." So he sat down to work again. A long time or a short time, much time or little time passed until the agreed-upon date, and the moon came for the clothes. They fitted them and again they were too small. The tailor looked and looked and then said, "Apparently, I've again made an error."

And so again he sat down to cut out and sew. At the appointed time, for the third time, the moon came to the tailor for the clothes. The tailor saw that it was a fat moon coming to him, at least twice as wide as the clothing he had sewed for him. The tailor became frightened and thought, "What is to be done? I must flee!" No sooner said than done, and he tore off running.

The moon came, but there was no tailor. He searched and searched for him, but he still couldn't find him. And since that time there has been no tailor up there, and the moon still goes about the heavens naked and unclad.

A–T 294*

143. The Bladder, the Straw, and the Shoe

A bladder, a hay straw, and a shoe went to chop wood in the forest. They came to a river and did not know how to cross it. The shoe said to the bladder, "Bladder, let us swim across it on you."

The bladder said, "No, shoe, instead let's let the hay straw stretch itself from shore to shore, and we'll just walk over it."

The hay straw stretched itself across the water. The shoe walked onto it, and the straw broke. The shoe fell into the water, and the bladder laughed and laughed until it burst.

A–T 295

144. (The Bubble and the Beard)

Two old men were walking along a road, and they stepped into an empty hut to warm themselves by the stove. They were a bubble and a beard.

The bubble sent the beard off: "Go and get some fire!" So the beard went off and blew on a little fire, which set him alight, and then the bubble laughed and laughed, fell off the stove, and burst.

A–T 295

145. The Bun

Now an old man and an old woman lived together. He said, "Old woman, something makes me feel like eating some buns. You haven't any flour in your bin, have you?"

She went and scraped around and baked several buns. She pulled them out of the oven. One bun fell and started rolling away. And he said in a human voice, "I got away from the woman, and I got away from the old man!" And on he rolled.

A wolf chanced to meet him. "Bun, bun so sweet! I'm going to eat you."

"Don't eat me," he said. "I got away from the old man, and I got away from the old woman, and from you, wolf, I'll get away, too." And he rolled on.

A hare chanced to meet him. "Bun! Sweet little bun! I'm going to eat you."

"Don't eat me," he said. "I got away from the old man, I got away from the old woman, I got away from the wolf, and I'll easily get away from you, hare!" And he rolled on.

A bear chanced to meet him. "Bun! Sweet little bun. I'm going to eat you."

"Don't eat me," he said. "I got away from the old man, I got away from the old woman, I got away from the wolf, I got away from the hare, and I'll get away from you, bear." The bear took a swing with his paw, but the bun just rolled on.

A fox chanced to meet him. "Bun! Sweet little bun. You were baked with butter, made from the scrapings, sing me a little song, and I'll eat you!"

"Oh," he said, "don't eat me! I got away from the old man, I got away from the old woman, I got away from the wolf, I got away from the hare, I got away from the bear, and from you, fox, I'll get away easily."

The fox said, "Bun! Sweet little bun. Sit here on my nose and sing a little song."

"I'll sit and sing."

"Ah," she said, "I'm deaf, sit here on my tongue." The bun sat down and sang a little song as the fox widened her mouth and swallowed up the bun.

The old man went to look for the bun. He asked everyone whether they had seen a bun. "We saw him," they said. "He was sitting on the fox."

"Oh, that scoundrel, she's eaten him, so no one else could."

But she slept and slept, did the fox. So the old man loaded his rifle and shot the fox and tore open her belly, and there was the bun! He carried him home, brought the fox, too, and brought the bun and brought water. Could he be revived? He bathed him, he washed him, but the bun did not come to life. "Better we take the bun and eat it!" And they ate the bun, they drank some tea, and that's the whole tale.

A–T 296*

146. The Mushrooms

A mushroom thought it up; the pine mushroom, sitting beneath a little oak tree, gazing at all the other mushrooms, resolved it. He began to give orders: "Come here, you boletes, come and fight me!"

But the boletes refused: "We are noble lady mushrooms; we will not go to war!"

"Come here, you saffron mushrooms, come and fight me!"

But the mushrooms refused. "We are rich men, ill-equipped to go to war."

"Come here, you coral mushrooms, come and fight me!"

But these coral mushrooms also refused: "We are gentlemen's chefs; we do not go to war."

"Come here, you honey mushrooms, come and fight me!"

But the honey mushrooms refused: "Our legs are too thin; we cannot go to war."

"Come here, you milky caps, come and fight me!"

"We milky caps are a friendly lot; we'll go to war!"

And so that's how King Pea fought with the mushrooms.

A–T 297B

147. The Quarrel of Two Frosts

Once a frost froze a landlord in a bearskin and boasted about it before another frost, whereupon the latter answered him, "Just you try to freeze a barge hauler in a winter jacket."

So the first frost said to the latter, "That's no big deal; I'll freeze your barge hauler as quick as a wink." So he started freezing him. But the barge hauler resisted, hopping from foot to foot, and he reached the tavern, and there for a few coins he gulped down about a quarter of a measure, and after that he left the tavern, and the frost began freezing him harder than ever before. The barge hauler hopped from foot to foot, and then he took off his gloves and put them under his belt. When the frost started working on him even more fiercely than before, the barge hauler took off his cap, and so the frost left him alone.

A–T 298A

148. The Frost, the Sun, and the Wind

The frost, the wind, and the sun were walking along. They were walking, the three of them, down the road. And they met a peasant. He had a gray beard and white hair. "Greetings, little peasant!"

"Greetings."

"So, how long have you been living on earth already?"

"Oh, I've been living for seventy-five years."

"Well, today we've a pretty harsh frost, don't you think?"

"So what if the frost is harsh," said the peasant. "The frost won't do anything to a peasant. However much it frosts, a peasant can still warm himself. A peasant isn't much bothered by frosts. But," he said, "if there's frost and then the wind starts to blow, that's hard to deal with. But if the wind comes from the other direction, then it will cut through the frosts."

The frost questioned him once again: "Oh? How's that, how does it cut through the frosts?"

"Oh, it cuts through them easily," he said. "If it blows strongly, then it aids the frost, and it's a bit cold for the peasant. But if there's a frost, and the wind blows from the other direction, then the frost goes away. And then, too, there's the sun. If the sun's shining, then it takes on both the frost and the wind."

So the peasant went on toward the village. And the others went on ahead. But the frost was a little insulted. And he spoke: "Well, I'm going to freeze that little peasant. He won't get to the village."

But the wind said, "If you start freezing him, I'll turn and come from the other direction."

And the sun said, "I'll heat him, I'll bake him, so you won't have to do anything."

The peasant had walked off just a little way from them. The frost was already on his beard and on his hair, too. His hands in their mittens were starting to freeze, and his feet were beginning to freeze. It looked as though the peasant would perish. (The frost was really attacking him.) The peasant spoke: "It cannot be that you would kill me on the road! Even if my hands are frozen, I still have my blood." He pulled his mittens off his hands, took some snow, and began to rub it in his hands. He wiped the snow off and put his hands back in his mittens. It seemed warmer. And at the same time he went faster and faster. "The frost still hasn't done anything to me."

So the frost attacked him even more. The wind noticed that he was walking toward the peasant. He turned toward the peasant's back and began to drive him on. The peasant said, "The wind has turned to blow from the other direction, and now it's easier for me to walk. Those passersby just asked who was stronger: the frost, or the wind, or the sun. I answered them that you can save yourself from a frost if you don't fall asleep. But then the wind could knock you down if you dozed off, or it might carry you along as it is carrying me right now."

Then the righteous sun started shining. The peasant soon began to sweat (that means, the sun has won). But anyway, the frost had frozen one of his ears and a piece of his nose.

The peasant came into the village. He asked for a place to spend the night. He climbed up onto the stove to get warm. When he had gotten into his warm spot and sat there for a bit, his ear and nose started stinging. He said, "Oh, that damned frost! It froze me nonetheless."

In the morning the peasant got up. Those others appeared. "Would it be possible to warm up?"

"Of course you can, please do!" answered the host.

So they all sat down on the wooden benches—the wind, the frost, and the sun—and they started talking. And the frost asked, "Well, old man, where are you from? Are you a local?"

The old man answered, "I'm not local."

"But why are you sitting on the stove there?"

"I'm sitting on the stove until the sun warms up, then I'm going on. You see, yesterday I was walking; I'd walked about six versts, and it was warm, and then that damned frost got to me, and the wind blew in my face. Well, anyhow, I thought I'd perish. I had already rubbed by hands with snow, but still the frost got to me. He'd already gotten in my beard, and he'd gotten into my hair. It was like being hit from both sides. The wind would let up and then come back. Suddenly," he said, "the wind turned and blew from the other direction, almost carrying me away. It pushed me on ahead. And then the righteous one started shining. And I got warm. Then I halted, had a smoke, and said, 'That frost has gone off somewhere'!"

The passersby left the hut, and the old man remained inside. The sun began to shine. The old man once again got ready to set off. He came out, looked at the sun, and said, "Even though there is frost, there's sun, too, and so it'll be easier and I'll push off. Now I can walk bravely, for the frost will do nothing, and there's no wind, it's quiet outside."

The sun, the frost, and the wind went out onto the highway. And the sun spoke to the frost: "So, they believe more in me than in you."

And the wind said, "And they believe more in me than in the frost."

And the frost said, "How's that?"

So the sun spoke: "I light up in winter and summer. In winter I come out lower and I heat less. In the summer I come higher, so that I can almost bake even a man. Well, when I come, I bring gifts from the very highest, and then the wind gets up and cools everything off. Then suddenly clouds spring up and decide who will be hot and who will be cold. They tell the wind, 'Today some wind is needed,' but he's not there. The next day people say, 'It would be fine if there were no wind.' But the wind hears what people say, and he sticks out his thick lips and starts blowing quietly, and then stronger and stronger, and then to the point where he upturns trees and tears the boards off roofs and knocks people off their feet. But you, frost, are a force only in winter. You freeze the rivers, the land, and the trees. But then no one has any insults for you. No matter how you try, the wind can do everything, and you can do nothing. The peasants can always save themselves from you."

The frost said, "Watch how I freeze that landlord! That landlord has two fur coats on, but I'll freeze him!"

And the sun said, "Sure, you can freeze the landlord, but the peasant is anybody's guess."

The landlord rode out from his estate toward the city. He had a pair of horses. The frost crawled right into the landlord's fur coat. The landlord scrunched himself up and soon fell asleep. Frost froze that landlord. And then he said to the sun, "Just look! The landlord is finished! And I haven't even asked the wind to help me freeze him."

And then the sun said, "Well, now then, go on, over there's a peasant with his bullock going to the woods for firewood. His fur coat is ripped. There's room for both the frost and the wind in that fur coat! You go try to freeze him."

The frost set off toward the peasant in his ragged fur coat. It was still about a verst to the woods. The frost made his way into the holey fur coat. He made his way in and sat in the coat. The peasant was pretty cold already. He started driving his little bullock. But the bullock didn't go very fast. He drove into the woods. In the woods the wind quieted down. "Now in the woods it will be warmer," he said.

The peasant stopped his bullock, took off his fur coat, took his axe and started chopping wood. But the frost stayed in the fur coat. He kept thinking, "I'll still get you somehow."

The peasant chopped his wood. He went over to the coat. The fur coat was all white, like snow. He took a stick and beat it from one side. Then he turned to the other side. And he beat it from that side. He broke the sides of the frost, put on the coat, and set off.

And then the sun said, "Well, did you freeze the peasant?"

The frost was forced to admit, "One can never freeze the peasant and his horse."

A–T 298A + 298A*

149. The Sun, the Wind, and the Moon

There lived and dwelt this old man and his old woman. Now once the old man went to the barn for some grain, and he didn't see that there was a hole in the bag. The old man carried the bag home, but all the grain trickled out along the way. The old man thought, "If only the moon looked out now, I could gather up all the grain." He had just thought this when the moon suddenly looked out. And the old man promised to give him his oldest daughter in marriage if he did it. The moon looked out, and the old man gathered all the grain back up in the bag, carted it home, and the next morning handed over his eldest daughter.

A week, perhaps it was two, passed by, and the old man went to cut grass. He cut and he cut, and then there was such a downpour! And the old man said, "Oh, if only the sun would look out now, I would give my middle daughter in marriage to the sun!" He had just thought this when the sun looked out, bright and hot, and dried up all the old man's grass.

Well, maybe another week passed, but maybe it was two, and then the old man went to the field for the hay. He came and raked all the hay, and then he thought, "If only the wind were to blow, all my hay would fly home by itself!" He had barely thought this when a whirlwind came up! The old man's hay was lifted up and carried off home. And so the old man gave his youngest daughter in marriage to the wind.

He and the old woman were left alone, just the two of them. They lived, and life went on, but it was boring in the house, no one laughed, no one played. The old man said to the old woman, "Well, old woman, I'll visit my oldest son-in-law, the moon's son, and our eldest daughter."

So he went there, and the daughter asked him, "Well, father, perhaps you'd like to steam in the bath?"

"What do you mean, bath? It's night outside. Better give me a place to lie down and sleep."

"No, father, let's go to the bathhouse; you'll steam a bit after the journey."

So they went. The old man went into the bathhouse and said, "Give me a light, daughter, otherwise it's too dark to wash in there."

But the daughter said, "Don't worry about it, father, just go into the bathhouse."

The old man came to the bathhouse, and the moon's son stuck a finger in a crack, and it became as light as day in the bathhouse. The old man had a good wash and steam and then went home the next day. He came and demanded of his old woman, "Woman, heat up the bath."

"What do you mean, old one? It's already evening. How can we go to the bathhouse if it's so dark?"

"Heat it up," he said, "and don't chatter!"

So the woman heated up the bath, and she clambered in. She started to light a splinter, but the old man shouted, "Don't touch that splinter, don't waste it; just go into the bathhouse, take your birch branch, and climb up on the ledge."

So the woman climbed up onto the ledge, and the old man stuck his finger in the crack, but it was dark in the bathhouse! No matter how the old man tried—this finger, that one, he tried all his fingers—it remained dark in the bathhouse. The old woman started down off the ledge, but she fell and bruised herself. Well, there was enough cursing for a second day for the old man! Poor old man!

Well then, a week passed, and maybe it was two, but then the old man got ready to go to his middle daughter. And the old woman said, "Go, go on, old man, go!"

She packed up a satchel of bread for him, and the old man set off. He was behind the sun for a whole day. Toward evening, just as the sun was about to hide behind a hill, the old man finally caught up to him. The sun said, "Why have you come, old man?"

And the old man said, "It was boring in our house, so I've come to visit you."

And then his middle daughter ran out and greeted her father and said, "Well now, father, what would you like to eat? Perhaps you'd eat some hot pancakes?"

But the old man said, "What do you mean 'hot pancakes' if it's already evening outside?"

"Why not, father, we can make hot pancakes at any time."

The sun sat down on the floor, the daughter mixed up the pancake batter and poured it onto his head, and the pancakes just flew off the sun—they flew off so soft, red, and buttery! The old man ate his fill. He slept the night or maybe he spent a week, and then he went home. He came home in the evening and demanded some pancakes of his old wife, but the old woman said to him, "What do you mean, old man, where can I get hot pancakes, if I only heat the stove in the morning?"

"Never mind," he said. "You mix up the pancakes."

The old woman mixed up the pancakes in a mixing bowl. The old man sat down on the floor and said to the old woman, "Pour the batter onto my bald spot!"

The old woman said, "Have you gone mad, old man, or what?"

"Pour it," he said.

The old woman began pouring the pancake batter onto the old man, and she covered the old man all over, but not a single pancake did she cook. The next day she forced the old man into the river to bathe.

Well, another week went by there, and then the old man went off to visit his third daughter. He came to the wind. He visited and visited, but they didn't show him anything amazing at all, and so he started to get ready to go home. And then his daughter said, "Why should you walk, father? My husband will take you; you'll be home ever so quickly."

"And how will he take me?"

"Let's go."

The daughter came and told her husband that the old man was ready to go home. They went out onto the shores of a vast lake, and she threw a kerchief onto the water and said, "Get in, father!"

The old man got in, and the wind blew so that in an instant the old man turned up home. He came home and said to his wife, "Woman, let's go fishing."

"Where do you think you're going, old man, it's night!"

"Come on, listen to me."

So they went. The old woman started putting out the boat, she brought the oars up, and then the old man said, "Don't you dare touch anything. Let all that stay here. Just take that kerchief from your head and throw it onto the water."

The old woman said, "Have you gone completely crazy, old man?"

"Throw it down, I'm telling you!"

The old woman threw her kerchief onto the water, and the old man said, "Climb onto the kerchief!"

The old woman said, "No, I won't; you try to get in first!"

So the old man jumped and went right into the water up to his head. The old woman was forced to pull him out, and did she shake him up! Since then the old man hasn't gone visiting his sons-in-law, and he hasn't been performing any miracles at home either. And that's the whole tale; there are no more lies!

A–T 299* (552B)

150. Heaven and Earth

A peasant had some boots. The tops were whole, but underneath there were no soles. Heaven spoke: "The peasant is walking about in boots, and his boots are fine."

But the earth responded, "No, the peasant is going about barefoot."

"How barefoot, when he has boots on?"

The earth said, "I can see more than you can. You are looking from up above, but he's walking over me, and he is stepping so lightly because he has no soles, so he is barefoot."

A–T 299*

COMMENTARIES TO TALES

1. A–T 1 + 2 + 3 + 4 + 43 + 30 + 170 + 61. Recorded by A.N. Afanas'ev in Bobrov, Voronezh District, 1848. Published in Afanas'ev *Narodnye russkie skazki,* 1. Consists of A–T 1 (Fox steals fish from cart), A–T 2 (Wolf at the icehole), A–T 3 (Fox puts dough on her head), A–T 4 (Beaten carries unbeaten), A–T 43 (The bast or ice hut), A–T 30 (The wolf falls into a pit—thanks to the fox), A–T 170 (For a rolling pin—a goose), and A–T 61 (The fox as confessor). A–T 1 and 2 are often combined throughout the world. A–T 1, 2, 3, and 4 are combined by the Russians, Ukrainians, and Belarusians. Combining eight folktale types into one is unique to the Russians. Note that not all eight types are represented in the tale equally well.

2. A–T 6. Published in Shastina, *Russkie skazki vostochnoi Sibiri,* no. 40. Recorded in 1981 from F.A. Balagurov, village of Verkh Iag'e, Shelopugin District, Chita. Otherwise, unknown in East Slavic.

3. A–T 1 + 2 + 3 + 4 + 8. Published in XVI–XVIIIC. Tales, no. 54, from *Staraia pogudka,* 1794–95. Several unusual features mark this tale: a fishmonger rather than a peasant is the victim of the fox's trickery, the wolf attaches a basket to his tail and lowers it into the water, and the wolf wishes to turn into a bird. Scholars seem agreed that the tale is a rendering of an authentic Russian tale, however. In the eighteenth-century edition the tale is told in a rather florid literary style that is far removed from peasant speech.

4. A–T 9 + 154. Afanas'ev 24. Recorded in Lipetskii District, Tambov. Sometimes catalogued as A–T 1030 + 154, where the peasant divides the harvest with a devil.

5. A–T 15. Recorded in Pudozh Village in 1946 from F.F. Kabrenov, fifty-two years of age. Published in Pudoga Tales 23. Although the cunning fox is a common trickster of the North Russian tales, it is not often that a tale is entirely made up of one episode or type: several are usually woven together.

6. A–T 20A + 21. Afanas'ev 29. Of unknown provenance. The combination of 20A (Beasts in a pit) with 21 (Eating one's own intestines) is very common among the East Slavs.

7. A–T 20A + 21. From Balashov 99. Recorded from Mariia Fedorovna Zaborshchikova, fifty-three years of age, in 1961, in the village of Varzuga.

8. A–T 20A. Pomerantseva 17. Recorded in 1948 in Bashkiria by E.V. Pomerantseva from U.I. Peskova.

9. A–T 20C + 20A + 21. Balashov 70. Recorded in 1957 from Evdokiia Dmitrievna Koneva, fifty-nine years of age, in Varzuga.

10. A–T 20C. Mitropol'skaia 114. Recorded in 1967 from U.I. Pavlov, of the village of Burbiakliai, Lithuania.

11. A–T 20D*. Zelenin, Viatka Tales 111. This is the only recorded Russian version of this type. Recorded by a teacher, Aleksandra K. Shakhova, in the Orlov District of Viatka.

12. A–T 1 + 2 + 3 + 4 + 30. Originally published by Ivan Vanenko, *Narodnye russkie skazki i pobaski,* in two books, in 1847–49, reprinted in XIX C. Tales 38. Vanenko apparently enlarged his source by adding a host of details, but unlike many of his "revised editions," this one is relatively free of the patronizing, moralizing comments of its editor.

13. A–T 31. Published in Bardin, 191. Recorded by Stepan Afanas'evich Nalivkin from Agafiia Kireevna Dushkina in the village of Aleksandrovka, Buzuluk District (Orenburg).

14. A–T 33. One of the many stories told by Filipp Pavlovich Gospodarev and included in N.V. Novikov's 1941 edition of his tales, no. 76. This is the only version known in Russian.

15. A–T 35B*. Copied down in Stanitsa Umakhan-Iurtovskaia (Caucasus) by the teacher V. Kikot and published in Caucasian Miscellany, 1893, XV, p. II, no. 4, p. 189. The anticlerical humor is not typical of animal tales.

16. A–T 36. From the collection of censored stories, published by Afanas'ev in Geneva. Afanas'ev, Secret Tales 1.

17. AT 218B* + 1889K + 37 + 154. Published in Afanas'ev 21, but nothing is known of the origins. The type is well-known throughout Europe and Western Asia.

18. A–T 41. Published by Zelenin, Viatka Tales 119. A teacher from Elabug in 1914–15 set his pupils the task of recording one folktale each. These were then sent to Zelenin, who eventually published ten of the fifty or so he received. This charming tale was apparently recorded by B. Karasev in the Elabug District.

19. A–T 43 + 15 + 1. Published in Zelenin, Perm' Tales 88.

20. A–T 43*. Recorded in Efimenko, 7. This is the only known version of this variant among the East Slavs.

21. A–T 44*. Published in Afanas'ev 28. Recorded by O.L. Volkonidin in the Chernoiar District of Astrakhan. This is the only known Russian variant, although it is frequent in Ukrainian. This is the only tale in the Russian tradition in which the fox portrays a truly noble character. A similar plot lies behind the medieval Latin *Isengrimus.*

22. A–T 47A. Published in the journal *Zhivaia starina* in 1912, this is the only known Russian version of this tale. It is better known in Ukrainian and Belarusian.

23. A–T 47C*. The editors of SUS state that this is "a retelling from memory." It was published in Khabarovsk in 1939 by Kucheriavenko, pp. 58–59.

24. A–T 51A*. Published in BRFS, vol. I: 15, and in Komovskaia 5. Known only in this version among the East Slavs. Komovskaia's tales are from the Nizhnii Novgorod region of the upper Volga.

25. A–T 56A. Published in Akimova 414. Recorded in 1937 from Misha Ovsiannikov, eleven years old, in the village of Bel'shchino, Makarovsk District of Saratov.

26. A–T 56A*. Recorded in Chapama (White Sea coast) from Aleksandra Vasil′evna Strelkova in 1962 and published in Balashov 143.

27. A–T 56A. Recorded in 1956 in Konda, Trans-Onegin District, from K.A. Surikova and published in Zaonezh′e Tales 16.

28. A–T 56B. Recorded by a monk, Makarii (who was a member of the Russian Imperial Geographic Society), in Vasil′ev District of Nizhnii Novgorod. This is the only known Russian variant, although it is more common in Ukrainian. It is unusual in that the fox goes unpunished. The tale is believed to derive from the same source as 56A and likely is of Eastern provenance. An Arabic version, known from the eighth century, *Kalila wa Dimna,* was itself derived from the Sanskrit *Panchatantra.* It is worth noting that the three occupations the fox proposes to teach the young woodpeckers are all closely associated with magicians and storytellers, especially the *skomorokhi:* blacksmith, cobbler, and tailor. First published in Afanas′ev 32.

29. A–T 57. The only Russian recording of this tale was made in Perm′ in 1848 and published most recently in BRFS, vol. I: 25. The type is more common in Ukrainian.

30. A–T 60. Published in Afanas′ev 33, from a Tver′ District recording. A tale well-known throughout Europe, Africa, and North America and in the Near East, its written history may be dated from Aesop's collection.

31. A–T 61A. Published by Balashov 153, this version of the popular tale was recorded from Fedora Stepanovna Nizovtseva, sixty-two years of age, in the village of Pialitsa in 1962. It is very close to Afanas′ev 16. The subject can be dated from the seventeenth century both in written form and in a fresco surviving in the Holy Trinity Church of the Georgian Mother of God in Nikitniki, Moscow.

32. A–T 61A. Published in Afanas′ev 16, but originally from Perm′ where it was recorded in 1846 from a ninety-year-old skilled factory worker, P.S. Kazakov. The tale in a variant close to this was found objectionable by the imperial censors, who detected anticlerical themes.

33. A–T 61A. This tale is one of many recorded in the Voronezh District in the 1930s from "Kupriianikha" (A.K. Baryshnikova). Very similar to Afanas′ev's tale, it carries the imprint of the narrator in the rhythmical language of the original and the humor. Published recently by Pomerantseva 3.

34. A–T 61B. Published by Pomerantseva in *Russkie narodnye skazki* (Pomerantseva 20), from a version recorded in 1949 from U.I. Peskova in Bashkiria. This humorous telling of the tale owes much to printed versions.

35. A–T 62. Afanas′ev, 31. This tale was originally recorded in Tver′ District. Only one other version is known in Russian, but it is known in Belarusian, Ukrainian, and especially in several Caucasian traditions. The oldest written version is to be found in Aesop's collection.

36. A–T 60 + 68A + 1. Originally recorded in Tikhvin in 1853, this tale was published in Smirnov 69. The combination of tale types is not common. The ending of the tale has not survived.

37. A–T 68B. Published by Kretov (5) in a collection of recent tales from the Voronezh District. In Russian this tale type is often found in conjunction with other tales featuring the cunning fox.

38. A–T 2 + 3 + 158 + 68B. Smirnov's tale 225 was told by Praskovia Ploni in 1913 in Leka, Egor′ev District, Riazan District.

39. A–T 68C. This is another "recent" recording from the Voronezh District published in Kretov 3.

40. A–T 70. This little known tale was published by Chudinskii, p. 136b, in 1864. One Afanas'ev tale contains parts of A–T 70, but it is otherwise unknown in Russian.

41. A–T 70**. From Karnaukhova 99. The tale was told by Evdokim Sukharev, twelve years of age, in the village of Shotova-Gora, Pinega. Sukharev claimed he had read this and many other tales in schoolbooks. The tale is not known in any other East Slavic variant.

42. A–T 76. From Kupriianikha 31. This tale is known occasionally in Ukrainian, but this is the only Russian recording.

43. A–T 81. The only Russian recording is from the famous Samara storyteller Abram Novopol'tsev. Published in Sadovnikov 56 and more recently by Pomerantseva 15.

44. A–T 83*. The only East Slavic recording of this tale is by Pomerantseva in Bashkir Tales 9.

45. A–T 85. Unpublished. Recorded by T.I. Sen'kina and T.S. Kurets from I.P. Perkhina, fifty years of age, village of Avdeevo, Pudoga District, 1976. The manuscript is Archive of the Karelian Filial of the ANSSSR, Fond no 1, index 1 r.f., collection 98: 43, sheets 196–198, Petrozavodsk, Karelia. The tale is not listed in SUS. This is the first publication of the tale.

46. A–T 87A*. A unique rendering of this rare tale in Gospodarev 80.

47. A–T 88*. Not recorded in SUS. From Matveeva 37. Recorded in the settlement of Shelopugino, Chita District, from F.A. Balagurov.

48. A–T 100. Smirnov 68, has preserved this tale from Tikhvin, recorded in 1853. It is popular among the East Slavs, although the bear is the more common animal than the wolf. It is frequently in combination with A–T 101. Known in written tradition from the Aesop collection.

49. A–T 122A + 100. Nikiforov 34. He recorded this variant in the Zaonezh'e village of Ostrechovo from Marfa Rodionovna Kozniova, aged sixty-five, in 1926.

50. A–T 101. Mitropol'skaia 27. Recorded in Lithuania in 1972 from B.A. Bezzubova, sixty years of age.

51. A–T 102. Recorded in Eastern Lithuania in 1970 by Mitropol'skaia 3, from P.O. Vanagene, forty-eight years of age. This is the only Russian recording.

52. A–T 103. This version was recorded by F.V. Tumilevich 1961:1. It was told by D.E. Belikova, of the Novo-Nekrasovskii Khutor, in 1955.

53. A–T 103A. Nikiforov 33.

54. A–T 106* + 61A. Afanas'ev 17. This tale was recorded by the folklorist Iakushkin in the Tula District.

55. A–T 113*. Published in BRFS, I: 66, from Chistov, 197–98. Very likely borrowed into Russian from the West.

56. A–T 113C**. The vulgar nature of this tale prevented its publication until very recently. First published in the secret tales attributed to Afanas'ev, Secret Tales 7.

57. A–T 113G* (tent.) Not in SUS. Told by N. Boiarkin in 1980 and first published in Shastina 41.

58. A–T 116. Recorded in Elabug in the summer of 1925 by the student Sobornova and published in M. Vasil'ev, vol. IV, p. 221.

59. A–T 101 + 117*. This is a modern version told by the versatile Siberian storyteller "Magai," E.I. Sorokovikov 32.

60. A–T 118. Magai 33.

61. A–T 122A + 122M* + 121. Afanas´ev, 56. This tale was originally in the collection of the folklorist and lexicographer Vladimir Dal´. It is also included in Afanas´ev's collection of legends, 32.

62. A–T 121. Published by V.K. Sokolova in a collection of tales from Riazan´. Recorded in 1967 from Ekaterina Nikitichna Mezhdriakova, seventy-four years of age, largely illiterate.

63. A–T 122A. Recorded from Kupriianikha 32. Also published in BRFS I: 41.

64. A–T 122A + 122M*. Published in Afanas´ev 55, source unknown. The first tale type is attested from many parts of the world since the late Middle Ages, but the second is known only in the Baltic district (among Russians, Poles, Letts, Estonians, and rather oddly among the Uzbeks and Tatars of Central Asia). A–T 122M* is invariably found in conjunction with another type. The episode of the piglets' baptism is very typically Russian.

65. A–T 122D. Akimova published this Saratov tale (Akimova 430), which is the only known Russian version of it.

66. A–T 122M*/N*. Published in Kretov 2.

67. A–T 123. Published in Afanas´ev 54. Collected in 1848 in Lipetsk District, Tambov. The wolf's visit to the blacksmith is a popular feature of the East Slavic versions of this tale.

68. A–T 125 + 103. Published in Afanas´ev 44. Originally recorded in Gorokhovetsk District, Vladimir. An especially common tale in the Finnish tradition, but known sporadically throughout Eurasia and America.

69. A–T 125. Recorded by Onchukov 254, from Il´ia Nikolaevich Makarov, aged fifty-one in 1907, in the Arkhangel´sk District.

70. A–T 125E*. Kursk Tales, pp. 66–67. Recorded in Katyrinsk Village, Lenin District, Kursk. This is the only recording of this tale in East Slavic. It is odd that the great popularity of the hedgehog in literature, since the thirteenth century, is not reflected in folktales. The prickly little creatures make but rare appearances.

71. A–T 130D* + 126A*. Published in Afanas´ev 45, but the origins are unknown. The first part of the tale is rather uncommon except among the Latvians and Belarusians. The combination represented here is encountered in both Russian and Belarusian.

72. A–T 130 + 130B. Published in Afanas´ev 63. This version was recorded by the writer I.I. Lazhechnikov in the Tver´ District. Especially noteworthy parallels have been cited from the Sanskrit *Panchatantra* and *Shukasaptati* (Book of the Parrot).

73. A–T 130 + 130B + 130A. Published in Afanas´ev 65. This is a very rare combination of tale types, and especially odd is the marriage of the fool, the son of the owner of the animals.

74. A–T 130*. Karnaukhova 86. Recorded from a twelve-year-old girl, Dunia Riabova, in the village of Sura-Pogost, Pinega. No other East Slavic versions are known.

75. A–T 130**. This tale was recorded in the Kuibyshev District and is otherwise unknown in East Slavic. Kuibyshev Dialect 45.

76. A–T 130B. Onchukov 149. This tale was published from D. Georgievskii's manuscript of tales from the Petrozavodsk District dated 1890.

77. A–T 130D*. Viatka Tales 83. Collected by a teacher, E.A. Kostrova, in 1898 in the village of Sharanitsa of Viatka District.

78. A–T 151. Published by Zelenin in Viatka Tales 52. Recorded from A. Kh. Selezenov from the village of Kliuchi. This is a rare tale from the Russian north.

79. A–T 152. Published in part in Afanas'ev 48, and the Secret Tales 5. The Russian imperial censors permitted the publication of the first part only, for reasons that are obvious.

80. A–T 152C. From Afanas'ev's Secret Tales 3.

81. A–T 154. Published in Mitropol'skaia 25, in a version told by A.K. Korablikova, eighty years of age, in 1969. From the district of Vilnius, Lithuania. This is a very common tale throughout the East Slavic territory.

82. A–T 1030 + 154. Afanas'ev 23. From the Tula District. The oldest printed version is believed to be the Spanish tale in the collection *El conde Lucanor* compiled by Juan Manuel in the late fourteenth century.

83. A–T 154**. The only known version of this tale. Published in *Zhivaia starina,* 1911, I, 124–26. This tale contains some extremely archaic features (see vol. 1: *An Introduction to the Russian Folktale*).

84. A–T 155. Mitropol'skaia 13. Taken down in 1968 from A.M. Gidziunas, Zarasaisk District, Lithuania. There can be more than one victim. There are three distinct versions of this tale known throughout the world. In one a freezing serpent is revived by a human; in a second, a lion, tiger, or jackal is saved. The third version is found among the Slavs and some Asian peoples. In this a wolf or bear is the intended target of a fox, who falls victim to the human.

85. A–T 157. In Gospodarev 79. Gospodarev was a Belarusian who lived for many years in the north of Russia and came to tell his stories in Russian.

86. A–T 158. Karnaukhova 24. Taken down from Pelageia Nikiforovna Korennaia, Zaonezh'e.

87. A–T 159. From Pudoga Tales 4. Taken down from Irina Pavlovna Perkhina, Avdeevo, Pudoga.

88. A–T 160. In *Fol'klor narodov* 1977, p. 122. This is the only known Russian version of this tale. Single recordings are attested in Ukrainian and Belarusian.

89. A–T 160A*. In Kretov 17. This is the only known East Slavic rendering of this tale.

90. A–T 161A*. Afanas'ev 57. From Osin District of Perm'. This tale is almost entirely known from Russian versions, of which there are more than twenty. It reflects ancient, pre-Christian totemistic beliefs.

91. A–T 161A*. In I.A. Khudiakov 31. This version is originally from Zaraisk District of Riazan'.

92. A–T 161A*. Balashov 77. He preserves this North Russian version from Evdokiia Koneva, who was fifty-nine years old in 1957 and who lived in Varzuga, on the Tersk coast. "Looking around someone's head," searching for lice, is part of the Russian wedding rite. In folktales, and especially fairy tales, it often precedes sleep or death, both of which lead the hero to the otherworld. This version is quite remote from the more typical versions of 161A* and might well be regarded as transitional to the "fairy" tales.

93. A–T 161A**. Balashov 78, preserves this coarse version of the tale by Koneva (see 132).

94. A–T 162A*. In Bardin 193. This version of the tale is from Orenburg (Chkalov).

95. A–T 163. Morokhin 11 is the first publication of this tale. It was recorded from K.A. Toptaeva, born in 1914, in the village of Perevoz, Gor'kii District, 1972.

96. A–T 166A*. Afanas'ev Secret Tales 4 is the only Russian version of this type known.

97. A–T 170 + 158. Onchukov 127 recorded this popular tale from Velikaia Guba in Petrozavodsk District.

98. A–T 171. Afanas'ev 34. Also Pomerantseva 25. This tale was originally from Kaluga. (It is also numbered A–T 703*.) Ostrovskii's play *Snow Maiden,* with music by P.I. Tchaikovsky, and the opera by N.A. Rimskii-Korsakov are both broadly based on this tale.

99. A–T 176**. Zelenin preserved this tale in his Perm' Tales 62. It was originally told by E.E. Alekseev.

100. A–T 178A. This tale was published in the eighteenth century, Grandfather's Walks 4. It is otherwise unknown among the East Slavs. It is known elsewhere, especially in the Sanskrit *Panchatantra,* from which this version may well derive.

101. A–T 179A*. In Zaonezhe' 71; recorded in 1983 from Mariia Stepanovna Medvedeva, sixty-five years of age, in Shun'ga.

102. A–T 179B*. Balashov 157 is the only known East Slavic version. It was told by Pasha Kuznetsov, thirteen years of age, from Pialitsa, Tersk coast.

103. A–T 200. Gospodarev 81 is one of two sources for the Russian version of this tale, which is much more popular among Ukrainians and Belarusians.

104. A–T 210*. Afanas'ev 301. Taken down by direction of Afanas'ev in South Russia and known only in East Slavic. Afanas'ev's tale contains many fine examples of Russian proverbs.

105. A–T 212. Pomerantseva 19 is a reprint of Sadovnikov 55 from Samara District. It was told by Abram Novopol'tsev, one of the great storytellers of the turn of the century. Unlike most versions of this tale, Novopol'tsev's features short songs.

106. A–T 218B*. Zelenin: Viatka Tales 11 was told him by Grigorii Antonovich Verkhorubov, then thirty-eight, a peasant of Kotel'nicheskii District of Viatka. He was self-taught, and Zelenin described him as intelligent and eloquent. The ethnographer also noted that, despite his talents and intelligence, Verkhorubov believed absolutely in the *leshii,* the forest spirit "and other various sorts of devilishness." Verkhorubov was a carpenter and insisted that as such he had the power to let evil spirits into a house being constructed, a belief still common in the late twentieth century. This tale is in many respects akin to wonder tales, known in English as fairy tales.

107. A–T 219E*. This charming story from the Cossack tradition (Tumilevich 1961:3) was recorded from D.E. Belikova, from Novo-Nekrasovsk. She was born in 1882 in Turkey and returned to Russia with the other Nekrasovtsy (followers of Ignat Nekrasov) in 1912.

108. A–T 219E**. This story was recorded in the Caucasus at the end of the past century by a schoolteacher. It is the only known version of this variant. See Caucasian Miscellany 1893, XV(2), pp. 138–39.

109. A–T 220. Zelenin, in his Viatka Tales, pp. 509–10, reprinted this tale from

F. Pardalotskii, "Predanie o kukushke," from *Arkhiv Geograficheskogo Obshchestva,* vol. 24, pt. 6, pp. 71–74.

110. A–T 220A. Afanas'ev 74 preserves this tale, but without reference to its provenance.

111. A–T 221*. Zelenin published this tale in his Perm' Tales 89. It originally had appeared in the Perm' District *Vedomosti,* 1863, no. 44.

112. A–T 220 + 221B*. Zelenin: Viatka Tales 46. Collected from Andrei Ivanovich Blednykh, a soldier who had completed his twenty-five years compulsory service and was in his sixties at the time of recording his tales.

113. A–T 222B*. Zelenin, Perm' Tales 72. Another version from the Perm' District *Vedomosti,* 1863, no. 45. This one lacks the usual continuation of A–T 319B.

114. A–T 222C*. Mitropol'skaia 26. From L.E. Korubov, eighty-five years old, Vilnius District, in 1969. A version of the well-known children's tale "The Little Red Hen." This is the only version attested among the East Slavs, and it may well have come from further west.

115. A–T 225A + 61A. Onchukov 11. Recorded in the Russian Far North by Onchukov from Grigorii Ivanovich Chuprov of Arkhangel'sk District. Onchukov relates that Chuprov was an Old Believer who loved to tell stories, especially about the clergy. He was a carter, fisherman, and trader who also knew byliny (the ancient epics) and historical songs as well as many, many folktales. He was illiterate.

116. A–T 227*. Afanas'ev 73 is the only East Slavic version known. His source is not recorded, but the text is a mixture of Ukrainian and Russian, suggesting a southwestern Russian origin.

117. A–T 227**. Gospodarev 83 is the only Russian version known.

118. A–T 230. Gospodarev 82 is the only Russian source of this tale.

119. A–T 233D*. Afanas'ev preserved this bit of coarse humor in his Secret Tales 2. It is otherwise unattested in East Slavic.

120. A–T 241A (2021A). Balashov 9 published this anonymous tale, recorded in 1947 on the Tersk coast of the White Sea. The tale is frequently narrated as a song. It may also be classified as a cumulative tale.

121. A–T 243*. This is a Vologda text, Ivanitskii, p. 615, in the form of a song. It is quite popular throughout the East Slavic territory.

122. A–T 244A*. Afanas'ev 72. Recorded in Vologda, this is the only Russian text of the tale known, although it is known in Belarusian, Ukrainian, Lithuanian, and Latvian.

123. A–T 245B**. Tumilevich 1961:4, from D.L. Fateeva, of the village of Shevkitili, Georgia. This is the only East Slavic variant of the tale known.

124. A–T 246**. Published in Chudinskii 31. Otherwise unknown among the East Slavs.

125. A–T 247. Published in Tumilevich 1958:4. This is the only Russian version of the tale known, although it is known in Ukrainian and Belarusian.

126. A–T 248. Published in Afanas'ev 66. Of unknown provenance, with continuation in his Secret Tales 8.

127. A–T 20A + 21 + 248A*. Published in Afanas'ev 30 from a transcription made in Voronezh District by K.O. Aleksandrov-Dol'nik. This is a common combination of tale types, especially among the Russians.

128. A–T 248B*. Khudiakov 33 is the only version of this unusual variation of the 248 type in which a human is the victim of the old man's negligence.

129. A–T 254**. Pudoga Tales 39. Recorded in 1940 from Anna Mikhailovna Pashkova, a well-known keener and singer of the epics who was born in 1866. The version given here is interesting for the contemporary references to collective-farm workers and for the anticlerical conclusion.

130. A–T 275. Published in Afanas'ev 35. From Tambov District, before 1849. This is a widely disseminated tale that made its initial appearance in written form in Aesop. Probably from Asia Minor.

131. A–T 281A*. Mitropol'skaia 29 from the Vilnius District of Lithuania, from Danute Genovich, sixteen years of age, in 1969. This is the only known Russian rendering.

132. A–T 282A*. Sadovnikov 57 preserves this tale originally recorded from Abram Novopol'tsev. Only one other Russian variant is known.

133. A–T 282B*. Chudinskii 136a recorded this tale in 1864.

134. A–T 282B***. Mark Azadovskii 35 reprinted this tale from Shaizhin's prerevolutionary collection of 1903. Traditionally, Russian peasants referred to an occurrence as having taken place a certain number of days or weeks before, or after, a particular popular holiday. They also celebrated their "nameday," or day of the patron saint, rather than the actual date of birth. The personified holidays are given here.

Presentation: 2 February. Reception of Jesus in the temple, a minor holiday forty days after Christmas.

Annunciation: 25 March. The day when the Holy Spirit visited Mary to inform her of the advent of Christ.

St. George: 23 April and 26 November. Not just a dragon slayer but the patron saint of wolves, St. George's day was the day when livestock were driven out to green pastures for the first time. In the autumn, St. George's day until the end of the sixteenth century marked the day when peasants free from debt could move from one estate to another.

Nicholas: 9 May and 6 December. The most popular Russian saint.

St. Peter's Day: 29 June. The beginning of the haying season.

Il'ia the Prophet: 20 July, an important holiday at the end of haying and the beginning of the grain harvest. Originally dedicated to the thunder god, Perun, whose summer peace was sought by peasants concerned about wet hay or grain shattered from ripe heads by thunder.

Dormition: 15 August. The holiday corresponding to the Assumption in the Western church.

Frol and Lavr: 18 August. The patron saints of horses.

Ivan Postnoi: St. John the Baptist, 29 August, but popularly 24 June was celebrated as Ivan Kupala, which is midsummer and just before the Fast of St. Peter.

Pokrov: 1 October. The protective veil of the Mother of God, considered the beginning of winter in the North. "The shining white" is snow.

Autumn Kazan: 2 October. The day was devoted to the wonder-working icon of the Mother of God of Kazan, and the day young men were inducted into the army.

St. Michael's Day: 8 November. Associated with animal husbandry and cultivation. Patron saint of princes and the military.

135. A–T 283A*. Published in Afanas'ev 85, from a version taken down in Dalmatovo, Shadrin District of Perm' District by a state peasant named A.N. Zyrianin, around 1850. This tale, which is rather common in the Russian corpus,

seems otherwise to be unknown. It is very likely derived from a well-known song, which is reflected in the rhythmic quality of the original Russian text.

136. A–T 283A***. Students from a pedagogical institute in Kuibyshev (now once again Samara) collected this tale in the village of Nikolaevka Vtoraia, Kuibyshev Rural District as part of a linguistic field trip (Kuibyshev Dialectal Materials 143). It is otherwise unknown.

137. A–T 283B*. Onchukov 135 was collected in the Olonetsk District by A.A. Shakhmatov as part of this study of the North Russian dialect.

138. A–T 284*. Anisimova 86/87 recorded this from B.V. Kazachenko, Penza, in 1953. There are no other Russian variants, but the tale is known in Ukrainian.

139. A–T 393E*. From I.P. Sakharov, p. 201. The "sun" is where the gold is born. This is the only East Slavic version of this subtype known.

140. A–T 293G*. Mitropol'skaia 115 has the only version of this tale recorded in East Slavic. Hers is from Varensk District of Lithuania and was told by E.S. Borisova, who was sixty-nine years old in 1971. The tale was apparently originally Lithuanian, although the Russian version differs from the printed Lithuanian tale in a number of respects. The language of the Russian evinces no discernible Lithuanianisms.

141. A–T 294. Sokolova 70 published this tale from the Riazan' District. It was recorded in 1968 from Prokopii Stepanovich Pron'kin, born in 1901. No other versions are known in Russian although there are two recordings in Ukrainian.

142. A–T 294*. Sokolova 69 recorded this tale in 1966 from Praskov'ia Nikiforovna Gromova, a literate peasant born in 1887 and living in the Shatsk area of Riazan' District. No other East Slavic versions are known and Sokolova considers the tale to be of literary origin.

143. A–T 295. Afanas'ev 87. The origins of this tale are unknown. It could well be an adaptation of Aesop's tale about the clay and bronze pots, perhaps through the intermediacy of LaFontaine's version or even one of the Russian versions, well known since the eighteenth century, by Sumarokov or Krylov.

144. A–T 295. Afanas'ev 88. Collected in 1848 in Perm' District by the state inspector of the Kungursk School, S. Buevskii.

145. A–T 296*. Balashov's version (115) of this tale was collected in Chavan'ga, on the Tersk coast of the White Sea, from Mar'ia Andreevna Semenikhina in 1961, when she was seventy-one years of age. All these variants of "The Gingerbread Boy," as Americans know the tale, are usually classified with the cumulative tale, A–T 2025.

146. A–T 297B. Afanas'ev 90 retains this Orenburg tale. It is localized in northern and central Russia, with one recording in Estonia. The Russian versions are often rhymed.

147. A–T 298A. Smirnov 147. The tale was apparently collected in the 1850s in Iaransk District of Viatka.

148. A–T 298A + 298A*. Told by Gospodarev to N.V. Novikov, Gospodarev 26.

149. A–T *299. From Pudoga Tales 5. Recorded from Irina Pavlovna Perkhina in 1976 when Perkhina was fifty years old. The tale is closely related to the "Three Brothers-in-Law," A–T 552B, and in this version shows signs of literary origins. It is otherwise unknown in East Slavic.

150. A–T 299*. From the repertoire of F. Gospodarev 84. This tale is otherwise unknown in East Slavic.

BIBLIOGRAPHY

Short Citation	Source
Afanas'ev	Afanas'ev, A.N., comp. and ed. *Narodnye russkie skazki A.N. Afanas'eva v trekh tomakh.* Moscow, 1984.
Afanas'ev: Secret Tales	Afanas'ev, A.N. *Russkie zavetnye skazki.* Geneva, 1872, Moscow and Paris, 1992.
Akimova	Akimova, T.N., ed. *Fol'klor Saratovskoi oblasti.* Saratov, 1946.
Anisimova	Anisimova, A.P., ed., *Narodnoe krasnoe slovo.* Penza, 1959.
Azadovskii	Azadovskii, M.K., ed. *Russkie skazki v Karelii (starye zapisi).* Petrozavodsk, 1947.
Balashov	Balashov, D.M., ed. *Skazki Terskogo berega Belogo moria.* Leningrad, 1970.
Bardin	Bardin, A.V., ed. *Fol'klor Chkalovskoi oblasti.* Chkalov (Orenburg), 1940.
Bashkir Tales	Pomerantseva, E.V., ed. *Russkoe narodnoe tvorchestvo v Bashkirii.* Ufa, 1957.
BRFS	Kruglov, Iu.G., ed. *Biblioteka russkogo fol'klora. Skazki.* Moscow, 1988–1989.
Caucasian Miscellany	*Sbornik materialov dlia opisaniia mestnostei i plemen Kavkaza.* Vols. 1–46, Tiflis-Makhachkala, 1881–1929.
Chistov	Chistov, K.V., ed. *Perstenek-dvenadtsat' staveshkov.* Petrozavodsk, 1958.
Chudinskii	Chudinskii, E.A., comp. *Russkie narodnye skazki, pribautki, i pobasenki.* Moscow, 1864.
Efimenko	Efimenko, P.S., comp. *Materialy po etnografii russkogo naseleniia Arkhangel'skoi gubernii,* part 2. Moscow, 1874.
Fol'klor narodov	*Fol'klor narodov RSFSR. Mezhvuzovskii sbornik.* Ufa, 1976, 1977.
Gospodarev	Novikov, N.V., ed. *Skazki Filippa Pavlovicha Gospodareva.* Petrozavodsk, 1941.
Grandfather's Walks	anon. *Dedushkini progulki, soderzhashchie v sebe 10 russkikh skazok.* Moscow, 1819, 1st ed., St. Petersburg, 1786.

Short Citation	Source
Ivanitskii	Ivanitskii, N.A., ed. *Materialy po etnografii Vologodskoi gubernii. Sbornik svedenii dlia izucheniia byta krest'ianskogo naseleniia Rossii.* Vol. 2, Moscow, 1890.
Karnaukhova	Karnaukhova, I.V., comp. *Skazki i predaniia Severnogo kraia.* Leningrad, 1934.
Khudiakov	Khudiakov, I.A., ed. *Velikorusskie skazki v zapisiakh I.A. Khudiakova.* Moscow-Leningrad, 1964.
Komovskaia	Komovskaia, N.D., ed. *Predaniia i skazki Gor'kovskoi oblasti.* Gor'kii, 1956.
Kretov	Kretov, A.I., ed. *Narodnye skazki Voronezhskoi oblasti. Sovremennye zapisi.* Voronezh, 1977.
Kucheriavenko	Kucheriavenko, D., ed. *Skazy Dal'nego Vostoka.* Khabarovsk, 1939.
Kuibyshev Dialect	anon. *Dialektologicheskie materialy Kuibyshevskoi oblasti.* Kuibyshev, 1957.
Kupriianikha	Novikova, A.M., and I.A. Ossovetskii, eds. *Skazki Kupriianikhi.* (A.K. Baryshnikova). Voronezh, 1937.
Kursk Tales	Aristova, A., and M. Pavlova, eds., *Fol'klor. Chastushki, pesni, skazki, zapisannye v Kurskoi oblasti.* Kursk, 1939.
Magai	Eliasova, L., and M. Azadovskii, eds., *Skazki i predaniia Magaia* (E.I. Sorokovikov). Ulan-Ude, 1968.
Matveeva	Matveeva, R.P., and T.G. Leonova, eds. *Russkie skazki Sibiri i dal'nego Vostoka: Volshebnye i o zhivotnykh.* Novosibirsk, 1993.
Mitropol'skaia	Mitropol'skaia, N.K., ed. *Russkii fol'klor v Litve.* Vilnius, 1975.
Morokhin	Morokhin, V.N., ed. *Prozaicheskie zhanry russkogo fol'klora. Skazki, predaniia, legendy, bylichki, skazy, ustnye rasskazy.* Moscow, 1977.
Nikiforov	Nikiforov, A.I., comp. *Severnorusskie skazki v zapisiakh A.I. Nikiforova.* Moscow–Leningrad, 1961.
Ogarev	Ogarev, N.P., ed. *Baiki, basenki, pobasenki i skorogovorki.* Moscow, 1867.
Onchukov	Onchukov, N.E., ed. *Severnye skazki.* St. Petersburg, 1908.
Pomerantseva	Pomerantseva, E.V., ed. *Russkie narodnye skazki.* Moscow, 1957.
Pudoga Tales	Razumova, A.P., and T.I. Sen'kina, comps. *Russkie narodnye skazki Pudozhskogo kraia.* Petrozavodsk, 1982.
Sadovnikov	Sadovnikov, D.N., ed. *Skazki i predaniia Samarskogo kraia.* Zapiski RGO. St. Petersburg, 1884.
Sakharov	Sakharov, I., comp. *Skazaniia russkogo naroda, sobrannye I. Sakharovym.* Vol. I, books 1–3, 3rd ed., St. Petersburg, 1841; Moscow, 1989.
Shastina	Shastina, E.I., comp. *Russkie skazki vostochnoi Sibiri.* Irkutsk, 1985.
Smirnov	Smirnov, A.M. *Sbornik velikorusskikh skazok arkhiva Russkogo geograficheskogo obshchestva.* Petrograd, 1917.
Sokolova	Sokolova, V.K., ed. *Skazki zemli Riazanskoi.* Riazan,' 1970.

Short Citation	Source
Tumilevich 1958	Tumilevich, F.V., ed. *Skazki kazakov-nekrasovtsev.* Rostov-na-Donu, 1958.
Tumilevich 1961	Tumilevich, F.V., ed. *Skazki i predaniia kazakov-nekrasovtsev.* Rostov, 1961.
Vasil'ev	Vasil'ev, M., intro. *Materialy po fol'k loru. Nauchno-pedagogicheskii sbornik.* Vostochnyi pedagogicheskii institut. Kazan.' II. 1927, pp. 129–145. IV. 1928, pp. 211–231.
XIX C. Tales	Novikov, N.V., comp. *Russkie skazki v zapisiakh i publikatsiiakh pervoi poloviny XIX v.* Moscow–Leningrad, 1961.
XVI–XVIII C. Tales	Novikov, N.V., comp. *Russkie skazki v rannikh zapisiakh i publikatsiiakh (XVI–XVIII v.).* Leningrad, 1971.
Zaonezh'e Tales	Onegina, N.F., ed. *Skazki Zaonezh'ia.* Petrozavodsk, 1986.
Zelenin: Perm' Tales	Zelenin, D.K. *Velikorusskie skazki Permskoi gubernii.* Moscow, 1991. See also, edition by T.G. Ivanova, St. Petersburg, 1997.
Zelenin: Viatka Tales	Zelenin, D.K. *Velikorusskie skazki Viatskoi gubernii.* Zapiski RGO. Petrograd, 1915.
Zhivaia Starina	*Zhivaia starina.* 1890–1916. St. Petersburg.

Jack V. Haney received bachelor's degrees in Russian language and literature from the University of Washington (1962) and Oxford University (1964), where he was a Rhodes Scholar. In 1970 he completed a D.Phil. in medieval Russian literature at Oxford with a dissertation on Maxim the Greek. He is professor of Slavic languages and literatures at the University of Washington, Seattle, where he teaches medieval Russian literature, Russian folklore, and the Russian language, and is chairman of the department.